CHRISTOPHER MARLOWE

AND

HIS ASSOCIATES

Edward Alleyn.
From the portrait in Dulwich College.

CHRISTOPHER MARLOWE

AND

HIS ASSOCIATES

BY

JOHN H. INGRAM

ILLUSTRATED

COOPER SQUARE PUBLISHERS, INC.
NEW YORK
1970

To

THE MASTER

FELLOWS

AND SCHOLARS OF

Corpus Christi College

CAMBRIDGE

THIS RECORD OF AN ILLUSTRIOUS SON

OF THAT ANCIENT HOUSE

IS INSCRIBED BY

THE AUTHOR

Originally Published 1904
Published by Cooper Square Publishers, Inc.
59 Fourth Avenue, New York, N. Y. 10003
Standard Book Number 8154-0326-7
Library of Congress Catalog Card No. 70-116374

Printed in the United States of America

PREFACE

FOR upwards of three centuries the brightness of Marlowe's name has been dimmed by libel and slander. One writer after another has copied the legends of his predecessors, generally adding his own myth to the mixen, until a long list of authorities can be adduced as testimony against the poet; but repetition is not confirmation, and the only basis for imputing 'hellish sins' to him is puritanical malice—supported by libel and forgery.

The following pages will show that the remembrance and references of every one who knew Marlowe personally are favourable to his character. He is seen moving in all that was best, noblest, and most intellectual of English society of those days. Received as a friend in the Raleigh and Walsingham households; mixing with the scientific and learned men of the time; on intimate terms with Chapman, Drayton, and such men of honoured and honourable position; apparently working with, and certainly deeply admired by, Shakespeare, and respected or envied by his literary contemporaries. Could such a man, 'haughty man,' as the vapid Gabriel Harvey styles him, have been leading a profligate life, disregarding the decencies of society, and herding with rogues, vagabonds, and outcasts, such as were the associates of Robert Greene? During Marlowe's lifetime Greene alone ventured to try and depreciate his merits, and then only by innuendo and sneers. The slanders on his fair name were invented by succeeding generations.

Biographers of Marlowe have been startled and unnerved by the term of 'Atheist,' applied so freely to the poet by those who hated his freedom of thought and speech. All who read in the literary and political writings of Elizabeth's reign must know how lavishly this appellation was bestowed upon opponents by all sects and parties, irrespective of belief, and that to deny any dogma of the Church as by State established, was atheism and treason; and either crime punishable by death.

Although not an atheist Marlowe was a freethinker, a would-be-reformer, and, by the mouths of his *dramatis personæ*, dared to say what others scarcely ventured to whisper. He was no respecter of persons: even 'the round and top of sovereignty' did not shield the wearer from his keen shafts; nor did he falter when priestcraft was in question. He represents the revolutionary spirit of his age.

My purpose is not to deck the poet in the garb of the Pharisee, but to cleanse a noble character from the slime with which libellers and forgers have besmirched it. Of late years a revulsion of feeling has set in with respect to the estimate of Marlowe's personal character, a change which if not initiated has certainly been accelerated by my paper, 'A New View of Marlowe,' in the *Universal Review* for July 1889, wherein new *data* were given and a different complexion put upon the old; but the recent outburst of admiration for Marlowe's genius has—who can doubt it?—been largely instigated by the glowing eloquence and critical acumen which our greatest living poet has displayed in his recognition of its pre-eminence.

'Marlowe and his Associates' may be considered the most descriptive title for this work, much of the volume being concerned with his contemporaries, but my aim all through has been to represent the poet as he was—as I feel he must have been—as the companion, the compeer, and the admired of all that was best of his time; and my references to other men, to their words, their works, or their deeds, are only intended to give a better insight into the characteristics of the period and to infuse more contemporary colouring into the narrative.

'Conjectures,' says Fuller, 'if mannerly observing their distance, and not imprudently intruding themselves for certainties, deserve, if not to be received, to be considered.' Biography, like history, must owe something to conjecture. Reason requires that from the known we adduce the unknown, and suggests how certain given causes produce certain results. Into this work my idea has been to introduce such inferences only as shall really illustrate the poet's personality and place his mental quite as much as his incidental career before the reader.

Necessarily the information herein given has been derived from authorities, consequently quotations are numerous. In nearly every instance the books, deeds, letters, registers, manuscripts, and places referred to have been personally inspected by me, so that I have not only been enabled to confirm but in many cases to correct and considerably modify the information furnished by my predecessors and, after several years of patient research, to give much fresh material, chiefly from manuscript sources, which will be new to all, even to the most experienced students and bibliographers. Amongst the material now first published, special attention may be drawn to the information furnished about the King's School, Canterbury, and its scholars contemporary with Marlowe ; to the facts of the poet's university career, and to the Wills given in *Appendix C*: that of the poet's mother is not only interesting on account of the relationship of the testatrix to the poet, and as evidence of her social position, but from the realistic picture it presents of the home life of the period.

There is no known portrait of Marlowe : the truly 'counterfeit presentment,' which has done duty for some years past on the title-page and cover of Colonel Cunningham's edition of Marlowe's Works as one, is a likeness of Lord Herbert of Cherbury, the eccentric Elizabethan nobleman.

My impugnment of the authenticity of the Harleian MSS. referred to in the course of this work, may furnish matter for controversy, but before any one attempts to defend the genuineness of those documents, it is trusted that full consideration will be given to the many reasons now adduced for doubting it.

Readers are requested not to overlook the fact, as it vitally affects many circumstances in this narrative, that money in the reign of Elizabeth was worth eight or ten times as much as it is at the present day.

In taking leave of the work which has for several years occupied so much of my mind and time, it is requisite that I should offer my grateful thanks to the many kind correspondents who have borne with my inquiries and have endeavoured to comply with my requests. For information derived from printed works my obligations are manifold, and, in addition to the acknowledgments made in various parts of my book, I wish to gratefully refer to the publications of the Rev. Alexander Dyce, of Mr. A. H. Bullen, of the late Richard Simpson, of Professor Masson (*Life of Milton*), the late James Broughton, C. H. Cooper, and Thompson Cooper, Dr. Masters, Howard Staunton, and Charles Knight, of Mr. F. G. Fleay, to the contributors to *Notes and Queries*, to the Reports of the Royal Commission on Historical MSS., and to the *Dictionary of National Biography*. Other literary and bibliographical information, from printed or manuscript sources, has been acknowledged in the *Notes* at the end of this work.

For courtesy and assistance of various kinds I am indebted to the late Dr. J. B. Sheppard of Canterbury, and the late Dr. A. B. Grosart, to the Rev. Dr. Perowne, Master of Corpus Christi College, Cambridge, and to Mr. Arnold Wallis, of that College, to Mr. J. W. Clark, Registrary of that University, to the Rev. A. J. Galpin, Headmaster of King's School, Canterbury, for much kind help and useful suggestions, to the late Rev. Francis T. Vine, Rector of St. George's, Canterbury, to the Rev. A. Shirley, in charge of St. Nicholas Church, Deptford, to Mr. J. R. Dasent, C.B., Mr. Arthur Hussey, Mr. A. F. Leach, Mr. P. D. Eastes, editor of *The Kentish Gazette*, Canterbury, and Mr. Henry Mead, of the Canterbury Museum and Library, to Miss Butler and her father, late tenants of Marlowe's alleged birthplace, to Mr. Stanley Cooper, F.R.S.L., Mr. J. H. Allchin, Maidstone Museum and Library, Mr. J. E. S. Pickering, Inner Temple Library, Mr. E. W. Lockhart, St. John's College Library, Cambridge, Mr. E. W. B. Nicholson, Bodleian Library, Oxford, Mr. H. R. Oswald, the Coroner for South-Eastern London, and others whose kindness if not here named is none the less appreciated. Also, for personal aid and courtesy I have to thank the Officials of the British Museum, the Lambeth Palace, and the Guildhall Libraries, the Record Office, the Will Department, Somerset House, the Clerk of the Peace and the Officials of Westminster Guildhall, of Corpus Christi College, and of the University, Cambridge, and of other public institutions.

Finally, my most grateful thanks are due and are hereby tendered to Mr. J. M. Cowper, author and editor of so many works of historical value, for the inexhaustible patience with which he has endured my many inquiries and for long-continued kind assistance, and, if last, by no means least, to the Rev. Dr. H. P. Stokes, author of the *History of Corpus Christi College*, Cambridge, who has furnished me with so much friendly aid and valuable information during a lengthy series of years, and to whom I am deeply indebted for many interesting items in elucidation of Marlowe's career, amongst others for the fact that the poet was elected to at least one and

apparently, a second scholarship at Corpus Christi
College.   This last discovery disposes for ever of
the surmise that Marlowe was a pensioner at the
University, and dependent upon a patron's bounty.

JOHN H. INGRAM.

CONTENTS

ILLUSTRATIONS

CHRISTOPHER MARLOWE

CHAPTER I

CANTERBURY : CHILDHOOD

IN the midst of verdant valleys and well-wooded hills reposes Canterbury, capital of the ancient kingdom of Kent. Branches of the sleepy Stour intersect the plain in all directions, and one of these branches dividing, clasps two arms round the ancient city—a city claimed by one of its many renowned sons to be older than Rome itself![1] Steeples and spires and time-tinted turrets rise from out the plain, whilst far above them all, soar into mid-air the lofty towers of the Cathedral, the guardian of this erstwhile sacred city.

Canterbury, in many respects the second and in some even still the first city of the kingdom, in the latter half of the sixteenth century was gradually recovering from the shock it had received in the reign of King Henry the Eighth. It was not so much the spoliation of its enormous wealth—and six-and-twenty wagons had been employed in carrying off its gold and jewels[2]—as the blow given to its sanctity by the desecration of its shrine, the decanonisation

A

of its patron saint, and the overthrow of its religious pre-eminence. The loss of the miracle-working reputation which Henry had deprived the city of did more to impair its position than did the loss of its material possessions.

With the succession of Elizabeth, in 1558, brighter days seemed dawning on the distracted land, and 'the fair city of the East' shared in the general resuscitation. Civic prosperity, which had fluctuated sadly during the last two reigns, was, for a time at least, partially restored, and Canterbury smiled once more. Princes and ambassadors and other notabilities again made the city their halfway resting-place on the journey to London, and to some extent Canterbury resumed its wonted aspect. The prophets and the martyrs of the new mental era were born, but as yet they had neither preached, nor prophesied, nor had they yet suffered for the crime of knowledge. At present all went merrily, and men knew not the penalty of too much learning.

Freed from internal and foreign strife the citizens of Canterbury reverted to the love of the good things of this world, and appeared to concern themselves little with the mental problems which so violently agitated people in some parts of the kingdom. The misdeeds and offences which had been ascribed to the rule of priestcraft continued, or rather revived with renewed prosperity, and the city was a hotbed of vice. Wealth and poverty still elbowed each other in the streets, and extravagance and usury still held

CANTERBURY

PLATE II.

their carnivals. Midnight outrage and drunken brawls were anything but infrequent, and as the severity of punishment increased so did the number and nature of crimes. The civic records show that men literally carried their lives in their hands, for no one paraded the streets without a weapon, and daggers were used on the slightest provocation.

For the many pilgrims who in this latter half of the sixteenth century still thronged the thoroughfares, some merely to view, others to secretly worship at, England's holiest but desecrated shrine, what a vision was conjured up! Narrow streets overshadowed by lofty buildings already sombre with age ; strange public edifices decorated with marvellous heraldic signs in colours more or less faded ; ancient churches and quaint dwelling - places unfolded to view in confused, picturesque succession. Grotesque and gloomy as that city seemed to the stranger, it was still less darksome than many a contemporary city of even less antiquity, and was well cared for by its citizens. As early as 1474, in the thirteenth year of the fourth Edward's reign, an Act had been passed for paving the principal thoroughfares, in which it had been stipulated that they should be properly pitched with boulders and Folkestone stone and, in order to have the work properly carried out, it was enacted that every proprietor should pave that portion of the street upon which his burgage (tenement) abutted.[3] Many other equally useful local regulations were made by the corporation, such as those for lighting the streets and alleys at night by means of lanterns, although it is feared they were not always complied with.

Numerous quaint roomy hostelries and thickly populated houses, of all kinds of curious architectural development, shouldered one another into the street and overhung the shadowy thoroughfares. The eaves of the more pretentious buildings were supported by grotesque figures called 'telamonies,' by goblins, and grinning monsters ; whilst runic-knots, scrolls and zigzags were much in evidence amid what was intended to be considered ornamental. 'Here were lanes, odd nooks and corners, queer old buildings with some monster or elfin carved upon the massive beams, at which the pilgrim stared, hardly knowing whether to cross himself or not, whether it betokened a saint duly canonised, or a devil, or a punchinello who owed his existence to that comic spirit which the genius of ecclesiastical architecture and art invoked in the middle ages, in strange contrast to (*sic*) its devotional tendencies.'[4]

The citizens of this ancient metropolis, wealthy and long accustomed to the good things of this life, and well endowed with municipal privileges, nourished a love of independence and an attachment to liberty which rendered them sturdy in the maintenance of their civic rights and less amenable to the restrictions under which many of their classes lived elsewhere. 'All the bodies of Kentish men be free,' proclaims the *Custumal of Kent*, and although for many centuries this was not a fact as regards the agriculturalist, it applied pretty generally to the burgher of proud Canterbury.[5]   The corporation maintained its freedom, as well as its other privileges, and passed stringent decrees to deter any of its members from attaching themselves to, or becoming retainers of, any 'worshipful man' outside their own circle.   At a court of Burghmote, as the civic governing body was designated, held in 1572, it was decreed: 'That if any Alderman or Common Councilman shall take *any livery*, or be retained as servant to any Nobleman or man of worship, then every such Alderman or Common Councilman shall be discharged from his office and from this Court.'   And their records prove that the rules of these independent-minded burghers were duly enforced.[6]

This high and mighty Canterbury, this revered shrine of the martyred A'Becket, had been for centuries the resort of the people of all Christian lands.   Mighty princes and haughty prelates had journeyed thither, and had been jostled in its narrow thoroughfares by the superstitious and the needy; the rich and the poor, the halt, the maimed and the blind, all pilgrimaged to this miracle-pervaded city in the hope that their prayers might be granted or their wishes accomplished.   Many resorted to it as the probable scene of living adventure, fashion, folly, and, peradventure, with a prospect of earning a penny more or less honestly.   Wealth flowed into the city, and its citizens became men of importance, gaining fortunes, reputation, and even titles. In the second half of the sixteenth century, it is true, the pillage of its treasures and decanonisation of St. Thomas A'Becket undoubtedly deterred many pilgrims from visiting his shrine, and facilitated the decadence of Canterbury, but, as yet, the city held its head high among the cities of the land; its archbishop kept sway over all the prelates of England, and its corporation continued to receive and entertain in lordly style not only foreign potentates but the rulers of our own country. All these things—memories of a high, mighty, and marvel-haunted past—a recent martyr-making era of persecution, and an independent but pastime-loving present—combined to form and influence the minds of such of the upgrowing generation as were suitably formed for impression.

For several generations a family of the name of Marlowe or Marley had dwelt in this city. Out of Canterbury and its vicinity the name has never been common. Here and there about England the cognomen of Marlowe occasionally crops up, but outside the county of Kent it has never been of frequent occurrence. Early in the fifteenth century there are traces at Wisbech, it is true, of a certain Marlowe family, but it soon terminated in one of them known in local records as a 'musicianer';[7] in 1409 a Richard Marlow was Lord Mayor of London, and according to Weever, in his 'maioraltie there was a play at Skinner's Hall, which lasted eight dayes, to heare which most of the greatest Estates of England were present. The subject of the play was the sacred Scriptures, from the creation of the world.'[8]   Such plays, the reader may be reminded, were performed in various parts of the kingdom under the title of *Corpus Christi* plays.

Early in Queen Elizabeth's reign there was an Edward Marlowe of some local importance residing at Clifton, Bristol, who got into trouble for taking unlawful possession of a salt-laden vessel belonging to Denmark, a country with which England was at peace.[9]   John Marlowe, of Merton College, Oxford, who died in 1543, was thought to have been a scion of the Kentish Marlowes.   He became treasurer of Wells Cathedral and canon of the King's Chapel of St. Stephen within the palace of Westminster, and was evidently a person of some importance in his days.[10]   Anthony Marlowe, of whom more hereafter, was a wealthy and influential Deptford merchant, and probably a connection of the Canterbury Marlowes.[11]   Captain Edmund Marlowe, who lived till 1615, is mentioned in Purchas's *Pilgrims* as 'an excellent man, and well skilled in the mathematics and the art of navigation,' and may have belonged to Kent.   In 1571 a Richard Marlow was master of the Grammar School of St. Olave's Parish, Southwark, London, and about twenty years later a Thomas Marlow was living in the neighbouring parish of St. George in the same borough, and was assessed on property of some considerable value.[12]   With these few examples may end the tale of the non-

Kentish Marlowes ; some, if not all of them, were probably of the Kentish stock.

In the records of Canterbury the Marlowes can be traced back to the early part of the fifteenth century. They all belonged to the trading community, and occasionally gave evidence of being not only wealthy but regardful of the public weal.   The earliest trace of a public bequest by any of the family is contained in the will of one Richard Marley.   This Richard Marley, who, in 1514, is described in the accounts of the chamberlain of the city as a son of John Marley, tanner, and as a freeman and tanner of Westgate Street,[13] was apparently the great grandfather of the future poet.   In his will, dated 1521, after giving directions for his own burial in the churchyard of Holy Cross Church, 'before the Crucifix of our Lord, as nigh the coming in of the North door there as conveniently can be,' he directs 'his executors to see gilt well and workmanly the Crucifix of our Lord, with Mary and John standing upon the Porch of the said North door.'   This crucifix, which Richard Marley wished 'gilt well and workmanly,' as it stood in the porch of the church by Westgate, to arouse the devotion of communicants, did not stand long in that position, for even in the next century Somner had to record that it had gone, 'and the King's Arms was set up in place of it.'[14]   Others of the family founded hospitals and in various ways provided for the benefit of their fellow-beings.

A certain Christopher Marlowe belonging to the

CHURCH OF ST. GEORGE THE MARTYR, CANTERBURY,
BEFORE THE TOWER WAS TORN DOWN

PLATE III.

tanners, a trade which combined with the shoe-makers in forming a guild, appears by his will, made in 1550, to have been possessed of some property. The date of his death is unknown.[15] Another Christopher Marlowe of this district who was 'presented' (*i.e.* reported) to the archbishop for some breach of morality, was probably his son. This Christopher, who lived into the seventeenth century, left two daughters only, but it is necessary to refer to him, so that his record may not be confused with the poet's.[16]

A John Marlowe, to whom various church register references are made in connection with the christening and burial of his children, was probably the poet's paternal grandfather.[17] His occupation and the date of his death have not been traced, but it is surmised that the next John Marlowe was his son, and he was, as is known, the poet's father. This last John was married on the 22nd of May 1561, at the parish church of St. George the Martyr, by the Rev. W. Sweetinge, the rector, to Catherine Arthur, the daughter, in all probability, of the Rev. Christopher Arthur, at one time rector of St. Peter's, Canterbury, and, apparently, a scion of an ancient Kentish family entitled to bear arms.[18]

Like her contemporary Mary Arden, the wife of John Shakespeare of Stratford-on-Avon, Catherine Arthur seems to have belonged to a family somewhat higher in the social scale than her husband's. But the marriage would scarcely have been an unequal one. The Rev. Christopher Arthur was one of

those clergymen ejected by Queen Mary on her
accession as a ' reforming ' minister and, presumedly,
for having married.   Even if alive at the time of his
daughter's wedding, and this is doubtful, the dis-
gowned priest might not have been dissatisfied to
see his child become the wife of a respectable trades-
man.   By birth or by apprenticeship, John Marlowe
the younger had evidently already acquired the
freedom of the city, whilst later on he became a
member of the Guild of Shoemakers and Tanners,
a guild to which other members of the family had
already been admitted, a proof that they were not
without some standing in the city of Canterbury.

In accordance with an old decree of Burghmote it
was enacted, ' That if any of the seide fraternite
Guild of Shoemakers dwelling in the liberties of
the seide citie, intende to be married, then he shall
give knowledge of hit to the wardeyns of the seide
fraternyte three daies before the marriage, and then
the seide wardens to give a commandment to the
bedill of the same fraternite to name the brethren in
due time to go with him from his dwelling place
unto the parisshe church where the matrimony shall
be solemnised, and to offer with him ' ; [19] and as John
Marlowe, although evidently a very young man, is
seen in various ways complying with his civic obligations, it may be assumed that he readily carried out
this instruction of his guild, evidently a highly
prosperous and important body of citizens.

In May following the year of the young couple's

THE FONT AT ST. GEORGE'S CHURCH, CANTERBURY, AT WHICH
CHRISTOPHER MARLOWE WAS CHRISTENED

PLATE IV.

marriage their first child, Mary, was christened at
St. George's, and on February 6, 1564, their eldest
son was born.[20]   He was christened Christofer, on
the 26th of the same month, at the church of St.
George the Martyr,[21] and apparently by the rector,
Mr. Sweetinge, at a font still doing service in the old
parish church.   Several other sons and daughters
were born to the young couple, were christened,
some married, and in due course all were buried; but
although the parish registers record these events,
history only concerns itself with the first-born boy—
with Christopher.

On the 20th April, 1564, being the sixth year of
Queen Elizabeth's reign, the poet's father is thus
referred to in the city's records : 'John M'lyn of
Canter. Shomaker, was admitted and sworn to ye
lib'ty of ys citte for ye whitche he pd, but 11 11s. 1d.
becaus he was inrowlyd w'thyn ys citte acordyng to
ye customes of ye same.'[22]   Having by birth or
apprenticeship already acquired the freedom of the
city, John Marlowe, in accordance with ancient custom, was now enabled by payment of the customary
reduced fee to become a duly recognised citizen,
empowered to start in business on his own account.
Apparently he had only just reached manhood, but he
had powerful incentives to become a burgher and to
acquire a right to be a masterman, in consequence of
his marriage and a rapidly increasing young family.

Although John Marlowe may never have been a
wealthy man, he was a freeman and a member of an

influential guild; from time to time he took apprentices, and was evidently in decent circumstances.
For several years, it is seen from civic records, he
was deemed a man of substance. He, or perhaps
still more his wife, was ambitious enough to obtain
for the first-born son educational advantages not
generally attainable in those days, save by children
of the higher classes. It would, indeed, be interesting to trace the earliest development of the boy's
mind, and, were it possible, to behold the foreshadowings of his genius; but as there is no guide to such
knowledge, whence and how his poetic temperament
and aspiring spirit grew can only be surmised.

Christopher Marlowe entered the world at a stirring period, when the old times were rapidly passing
away and a new era of mingled hope and doubt was
dawning upon his country. England was just recovering from internal and foreign conflicts, and
during the lull a partial truce was patched up between
followers of the rival creeds. The rapid diffusion of
printed books was creating a revolution in every
branch of learning, and the new knowledge thus
gained aroused men to dare in thought and deed
things hitherto undreamt of. A feeling of new-born
hope permeated the nation. The time was ripe for
thinkers and actors. There was a stir and excitement in the mental atmosphere of the age, influencing
and moulding the minds of the new generation, which
seethed in a turmoil of speculative thought, and by
its aspirations and actions reacted upon and controlled

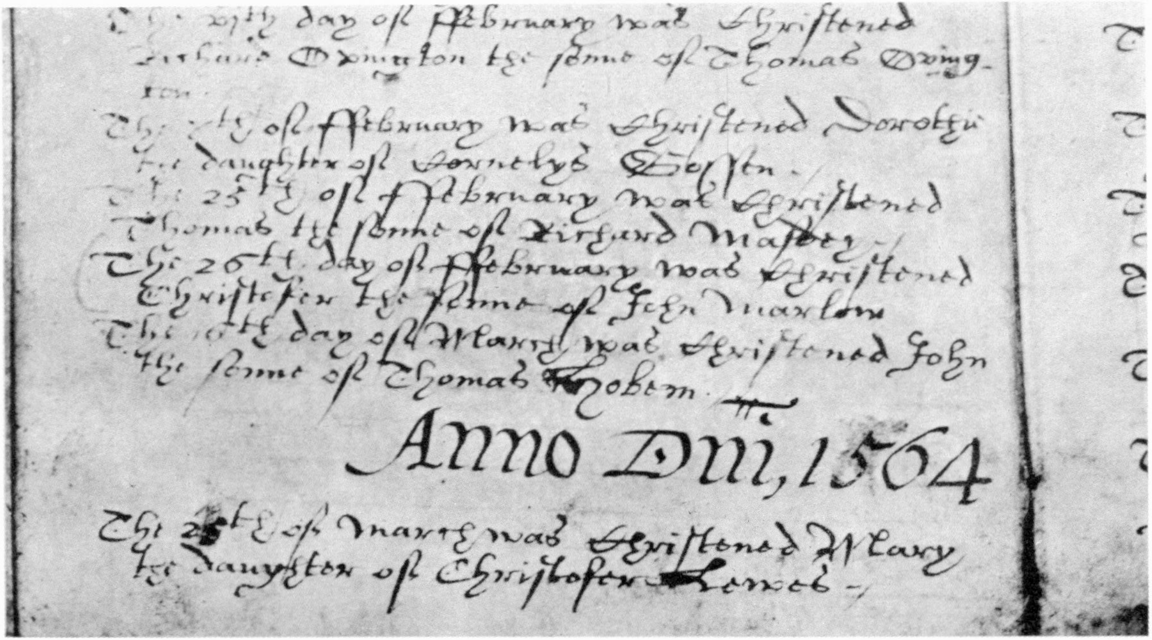

PLATE V.

EXTRACT FROM THE CHURCH REGISTER OF ST. GEORGE THE MARTYR, CANTERBURY,
OF CHRISTOPHER MARLOWE'S CHRISTENING, 26th FEBRUARY 1564

not only those who lived in it, but those who came after it.

As a matter of fact, however, Canterbury appeared to concern itself little with such things; its citizens busied themselves more about civic feasts and public shows; eating and drinking was the order of the day, and plays and pageants of constant occurrence. Little Christopher may well have had his share of these pastimes, and even have laid the foundation of his dramatic proclivities in viewing the spectacles produced, as they then were, for public gratification at the public expense.

To comprehend the formation of a child's mind more than the building up of his physical body, it is necessary to study closely the nature of his time and of his surroundings. Who were his guides and his companions? What were his occupations and amusements? Among the latter, in Marlowe's case, would be the miracle plays such as 'Abraham and Isaac,' payment for the public presentation of which religious drama is recorded in the accounts of St. Dunstan's parish, Canterbury, or the Corpus Christi plays. 'To the Guild of Corpus Christi in particular, was assigned the drama or Mystery in forty acts, which traced the whole progress of Bible history, beginning with the Creation and ending with the Last Judgment.' This guild was held in Holy Cross Church, just outside the West Gate, at the very spot where Richard Marley had provided for the embellishment and upkeep of the crucifix. It was not many minutes' walk from Marlowe's native parish of St. George the Martyr, and little Kit would certainly be taken to witness it.

The performance of these sacred dramas was assigned in some cities to the various guilds or companies, each guild undertaking a separate section or play. In Canterbury a special guild, known as that of 'Corpus Christi,' was instituted by a decree of the Burghmote, in 1504, for acting these plays, and it gave performances during Lent and upon certain festivals. 'These performances, which dealt with the most sublime subjects in a manner which appeared from their style, dialogue, and scenery, to exhibit a combination of the ludicrous, the sacred, and the familiar, were a source of immense attraction to the people of England. . . . The ancient mysteries performed by the Guild of Corpus Christi frequently exhibited the august personages of Holy Writ in a sort of comic burlesque; and one strong part was Noah and his wife fighting, previous to their entry into the ark—a point which not only awakened the undisguised glee of the diabolic personages of the drama, but called forth the unbounded applause of . . . the devout audiences of Canterbury.'[23]

For some children this method of instilling scriptural story into their minds would have more the appearance of study than amusement, and, doubtless, pastors and parents did try to make them profit by the opportunity; but over a child with such an imaginative faculty as young Marlowe must have been endowed with, the dramatic air of the proceeding would exercise a strange fascination, and strongly influence his boyish brain. He had no books, save those used for lessons, to beguile his boyish fancy, and his mind had to feed upon itself. He had no collections of ballads, nor of poems, songs, or adventures, no pictures and no toys. His imagination had to be aroused and sustained by songs and ballads sung by the older members of the family, or by the minstrels and glee singers of the city, who were duly licensed and paid by the corporation for their performances. Curious items of folklore he would gather from the country people, and from relatives residing without the walls of Canterbury, but such matter of old-time superstitions appear to have left little imprint on the mind of this city born and bred boy; unlike his contemporary, William Shakespeare, who, having passed his earlier life in the country, was strongly influenced by rural mythology. What impressed Kit's thoughts most deeply were those weird semi-theological plays in which sins and virtues were personified, and wherein the personages of the Christian hierarchy were brought on to the stage and presented bodily before his boyish eyes.

Besides plays and pageants, music and glee singing, other less edifying entertainments were provided for the people's pleasure and, also, at the people's expense. Bull-baiting, cock-fighting, and even dog-fighting were popular sports. The children, it is hoped, were kept away from the atrocities of the

' Bull's Stake,' in the Canterbury Butter-Market ; yet it is difficult to understand how a boy having the use of his eyes and limbs could, in those days, be unacquainted with the horrors and miseries of the hapless bulls, whose flesh, by special order of the Burghmote, was not allowed to be sold unless the unfortunate beast had been baited before it had been slaughtered. ' Now and then an infuriated animal broke from the stake, carrying terror and confusion before him as he franticly rushed through the narrow thoroughfares of the Mercerie, followed by shouting butchers and by yelling dogs, scarcely less savage or brutal than their masters.' [24]

Other reprehensible subjects occupied the attention of the citizens and naturally formed the subjects of the elders' gossip. The readiness with which daggers, the accompaniment of every freeman's attire, were drawn and made use of is exemplified in many quaint and tragic records of the time, and the rapidity with which the folks took the law into their own hands and stayed not for the law's reprisal, caused life to be held cheap. Sometimes such episodes not only ended in the death of one of the combatants, but also in the trial and execution of his slayer or slayers. To the execution it was usual for parents to take their children, not only as an outing for themselves and the youngsters, but because to witness the sending out of life of the more or less unfortunate criminal was regarded as a salutary warning for the youthful spectator. What object-lessons for a child! What tales of terror for an imaginative boy! What inducements to succumb to passion for a hasty youth! What disregard of danger for an impulsive man! What subversion of one's ideas of justice was everywhere prevalent!

Entertainment of a different character, but generally more expensive for the townsfolk, was afforded by the visit of somebody of note, perhaps even the sovereign in person, in which case the archbishop or the corporation had to play the host. In 1573, when little Kit was in his tenth year, Queen Elizabeth paid one of her visits to Canterbury, and was magnificently entertained, the usual costly gifts being made to her and the members of her suite during her stay. To meet her on her arrival it was arranged that 'Mr. Mayor, the Aldermen, and every one of them, ride in their scarlet gowns to meet the Queen; and the Common Council be on foot with their best apparel, and likewise as many of the chief Commoners as have gowns.'[25]

The Church vied with the corporation in honouring the queen. Archbishop Parker and other high dignitaries met her Majesty at the west door of the cathedral, to which she had ridden on horseback, and when her 'grammarian,' who was one of the scholars of the King's School, had finished his oration to her, she alighted and went into the cathedral to evensong.[26] During her visit the queen resided at the monastery of St. Augustine, which her father, Henry the Eighth, had seized and turned into a palace.

B

Here she kept her court, attending service at the cathedral every Sunday during her stay at Canterbury, and affording the citizens a continuous jubilee during the whole of her visit.   On her birthday, which she kept at the archbishop's palace, the queen and her attendants, together with a large company of distinguished visitors, were entertained by Archbishop Parker at an enormous expense to the worthy if wealthy ecclesiastic.   The corporation at her departure presented the queen with a costly piece of plate, and made presents to all her attendants, including heralds, trumpeters, sergeants-at-arms, and 'gentlemen surveyors of the ways.' [27]

It cannot be doubted but that young Kit was among the crowd which from time to time gazed on the queen and her gorgeous retinue, and that he was amid the spectators, even if he took no active part as a performer, at the fêtes and pageants devised for her Majesty's amusement.

Later in the year 1575 occurred a still more memorable matter for Canterbury.   The visit of the queen was followed by the arrival of a still more mighty monarch, the terrible Plague reaching the city and committing dreadful ravages.   Whether the home of the Marlowes had to have its door marked with the portentous sign of the red cross and the inscription which accompanied it, 'Lord have mercy upon us,' to signify death had been busy there, is unknown, but among the places affected was the King's School, which was closed until the 1st of

September of that year in consequence of the terrible
epidemic. If the Marlowe family lost none of its
own members it must have had to bewail the loss of
some kindred and friends amongst the many victims.
Amid all the impressive events of those days nothing
could have affected an imaginative boy's mind more
than the ghastly sights and sickening incidents which
attended a visitation of the Plague; the effects of
which were to weaken all human ties, to dull all
earthly pleasures, and to carry off young and old,
rich and poor, indiscriminately.

The magnificent architectural antiquities of his
native city cannot fail to have made lasting impression upon Marlowe's plastic mind, and to have
excited his boyish wonder and admiration. Canterbury could not fail to have ever been a city of marvel
for him. Every evening when the sounds of the
busy streets began to wane, and the mystical hour
of eight rang out from the several steeples, how
breathlessly must he have waited for the sound of
the curfew from the lofty ' Bell Harry ' tower, telling
him of bed-time. How solemnly must have sounded
to him the knell from that bell as, in 1575, in accordance with custom immemorial, it tolled out to the
saddened city the news that an archbishop, a noble
benefactor, had passed away. Little Kit could not
then have foreboded that that sullen sound betokened in the death of Parker the loss of the best
friend this world had given him.

All things considered, it may be deemed that

Marlowe's boyhood days were neither unhappy nor unprofitable. Sometimes death broke in upon the family circle, and from time to time bore away first a sister and then his little brothers; but these things often happen, and rarely cause more than a passing cloud in the morning of life. The child saddens for a time over the loss of a playfellow, but others gradually take its place, and the wound closes, scarcely leaving a scar.

If Kit lived in the two-story timbered building, still standing in the parish of St. George, which has been suggested as his birthplace,[28] and which even in his days must have been very ancient, one can easily conjure up a picture of him as the leader of a troop of children pattering up and down the dimly lighted stairs and running in and out of the many tiny rooms of their quaint old home; sometimes mixing in the sports and gambols of the four sisters left to him, or of other relatives and companions, helping with his childish treble to make music in the darksome corridors. Or, as he grew in years, he may be fancied gazing out dreamily at the antique church opposite, where the only recorded incidents of his early life happened; where his parents were wedded, he and his brothers and sisters were christened, and some of them buried. Or, as he grew older and pondered more earnestly over the causes and consequences of things, he would have gazed from the rear of the old dwelling far away into the fairyland of Fancy, catching perchance

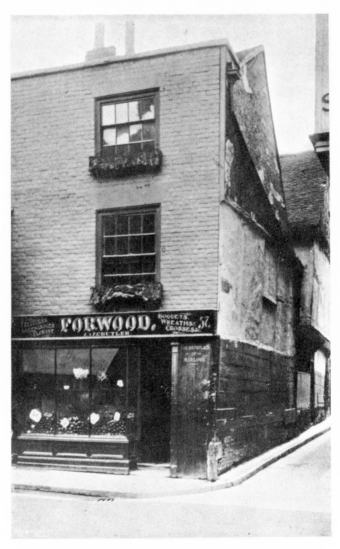

THE ALLEGED BIRTHPLACE OF CHRISTOPHER MARLOWE IN
ST. GEORGE'S STREET, CANTERBURY

THE FRONT HAS BEEN 'MODERNISED' RECENTLY

From an original photograph.

PLATE VI.

glimpses of the distant meadows and cloud-capped hills, or, without having to lose himself in such childish speculations, his boyish bewilderment, and even awe, must have been aroused by the weird carved figures, half-humanised fiends in appearance, which then projected, as even now they project, from the back of the quaint parental abode.

In these early years from whom was the little lad obtaining the rudiments of his education? Was his mother directing his childish aspirations, or was his father, who must have had a little more scholarship than his neighbours, as he ultimately became parish clerk of St. Mary's Bredman, or was the teacher one who more from kinship of spirit than of race, lured him through the early stages of his studies in quest of 'learning's golden gifts'? In wealthy families private tutors could be found to remove the stumbling-blocks on the road to learning and to stimulate every spark of talent discernible, but the case must have been different for one of the shoemaker's many children. Yet the fathers of the city had been mindful in various ways of their children's educational needs, and all classes were provided for. In 1544 they had decreed that the corporation's common clerk should have the shop adjoining the Court-hall, called the 'Fyle,' upon the understanding that there he should, 'or one for him, do the duty of his office and instruct children.'[29]

The duties of this office would have still been enforced in Marlowe's days, and it is very probable that the common clerk, 'or one for him,' gave the boy his earliest lessons in the 'shop adjoining the Court-hall,' in the High Street, not many minutes' walk from his home in the parish of St. George the Martyr. The lad would have learned to read and write and to gain an elementary knowledge of the 'parts of speech'; but he must have displayed greater aptitude for study than the generality of his comrades, for by the end of 1578 he had obtained a scholarship in the King's School, the chief educational institution of Canterbury.

Traditionally founded by Archbishop Theodore in the year 600, this ancient and famous grammar-school, after passing through many vicissitudes of fortune, had been restored and re-established by King Henry the Eighth, who bestowed upon it its present royal title. A limited number of lads, upon giving proof that they already possessed a certain quantum of learning, were admitted on the foundation, and each such scholar after admission received a quarterly stipend of one pound.[30] As scholars were only admitted between the ages of nine and fifteen, they must have given proof of age before admission. They were only admitted to the foundation at the November chapter, to fill such vacancies as might take place in the ensuing year, and as Kit was not admitted until January 14, 1579, that is to say, in the quarter terminating at Lady Day, he obtained his admission only just in time. His late entrance into the King's School may have been due to the

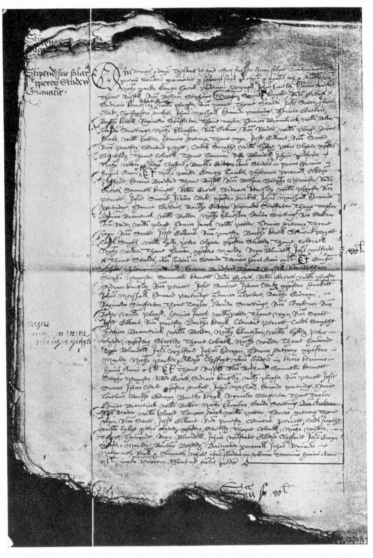

LEAF OF THE TREASURER'S ACCOUNTS OF PAYMENTS MADE TO THE
SCHOLARS OF THE KING'S SCHOOL, CANTERBURY, IN 1578/9

PLATE VII.

fact that no vacancy had occurred sooner, whilst his stay in the school was undoubtedly curtailed by his advanced age.

Nicholas Goldsborough, then the head-master, received a stipend of forty pounds per annum, whilst ten pounds were paid to his assistant, Robert Rose,[31] probably a relative of John Rose, who was mayor of Canterbury in 1574, and again in 1583.[32] The accounts of the King's School for that period, although still perfect, are very meagre, and do not afford much information beyond dates and names, although they, indeed, are by no means uninteresting nor unimportant. From other records, however, useful items about the school are obtainable. It is pleasant to learn and to see the result in Marlowe's person, that the King's School was not entirely restricted to the education of sons of what Hasted terms the 'best families.' In 1541 Cranmer, as archbishop, became first 'visitor' to the King's School. He took a great interest in the scheme prepared by King Henry for its re-establishment, and told the Commissioners who, when electing the first scholars, sought to restrict the scholarships to the sons of high-born wealthy parents, 'If the gentleman's son be apt to learning let him be admitted; if not, let the poor man's apt child enter his room.'[33] Happily Cranmer succeeded in carrying his point.

Archbishop Parker, who did so much for learning, was also of his predecessor's opinion: he deemed that the institution should be open to the sons of the poor man; and it is probable that, whilst several of Kit's fellow-pupils were the children of high-born parents, others were of the same rank of life as was Marlowe. Doubtless, indeed, the lad acquired there that indefinable air of education and courtesy seldom possessed by those not born in, or accustomed in early life to mixing with, the educated classes.

The curriculum of the school at this period would comprise a certain quantum of Latin grammar, the rules of which had to be learned by heart; any amount of Latin verse; probably a little Greek for the higher forms; and the study of certain prescribed classical authors. Marlowe doubtless entered on the school foundation with some knowledge of the Latin accidence, and had therefore been sufficiently grounded to begin the study of Lily's famous grammar and the *Sententiæ Pueriles*. He would have had to study and construe passages from Virgil, Terence, Cicero, and other Latin authors, and write themes both in prose and verse. Latin was the chief study, living languages being then much neglected amid the usual subjects of an Englishman's education. Although the curriculum thus provided may not be considered a very liberal one, it afforded a good, sound classical foundation for a lad preparing to enter one of the learned professions, and by this time it is certain that Kit was destined for the Church.

How proud Catherine Marlowe must have been when her son returned home daily from his studies, clad in his scholar's black gown, foreshadowing the apparel of the priest! She must have had maternal visions of the lad following her father's example, and filling a place in the pulpit as he had done; perhaps becoming—who knows how far a mother's proud affection may aspire?—even an archbishop, as had the sons of fathers in as lowly a position as John Marlowe—as, for instance, Archbishops Parker and Peckham—or, at any rate, rivalling the dignity of his supposed kinsman, John Marlowe, the Canon of Westminster, whose reputation was doubtless a household word in the Canterbury home. Perhaps at times the lad's quaint hauteur, or his studious eccentricities of temper, may have caused her misgivings, but, if so, like Mary of yore, she would doubtless have 'kept all these things, and pondered them in her heart.'

In his daily journeys to and from school young Kit must have beheld and treasured in his memory many visible prototypes of the fiends introduced in later days into his *Faustus*. There they still are, projecting from under the eaves of the city's ancient dwellings, beside the quaint water-ways, along the dusky streets, and under the niches of the public buildings. There would he behold those fiendish faces and distorted figures, whose semblance would be stamped for ever upon his 'mind's-eye': those complex shapes, half human and half demon; some as pompous prelates, or portly priests; some as misshapen sinners, or as martyred saints, with ghastly grins or sinister smiles; some glancing

benignantly, but more frequently sneering scorn-
fully, or sarcastically, on the stripling as he hurried
along.

The King's School appears in those days to have
already acquired a not undeserved reputation for the
good scholarship of both its tutors and its pupils.
Dr. John Ludd, appointed headmaster just as Kit
was leaving the school, was referred to by White
Kenneth, Bishop of Peterborough, as having 'had
at one time no less than thirty-seven Masters of
Arts of his own bringing up,' doubtless a rare feat
at that time; and it is recorded of Richard Boyle,
who became the famous Earl of Cork, one of Kit's
fellow-students, that he 'must have been well
grounded, for he was exceptionally accurate in his
syntax and orthography, and, when mindful, wrote
a fair hand';[34] all very unusual things for a nobleman of Elizabeth's days.

In scrutinising the records of the King's School
during the period that Kit was scholar there, it is
noteworthy to find amongst the naturally limited
number of his fellow-students the names of many
either connected with eminent men, or who became
eminent themselves. Some few of the lads signed
personally for their quarterly stipends—would that
Kit had done so!—and their calligraphy was worthy
of the school's reputation. Amongst the names
enshrined in these precious rolls are several belonging to the best Kentish families. The list included
two Mundeys, doubtless relatives of that Anthony

Mundey, the author, who, not being able at one period of his literary career to make a living by play-writing, made it by writing against plays. One of them was probably that John Mundey, B.D., Fellow of Corpus Christi College, Cambridge, who was elected, in 1626, to the mastership of his college. The election being soon after declared void, some one posted on the college gate the words, *sic transit gloria mundi.*

One of Marlowe's schoolfellows was W. Lyly, doubtless a brother of John Lyly, of Euphuistic renown, who was born in the Weald of Kent, and a descendant of the William Lyly whose far-famed Latin grammar was then being used in all the public schools. Another was Thomas Colvile, or, as the lad wrote it himself, in very neat handwriting, Thomas Coldwell, afterwards an author and publisher, and believed to have been a son of John Coldwell, Bishop of Salisbury. This unfortunate prelate was a native of Faversham, Kent, and notwithstanding his episcopal dignity, was so reduced by misfortune, that at his death in Canterbury, in 1596, he was indebted to charity for burial.[35] George Coldwell, the translator of Boethius, was doubtless a relative as well as a contemporary. H. Parrott, the future epigrammatist, author of *The Mastive or Young Whelp of an olde Dogge* and other curious works, was another contemporary at the King's School, as was Thomas Playfere, afterwards doctor of divinity, and an 'eloquent divine of famous memory,' whose sermons, although now buried under the dust of antiquity, are, for all that, very entertaining reading. They are strongly imbued with the prevalent Euphuism, and are remarkably quaint. One of them, heralded by the quotation '*Etiam mel se nemium,*' and dated from St. John's College, Cambridge, 1st day of February, 1595, is dedicated to Lady Elizabeth, wife of Sir George Carey, in these terms : 'Madame, it is reported that Demonax, having his head broken with a stone, and being advised to complaine to the Proconsull of that injurie, answered that he had more need to goe to a churgian to heale his head than to a Magistrate to redresse his wrong. I must also confesse I had rather have had my head broken than my sermon so mangled, for this sermon hath been twice printed already without my procurement or privitie any manner of way : yea, to my very great griefe and trouble.'

Another and still more noted fellow-pupil of Kit was Benjamin Carrier, whose name is so frequently misspelt Carier. He was a student at the King's School at the same time as Marlowe, and, subsequently, with other lads of the same period, rejoined him at Cambridge. A few more words may be devoted to Carrier later on, although, as his name and fame are European, but slight reference is needed to him here. Other contemporaries at the school bore the names of Shelley, Dobson, Lewes, Sydney, Russell, Playfair, Bentham, Scott ; designa-

THE KING'S SCHOOL, CANTERBURY, AS IT APPEARED IN 1611

PLATE VIII.

tions already then or since made renowned by their wearers. Stephen Gosson, author of the *School of Abuse*, left the school in 1572, of course before Kit went on the foundation, and William Harvey, discoverer of the circulation of the blood, did not enter until 1588, eight years after Marlowe had left, not matriculating at Cambridge until 1593.

Allusion has been made to Hasted's remark that the boys educated at the King's School were 'in general of the very best families of this part of the country,' and amongst such boys, it is stated, were John Boyle, afterwards Bishop of Cork, entered in 1578, and, in 1580, his brother Richard (born in Canterbury), who became 'the famous' Earl of Cork.[36] Their names do not appear in the school accounts, therefore they could not have received the usual quarterly stipend, although they were certainly at the school.

As has been stated, Kit entered the King's School on January 14, 1579, and was paid his stipend until Christmas. As the Accounts for 1580 are missing, it is uncertain when he left, but he probably remained at the school until he obtained a scholarship at Corpus Christi College, Cambridge.

Matthew Parker, the learned and liberal Archbishop of Canterbury, had not only founded various scholarships at Cambridge (including two for the King's School at Corpus Christi College, the place of his own education), but also maintained fifteen scholars there at his own expense.[37] All the qualifi-

cations Parker exacted from the scholars benefiting
by his generosity were that they should be the 'best
and ablest scholars' picked from certain Kentish
and Norfolk schools, should be well instructed
in grammar, 'and, if it may be, such as can make
a verse.' [38]   Kit's ability to comply with this last
qualification might be deemed certain if English and
not Latin verse were intended, for no one attained to
his dexterity in rhythm and command of language
who had not begun to versify early in life; but it
may be taken for granted that the lad's election to
one of the Parker scholarships for the 'best and
ablest scholar' was gained by his own talents.   No
patron was necessary, and, in his case, certainly not
needed.

In 1548 Archbishop Parker founded six new
scholarships at Corpus Christi College, and in May
1569 he arranged for a further two at the same
college for lads out of the King's School, no other
restriction being made save 'that the lads must be
of this school and natives of Kent.' [39]   These two
additional scholars, it was agreed between the Master
of the Eastbridge Hospital and the Keeper of
the College of Corpus Christi, Cambridge (then
Dr. John Pory), should be chosen, named, and
approved by the said Hospital Master and the Dean
of Christ Church, Canterbury, for the time being:
Dr. Thomas Godwin, it may be pointed out, being
then and till 1584 the Dean.   The last two scholars
were to be known as 'the Canterbury Scholars,' and

after their admittance at 'the said College, according to the Orders, Decrees, and Statutes of the said College, shall have the provision of the said Master or Keeper, Fellows or Scholars, and their successors.'[40]

On the archbishop's death in 1575, it was found that he had increased the number of 'the Canterbury Scholars' to five, by the addition of three more scholarships, 'the first of these to be taken out of Canterbury School,[41] being a native of the city,' and to be born 'of honest parents.' This was, undoubtedly, one of the scholarships to which Marlowe was subsequently elected.

The delight of his parents at Kit's success need not be questioned, nor the lad's own joy at the prospect of receiving the shelter of a famous college where he might indulge his aspirations 'after knowledge infinite.' The preparation for his journey and prolonged residence away from home must have caused much bustle and excitement in the Marlowe household. It is easy to picture Kit's mother striving to suppress her sorrow at the approaching departure of her only surviving son, and endeavouring to forget it by busily setting together the needed articles for his long journey and lengthy absence. She would have to see that his linen, not too plentifully supplied in those days, was not too scanty, and that the scholar's outfit should be as good as his parents were able to provide. Doubtless a roomy cloak-bag contained all the lad's outfit, even including his little store of books. His shirts and shirtbands, his girdle and knife, and numberless odds and ends, motherly love would provide, not forgetting of course the camphor-balls he should carry as a preventative against the Plague and the many other ills human flesh is subject to. Last, but by no means least, would be his stock of money, carefully put away in that wonderful invention, a purse. Possibly John Marlowe would not be able to spare his son many crowns, and the mother's store must have been wofully depleted in providing Kit's outfit; but the Chapter, as was customary when a scholar was sent from the King's School to the University, would make him a gift of a few pounds—of more money than he had ever had in his life before. The Chapter was most generous in assisting the King's School in all its requirements, not only helping the students proceeding to or residing at the University, but even aiding the headmaster when he had domestic trouble, and furnishing a considerable sum towards the expenses to be incurred in the setting forth of tragedies, comedies, and interludes, no unnoteworthy circumstances when considered in connection with the subsequent dramatic proclivities of several of the scholars of the school.[42]

It is pleasant to picture young Kit, just seventeen, in all the audacity of youth, forgetting, as he rode away from home, the wise admonitions of his father, the admiring looks of his sisters, and the envy of the apprentices—yea, even the sad glances of his mother

EXTRACT FROM THE REGISTRUM PARVUM AT CORPUS CHRISTI COLLEGE,
CAMBRIDGE

SHOWING THE ADMISSION OF CHRISTOPHER MARLOWE TO A SCHOLARSHIP IN PLACE
OF CHRISTOPHER PASHLY, 1581

PLATE IX.

—as he went forth into the unknown world to fight and conquer. Full of hope, health, and youth, what could mortal wish for more? And yet Marlowe was hoping for much more. With boundless ambition he was—who can doubt it?—seeking Fame if not Fortune, deeming all things possible for him who seeks. Seventeen years old! More money in his pocket than he had ever had before, and life all before him. Happy youth!

Kit would certainly have had company, and not unlikely one or more fellow-scholars from the King's School. If he rode the whole way to London he would have paid about three shillings or so for the use of his steed, but it is more than probable that he only rode as far as Gravesend, and then, according to the usual custom, would take the ferry on to complete what in those days was a long and arduous undertaking. Gravesend would probably be the termination of the young traveller's second day's journey, the first night from Canterbury having been spent in one of the many towns or villages on the way.

Good accommodation was obtainable at many of the numerous inns which Gravesend contained. Fynes Moryson, the famous traveller, passing through the town not long after Marlowe would have visited it, says, with respect to foreigners landing there, 'The World affoords not such Innes as England hath, either for good and cheape entertainment after the Guests owne pleasure, or for humble attendance on passengers ; yea, even in very poore villages. . . .

For as soone as a passenger comes to an Inne, the
servants run to him, and one takes his horse and
walkes him till he be cold, then rubs and gives him
meate, yet I must say that they are not much to
be trusted in this last point, without the eye of the
Master or his servant to oversee them. Another
servant gives the passenger his private chamber, and
kindles his fire, the third pulls off his bootes, and
makes them cleane. Then the Host or Hostesse
visits him, and if he will eate with the Host, or at
a common table with others, his meale will cost him
sixe pence, or in some places but foure pence. . . .
It is the custome and no way disgraceful to set up
part of supper for his breakfast. In the evening or
in the morning after breakfast (for the common sort
use not to dine, but ride from breakfast to supper-
time, yet coming early to the Inne for better resting
of their Horses) he shall have a reckoning in writing,
and if it seeme unreasonable, the Host will satisfie
him either for the due price, or by abating part,
especially if the servant deceive him any way, which
one of experience will soone find. . . . If Gentlemen
will in such sorte joyne together to eate at one table,
the expenses will be much diminished. Lastly, a
Man cannot more freely command at home in his
owne House, then hee may doe in his Inne, and at
parting if he give some few pence to the Chamberlin
and Ostler, they wish him a happy journey.'[43]

Doubtless Kit knew by instruction or report most
of what Moryson refers to, and it is to be expected

that parental admonitions had equally well prepared him for such casualities as the above experienced traveller cautions his readers against. 'In all Innes, but especially in suspected places, let him bolte or locke the doore of his chamber; let him take heed of his chamber fellowes, and alwayes have his sword by his side or by his bedside; let him lay his purse under his pillow, but always foulded with his garters, or something hee first useth in the morning, lest hee forget to put it up before hee goe out of his chamber. And to the end hee may leave nothing behind him in his Innes, let the visiting of his chamber and gathering his things together be the last thing he doth, before hee put his foote into the stirrup.'[44]

Having survived all the dangers thus far, our youthful traveller would be able next day to take a passage to London by water, for in those days at every tide, 'a man may pass for ye valew of two pence in ye common barge, and in a tiltbote for vi.d,' the distance being about twenty miles.[45]

Arrived in London, by whatever means he may have made use of, the lad would doubtless seek out and present himself to the wealthy and influential Mr. Anthony Marlowe, who could not well refuse shelter and a gracious reception to a clever young kinsman, bound for the University. Some few days would probably be spent in making an inspection of the most prominent sights of the mighty metropolis —'The Fair Queen of the West,' as her poets loved to style her—and then, ho, for Cambridge!

CHAPTER II

THE facilities for travelling between London and Cambridge were greater than between the metropolis and any other town in the kingdom : this advantage being due to the enterprise of one man. Thomas Hobson, supposed to have been a native of Bunting-ford, Herts, was born about 1544. Whilst yet a lad he had to drive a team of horses for his father, and when he arrived at manhood he started a team on his own account. His father left him a nice little property including, besides copyhold lands in Grant-chester, a wagon and eight horses and their harness and other belongings. By means of this, and by industry and thrift, Hobson amassed an independency and, notwithstanding the fact that he had a large family, became one of the richest men in Cambridge. He was farmer, maltster, inn-keeper, and carrier, the last-named occupation directing his attention to the profitable idea of letting horses on hire.

'Being a man that saw where there might good profit arise, though duller men overlooked it,' and 'observing that the scholars of Cambridge rid hard,' he contrived to get together 'a large stable of horses,

TOM HOBSON

After a painting at Cambridge.

PLATE X.

with boots, bridles, and whips, to furnish the gentlemen at once, without going from college to college to
borrow.' [46]

According to tradition Hobson was the first man
in England to let out hackney horses, and the same
authority has it that he had a stable of forty good
steeds always ready and fit for hire. When a
customer came for a horse he had always to take
the one nearest the stable door, the carrier's rule
being that every horse should be ridden in its turn.
From this rule no exception would be made, hence
the origin of the proverb of 'Hobson's choice.'
When Hobson let out a horse to go as far as
London he was careful to impress upon his
customers, many of whom were students and
frequently unaccustomed to riding, 'that they would
come time enough to London if they did not ride
too fast.' [47]

For upwards of sixty years Hobson had the traffic
between Cambridge and London entirely in his own
hands, and in those days of difficult travelling his
aid was a blessing to many. There can be but little
doubt that Marlowe availed himself of Hobson's
assistance to reach Cambridge, where he arrived
some time before his seventeenth birthday, that
is to say, when he was somewhat older than the
customary age of entrance in those days, many
students matriculating at sixteen, fifteen, and even
earlier. Marlowe's name was entered as 'Marlin'
in the Register of Admissions to Corpus Christi

College in 1580, last but one (Basingwhite's) for that year,[48] although he did not matriculate until March 1581.   There was nothing unusual in Marlowe's name being entered as ' Marlin' without any prefix. The 'obliging informant' who told Dyce that ' Scholars were entered with a "pomp and circumstance" not found in the notice of "Marlin,"' evidently knew nothing about the facts, as the list of admissions, still extant, shows that it was the custom to thus enter the names of scholars at Benets.[49]

In 1579 a special regulation had been passed at the University that students were to matriculate within a month of coming to Cambridge, but this rule does not appear to have been rigorously insisted upon, and it is evident from the manuscript records that Marlowe had already been admitted to Corpus Christi College, and was in residence there, some time before his matriculation was recorded in the Cambridge Matriculation Book.   It should perhaps be explained that whilst both admission into a college and matriculation in the University registers are necessary, they are two distinct acts. The college books contain the particulars of a student's connection with his college and of his residence there, but a student's position in the University, record of his degrees, and so forth, are preserved in the Cambridge Grace Book kept by the University Registrary.

Corpus Christi College, formerly known as Benets,

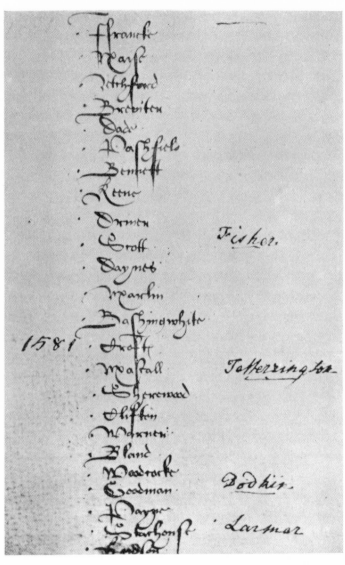

EXTRACT FROM THE ADMISSION BOOK OF CORPUS CHRISTI COLLEGE,
CAMBRIDGE, FOR THE YEARS 1580-1

PLATE XI.

from the adjoining church of St. Benedict, although
one of the most ancient was not one of the largest
colleges of the University. The number of persons
who were to be admitted was not fixed, but was
regulated according to its revenue. Archbishop
Parker, in remembrance of his own education there,
added largely to the number of its scholars, to the
revenue of the college, and to its wellbeing in
general; the other students there were maintained
by income partly derived from the original foundation
and partly acquired through the generosity of various
benefactors.

Marlowe, as has been seen, was not yet seventeen
when he arrived at Cambridge, and must have found
the new life into which he had entered wonderfully
strange. It was probably the first time the lad had
ever been any distance from home, and almost
certainly the first time he had to take up his residence in a strange abode. The same feeling of
strangeness and isolation, despite the hundreds of
similarly circumstanced lads about him, which
thousands of youths must have felt would have
affected young Marlowe, despite his ambition and
proud anticipations, and for the time must have
chilled his aspirations.

On the 17th March 1581 Marlowe's name was
inscribed in the Matriculation Book of the University
as 'Chrōf. Marlen, Pensioner.' [50] The choice of
chambers at college is necessarily of importance to a
freshman, but in Kit's case there would be no choice.

Three lower chambers on the north side of the quadrangle had been assigned to the five former 'Canterbury' scholars, but if Marlowe kept on the ground floor, says the Rev. Dr. Stokes, as he would have to do, his chamber would be 'on the right-hand side of the old court staircase, now lettered R. This room had long been used as the store-house, but it had been lately fitted up as a chamber, where three of the Parker scholars might live';[51] and it is almost in the same condition as it must have been in when Marlowe occupied it.

The following extract from Archbishop Parker's will renders the identification of the chamber clear: '*Item. Volo quod Executores mei paratum reddant cubiculum in eo Collegis jam vocat* "a Storehouse" *pro tribus aliis meis scholasticis inhabitandis pro quibus singulis volo tres libras sex solidos et octo denarios per annum dari juxta formam quam Executores meos in scholia Cantuariensi, et in ea Urbe oriundum; secundum electum volo e schola de Aylsham; et tertium e schola de Wymondam in his duabus villis oriundos.*'[52]

In connection with the above occupation of rooms, it should be understood that at that period, although separate beds were allowed for all scholars above the age of fourteen, separate rooms, even for Fellows, were rarely allowed. Two or three scholars occupied the same chamber, and in the full colleges, all kinds of devices, such as 'truckle beds' and the like, were used to supply extra accommodation. The original

MARLOWE'S ROOM AT CORPUS CHRISTI COLLEGE, CAMBRIDGE.

PLATE XII.

statutes of Christ's College, and they may be regarded as representative of the other colleges in this respect, show how the chambers were allocated: 'Our wish is,' says the founder, 'that the Fellows sleep two and two, but the scholars four and four, and that no one have alone a single chamber for his proper use, unless perchance it be some Doctor, to whom, on account of the dignity of his degree, we grant the possession of a separate chamber.'[53] Although all the colleges, as was the case at Corpus Christi, were not so crowded, it is stated that both in Trinity and St. John's Colleges, four students, or one Fellow and two or three students, used originally to have one chamber in common.   In none of the colleges was it the practice for less than two students to occupy one room, and it is possible, from Marlowe's reference to a 'sweet chamber-fellow,' that he was not obliged to share his small bedroom with more than one, and that one not uncongenial.   This chamber-fellow's name, if never known with certainty, may still be conjectured. The room is very small, and does not appear fitted to hold more than two small bedsteads.

The first of the three new 'Canterbury' scholars was to be chosen within three months after a vacancy at the college from such lads at the King's School 'as should be competently learned in grammar, born of honest parents, and be of such qualities as should be thought meet, and of such as were thought likely to proceed in Arts, and afterwards to make Divinity their study.   Upon which conditions he was entitled to this exhibition for six years, otherwise it was to cease after three.' [54]

There can be no doubt Marlowe held one of these exhibitions, and it is almost certain that at the University he obtained another scholarship. When he went to Cambridge it was with the full intention of taking Holy Orders, and his chamber-fellow, from the way Marlowe alludes to him, was doubtless inspired by a similar intention, but unless his name be identified, it is impossible to know whether he succeeded in his desire.

At Cambridge, Kit must have met several of his old schoolmates from King's, some at Corpus, and some at other colleges ; among these lads and young men were many who subsequently acquired considerable reputation in literature and science; of them, probably, Benjamin Carrier, son of Anthony Carrier, a learned minister of the Church of England, attained the greatest contemporary fame. Born in 1566, he was two years younger than Marlowe, but he did not obtain his admission to Corpus until 1582. After a brilliant career at the University, Benjamin Carrier created no slight sensation in the leading theological circles of Europe by forsaking the English Church, in which he had gained a great reputation, for that of Rome. After a lifetime of religious strife he died at Paris in 1614.[55]

In 1582 another distinguished member of a Kentish family, and a fellow-pupil of Marlowe at King's School, John Boyle, subsequently Bishop of Cork, was admitted into Corpus Christi College; his

Corpus Christi and St Maries College was founded in the year 1351 by the contributions of 2 Religious Societies viz of Corpus Christi and of St Marys, united under ye Protection of Henry ye First Duke of Lancaster. Abp Parker presented this college with a valuable Collection of Books selected from ye Remains of ye Old Abby Libraries &c. they chiefly relate to ye History of England & are frequently referd to by writers on yt Subject. this College has a Master 12 Fellons and 40 Scholars.

CORPUS CHRISTI COLLEGE, CAMBRIDGE, IN THE SIXTEENTH CENTURY

PLATE XIII.

still more celebrated brother, Richard Boyle, afterwards the famous Earl of Cork, not being admitted until 1583, in which year also was admitted Thomas Hamond, another of Kit's old schoolfellows, as was also Edward Parker, doubtless a relative of the late archbishop.[56]

The 'Canterbury Scholars' who benefited by Parker's thoughtfully worded agreement with the college authorities were allowed eightpence (afterwards increased to one shilling) a day for Commons, and in addition to their education were to be provided with convenient chambers, ' Laundery,' barber, and other necessaries, together with reading in the Hall free.[57]

If contemporary accounts of the style of living then prevalent in the University are not exaggerated, the lad newly arrived from the comforts of home-life must have found college fare barely endurable. A Fellow of St. John's, describing the studies and mode of existence then pursued at Cambridge, at least by the poorer students, says : ' There be divers there which rise daily about four or five of the clock in the morning, and from five till six of the clock use common prayer, with an exhortation of God's Word, in a common chapel ; and from six until ten of the clock use ever either private study or common lectures. At ten of the clock they go to dinner, whenas they be content with a penny piece of beef among four, having a pottage made of the broth of the same beef, with salt and oatmeal, and nothing else. After this slender diet they be either teaching or learning until five of the clock of the evening ; whenas they have a supper not much better than their dinner.   Immediately after which they go either to reasoning in problems or to some other study, until it be nine or ten of the clock ; and then, being without fires, are fain to walk or run up and down half an hour to get a heat on their feet when they go to bed.' [58]

Similar doleful accounts are given by other residents of the University about that date, some recording that the students had to make their own beds and sweep out their rooms.

According to official records, the daily routine of college life at Cambridge at that period was as follows : ' In the morning, at five o'clock, the students were assembled by the ringing of the bell, in the College-chapel, to hear the morning service of the Church, followed on some days by short homilies by the Fellows. These services occupied about an hour ; after which the students had breakfast. Then followed the regular work of the day. It consisted of two parts : the *College Studies*, or the attendance of the students on the lectures and examinations of the College-tutors or lecturers in Latin, Greek, Logic, Mathematics, Philosophy, etc. ; and the *University Exercises*, or the attendance of the students, together with the students of other Colleges, in the Public Schools of the University, either to hear the lectures of the University-professors of Greek, Logic, etc.

(which, however, were not incumbent on all students), or to hear and take part in the public disputations of those students of all the Colleges who were preparing for their degrees.

'After four hours or more so spent, the students dined together at twelve o'clock in the Halls of their respective Colleges. After dinner, there was generally again an hour or two of attendance on the declamations and disputations of contending graduates either in College or in the Public Schools. During the remainder of the day, with the exception of attendance at the evening service in Chapel, and at supper in the Hall at seven o'clock, the students were free to dispose of their own time. It was provided by the statutes of Christ's that no one should be out of College after nine o'clock from Michaelmas to Easter, or after ten o'clock from Easter to Michaelmas.'[59]

The rules governing the daily conduct of the students were extremely strict. 'While in residence, the students were confined closely within the walls of their respective Colleges, leaving them only to attend in the Public Schools. At other times, they could only go into the town by special permission; on which occasions no student below the standing of a *B.A.* in his second year was suffered to go unaccompanied by his tutor or by a Master of Arts. In their conversation with each other, except during the hours of relaxation in their chambers, the students were required to use either Latin, or Greek, or Hebrew.

When permitted to walk into the town, they were forbidden to go into taverns, or into the sessions ; or to be present at boxing-matches, skittle-playings, dancings, bear-fights, cock-fights, and the like ; or to frequent Sturbridge fair ; or even to loiter in the market or about the streets.

' In their rooms they were not to read irreligious books ; nor to keep dogs or "fierce-birds" ; nor to play at cards or dice, except for about twelve days at Christmas, and then openly and in moderation. To these and other rules obedience was enforced by penalties. There were penalties both by the College and by the University, according as the offence concerned the one or the other. The penalties consisted of fines according to the degree of the offence ; of imprisonment for grave and repeated offences ; of rustication, with the loss of one or more terms, for still more flagrant misbehaviour ; and of expulsion from College and University for heinous criminality. The Tutor could punish for negligence in the studies of his class, or inattention to the lectures ; College offences of a more general character came under the cognisance of the Master or his substitute ; and for non-attendance in the Public Schools, and other such violations of the University statutes, the penalties were exacted by the Vice-Chancellor. All the three— the Tutor and the Master as College authorities, and the Vice-Chancellor as resident head of the University —might, in the case of younger students, resort to corporal punishment. . . . In Trinity College there was a regular service of corporal punishment in the Hall every Thursday evening at seven o'clock, in the presence of all the undergraduates, on such junior delinquents as had been reserved for the ceremony during the week. The University statutes also recognised the corporal punishment of non-adult students offending in the Public Schools. At what age a student was to be considered adult is not positively defined ; but the understanding seems to have been, that after eighteen corporal punishments should cease, and that even younger students, if above the rank of undergraduates, should be exempt from it.'[60]

Corpus Christi College was not so badly provided with creature comforts as were some of the other colleges. Archbishop Parker, mindful of the hardships of his own times at the University, did not forget either the necessities, comforts, or even recreations of the students. From time to time he gave large gifts of money for firing, food, and other needful things, not even forgetting to have the college precincts paved, so that the students had not to take their walking exercise on the bare and muddy earth. He also gave money to provide the students with an annual feast, evidently not deeming merriment incompatible with scholastic training.[61] He presented his valuable library of books and manuscripts to the college, and, to ensure its safe-keeping and preservation there, coupled the gift with some costly plate which was only to be retained as long as the manuscripts remained in possession of the college. The indenture of the gift stipulates that 'if six manuscripts in folio, eight in quarto, and twelve in a lesser size, should at any time be lost through supine negligence and not restored within six months, then, with the consent of the Vice-Chancellor and one senior Doctor, not only all the books, but likewise all the plate he gave, shall be forfeited and surrendered to Gonville and Caius College within a month following. And if they should afterwards be guilty of the like neglect, they are then to be delivered over to Trinity Hall, and in case of their default, he appoints them to revert back in the former order.'[62]

Thus carefully did the worthy archbishop not only think out his gifts, but provide for the preservation of his beloved books and manuscripts. So effective has been his safeguard that the presentation plate is still intact: it includes a set of 'Apostle' spoons, which are stated to be one of the only three complete sets known to exist.[63]

After the first feelings of loneliness had passed away the young student would begin to recognise his dignity in cap and gown, and to familiarise himself with the various colleges, especially with the appearance in their midst of the majestic King's. He would behold and loiter by the banks of the famous Cam, and think of his own less-noted Stour at home. Within the precincts of his own college, Marlowe's daily walks would enable him to meet and associate and converse with his fellow-students with less reserve than in Hall. These companions, some

MATTHEW PARKER, ARCHBISHOP OF CANTERBURY

From an oil painting.

PLATE XIV.

known in the past and some to be more or less intimately known in the future, were from all parts of the kingdom, and with their different manners and various subjects of conversation would serve not only to interest but to educate and enlarge his mind.

The daily routine of college life in term time has already been described, but so severe a system of discipline was difficult to maintain. In some colleges it was probably never enforced, and in others was gradually relaxed. 'The rule of not permitting students to go beyond the walls of their Colleges was, also, much modified. Students might be seen wandering in the streets, or walking along the Trumpington Road, with very little security that they would talk Latin on their way, or that, before returning to College, they might not visit the Dolphin, the Rose, or the Mitre. These three . . . were the favourite taverns of Cambridge; "the best tutors," as the fast students said, "in the University." '[64]

Bathing in the Cam, which had been strictly prohibited, was a daily practice, and many amusements the collegians habitually indulged in were forbidden by old decrees, decrees which were forgotten or continually defied. Dramatic entertainments were by no means objected to, but were rather encouraged by the authorities, being 'held necessary for the emboldening of their junior scholars,' as says Thomas Heywood, who at this period was a Fellow of Peterhouse. He states that 'dramatic entertainments were publicly acted, in which graduates of good place and reputation have been specially parted' (*i.e.* given parts).[65]

Bearing upon the subject of dramatic entertainments encouraged by the college authorities, as also upon other matters concerning contemporary University life, such as corporal punishment, the following paragraphs from a Cambridge magazine article, entitled 'An Interrupted Performance,' are of exceptional interest [66] :—

'On the 23rd of February (1583) Dr. Bell, Vice-Chancellor, committed to the Tolbooth for three days, —— Mudd, B.A., of Pembroke Hall, because, in a comedy which he had composed, he had censured and too saucily reflected on the Mayor of Cambridge; and on the 26th of February, —— Mudd, at the command of the Vice-Chancellor, acknowledged his fault before the Mayor and asked his pardon, which was freely granted.

'The Vice-Chancellor also, on the first-mentioned day, committed Evance, a scholar of Pembroke Hall, to prison for three days, because he lay hid when sought for by the Bedel and had neglected to appear; and on the 25th of February he was beaten with rods before all the youth of the University in the Public School Street, because he had propounded scandalous, foolish, and opprobrious questions at the disputations of the questionists, and because he had made an assault with a club and had thrown stones when a play was exhibited in the College of Corpus Christi.'

In the paper from which the preceding paragraphs are extracted, the Rev. Dr. H. P. Stokes points out that the year when these interrupted performances were being held, 'was one of the years when Christopher Marlowe was in residence,' and it may be conjectured that 'he was the author of the dramas of which we unfortunately are not even told the titles.' In the same paper Dr. Stokes remarks how interesting it would be 'if some allusions to the student days of these great poets' (Marlowe and John Fletcher, both Corpus men) 'could have been unearthed from the college records; but when it is remembered that of old in such registers,

> " The evil that men do lives after them,
> The good is oft interred with their bones,"

we may say that "no news is good news."'

Then, as now, the University terms were fixed by the statutes of Elizabeth. The academic year began on the 10th of October, and the first, or Michaelmas term, from that day to the 16th of December. The Christmas vacation of four weeks followed. The second, or Lent term, began on the 13th January and ended on the second Friday before Easter. Then came the Easter vacation of three weeks; followed by the third, or Easter term, extending from the second Wednesday after Easter Sunday to the Friday after 'Commencement Day.' Commencement Day was always the first Tuesday in July, and being held after the great terminating

Assembly of the University, at which the candidates for the higher degrees of the year were said to 'commence' in those degrees. The University long vacation of three months then began.

It may be stated that the order of the curriculum, a very important item of the University career, which students had to comply with at Cambridge, in the Faculty of Arts, lasted over seven years. The first part covered the undergraduate period, extending from the date of admission to the obtaining the B.A. degree; and the second, the period of Bachelorship to the attainment of an M.A. degree.

According to the statutes, as they were then, four years' course of study, that is, twelve full terms of residence in a college, was necessary for the attainment of the B.A. degree, and each year of the four had its appropriate studies. During the fourth year of this period, and generally in the last term, the students who had qualified were required to keep two 'Acts,' or 'Responsions,' and two 'Opponencies,' in the public schools. These proceedings were arranged as follows :—

At the beginning of the academic year, one of the Proctors obtained the names of the students in the different colleges who were desirous that year of competing for the degree of B.A. Soon after the commencement of the Lent term each of these aspirants received notification that in about a fortnight's time he would have to appear as 'Respondent' in the Public Schools. This notification informed him that he must furnish three propositions, generally of a moral or metaphysical nature, which he was prepared to maintain in debate.   Three students of equal standing, from other colleges, were then elected by the Proctor to appear as 'Opponents.'   On the day appointed the Respondents and Opponents met in the Public Schools, and under the presidency of a Master of Arts, and in the presence of an audience of graduates, began the discussion.

A Latin thesis on the selected subject was read by the Respondent, and was answered, to the best of his ability and in the best Latin he could command, by one after the other of the Opponents.   When all the speakers had finished they were dismissed by the President, or 'Moderator' as he was called, with such remarks on their performance as he deemed necessary, and the 'Act' was over.

When a student had passed through two of these exhibitions of argumentative skill he underwent an examination by the officials of his own college, and, if successful, was 'sent up' as a candidate for the B.A. degree.   The selected candidates from all the colleges were then examined for three days, usually in the week before Ash Wednesday, in the Public Schools, before the Proctors and other members of the University.   Those who succeeded in passing this examination were furnished by their colleges with a *supplicat* to the Vice-Chancellor and Senate, praying that they might be admitted *ad respondendum quæstioni*.   A few days later the candidates from each college, headed by one of their Fellows, went up to the public schools, where they had to answer questions out of Aristotle's *Prior Analytics*, and then became 'determiners.' Between then and Palm Sunday they underwent a further course of exercises, and on this last-named day their probation ended, and they were pronounced Bachelors of Arts.[67]

Needless to say that many of the students never attained to this dignity, but after a year or two forsook the University for other occupations. It is a proof of Marlowe's perseverance, as well as ability, that he passed through the ordeal successfully, and in 1584, apparently as early as it was possible for him to have done so, obtained his B.A. degree. The Grace Book thus records the fact: 'Chrōs. Marlyn, *ex coll. corp. chris.* was admitted *ad respondendum questioni.*' His *supplicat* spells the name 'Marlin.' Thos. Harris signs as Prelector.[68]

Although there were, as already pointed out, certain vacations at Christmas and Easter, it was not usual for the students to leave the University at those times. The difficulties of travelling, and, probably, the youth of most of the collegians, caused the enforcement of much strictness in residence, and it was only during the long vacation that scholars from far-away homes had a chance of visiting friends or relatives. Archbishop Parker had, indeed, made a proviso in his agreement with Corpus Christi College that none of his scholars was to be absent

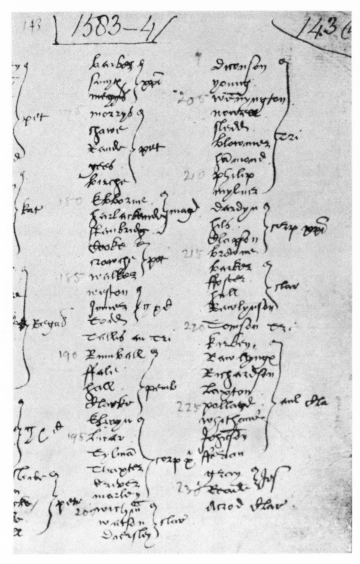

EXTRACT FROM THE GRACE BOOK OF THE UNIVERSITY OF CAMBRIDGE
FOR THE YEARS 1583-4

SHOWING THE B.A.'S OF THAT YEAR IN THEIR SENIORITY. MARLOWE IS NO. 199

PLATE XV.

above a month in the year, and then only with leave ;
and the provisions of the University did not permit of
a student being away from his college above one
month in the year (during the half of which time
only was he to have his allowance), without the
special leave of the Master and Fellows.

Although this restriction, like so many others
which the wisdom or experience of Founders had
made, was gradually allowed to lapse or become
obsolete, it is not probable that lads in the days
of Marlowe had the power, even if they had the
inclination, to disregard it.   That he contrived to
return home to Canterbury from year to year until
he attained his first degree is almost certain, but it
is equally certain that there is no record of his
journey, or his home-coming, or of his reception in
his native city.   His sister Joan was married in
1583 to John Moore, who was in the same kind of
business as her father, and in the same year John
Marlowe took as a new apprentice Elnas (*sic* but perhaps Elias) Martyn or Marlyn.   No further record
of the family is discoverable for some few years. [69]

At Cambridge Kit doubtless formed acquaint-
anceship with members of other colleges than his
own.   The suggestion that he then became friendly
with Thomas Nashe, the subsequent bitter satirist,
and with Robert Greene, the future author, has no
evidence to support it ; and although his name has
so often been coupled with theirs, it will be seen
later on that in all probability he never had any,

or only the slightest, personal acquaintance with either of them.

Hard as the living may have been, and dull the routine of college life in those days, there is plenty of evidence extant to prove that the students indulged occasionally in the fun and frolic natural to youth. Nashe, who took his B.A. degree at St. John's College, in 1584, doubtless referred to some real incident of University life, in which Gabriel Harvey, his long-time enemy, was concerned, when, after exclaiming in his characteristic manner, 'I have terms, if I be vext, laid in steep in aquafortis and gunpowder,' he proceeds to pour his corrosive flood of acrimonious verbosity over the head of the offending Harvey, that 'son of a rope-maker,' as he loved to term him, for having 'had'st thy hood turned over thy ears when thou wert a Batchelor, for abusing of Aristotle, and setting him upon the school-gates painted with ass's ears on his head.'[70]

Robert Greene, also a contemporary at St. John's, avers that deeds of much darker hue were not infrequently committed by Cantabs in his days, and he confesses to having been one of the worst offenders himself, but his catchpenny confessions and trumpery tracts, scribbled off for the purpose of obtaining a few shillings for the temporary relief of his chronic necessities, do not deserve the notice or notoriety they have received. That many of the University decrees and college regulations were set at nought there is abundant testimony; that in some colleges matters of costume were treated after the inclination or vanity of the wearer, instead of in accordance with rule, was self-evident; and that irregularities of many kinds were prevalent was notorious; but there is no proof that the criminalities hinted at by Robert Greene existed. Greene was so generally untruthful, and his descriptions so luridly coloured, that they need not be seriously regarded as typical pictures of University life. His statement that, after he had graduated B.A., he mixed with 'Wags as lewd as myself, with whom I consumed the flower of my youth,'[1] need not be accepted as the behaviour of Cantabs in general, and still less of Marlowe in particular.

The greatest trouble and grief to the authorities was caused by theological differences. On the one hand, says a historian, all serious people complained that 'nicknaming and scoffing at religion and the power of godliness,' and 'debauched and atheistical' principles, prevailed to an extent that seemed 'strange in a University of the Reformed Church'; whilst, on the other hand, the more zealous churchman had special cause of complaint in the increase of puritanical opinions and practices, more particularly in certain colleges, where the heads and senior members were puritanically inclined.

It was represented that upon Fridays and Fast-days, the victualling houses prepared a good store of meat 'for all scholars that will come or send unto them'; that in the churches, both on Sundays and

other days, there was little decency of behaviour,
and the regular forms of prayer were in many cases
avoided; 'instead whereof we have such private
fancies and several prayers of every man's own
making vented among us . . . that our young
scholars are thereby taught to prefer the private
spirit before the public, and their own invented and
unapproved prayers before the Liturgy of the Church.'
In Trinity College it was found that the scholars
'lean or sit or kneel at prayers, every man in a
several posture as he pleased; at the name of Jesus
few will bow; and when the Creed is repeated, many
of the boys, by some men's directions, turn to the
west door.'[72]

In most of the colleges something was always
discoverable by critical observers calling for
animadversion. Some of the collegians were too
puritanical and others too free-thinking. 'Atheist'
was the favourite appellation to bestow upon every
one whose theological views did not coincide with
the speaker's, or the writer's, as the case might be.
Roman Catholic so styled Protestant and Protestant
termed Roman Catholic so, whilst all Dissenters
from the Church as by State established, obtained
the same cognomen. The result of all this was
that the students who thought for themselves
became Freethinkers, or Roman Catholics, or
Puritans, as they were led by their natural instincts,
or were influenced by their favourite authors or
leaders.

In the midst of all this conflict of opinion and seething mass of speculative theology what was Marlowe doing? The attainment of his B.A. degree naturally allowed him somewhat more licence of word and deed than in his undergraduate days, but, if he intended to commence Master of Arts, there was still much to be done, and without it his original idea of taking Holy Orders might have to be abandoned.

By the original statutes of the University those students who intended to advance beyond the B.A. degree were required to reside three more years there, and during that time to go through certain higher courses of study, and perform certain fresh Acts in the Public Schools and colleges. These regulations having been complied with, the scholars were, after being examined and after having performed certain other formalities, ceremoniously created Masters of Arts.

It was not often possible, as authorities admit, 'consistently with the demands of the public service for men of education, that all scholars who had taken their B.A. degree should thereafter continue to reside as punctually as before during the three additional years required for their M.A. degree . . . hence, despite of oaths, there had been gradual relaxations,'[73] but, although these relaxations may have commenced in Marlowe's time, there is really nothing to show that he did not continue residence in his college until the expiration of the six years or so allotted to him. It is possible that during the whole of that period he may not have been the immaculate plodding scholar that the most exacting tutor might have desired, but there is nothing known or shown to the contrary. That he was a devoted student, thirsting 'after knowledge infinite' his labours prove, whilst the degrees he acquired show also that he conformed with the rules and regulations of the University.

Marlowe's academic studies must have been alternated and supplemented by translations from Latin poets, and in the composition of English verse, for which latter he had but few models to follow. Chaucer and his following were too antiquated; the dramatists, predecessors or contemporaries, were too stilted, rough, and essentially unpoetic to attract him ; whilst Spenser had done nothing to make himself known to him as yet. Naturally, he turned to the Latin and Greek poets, and for a time must have lovingly studied both them and their versification. His translation of Ovid's *Elegies* has indeed been thought to be due to this early period of his career, and some of his poetic productions must have been executed during his residence at Cambridge ; the *Amores* was doubtless one of the earliest.

Dyce considers 'this version of the *Amores* does little credit either to Marlowe's skill as a translator, or to his scholarship,' yet is forced to acknowledge that it 'is occasionally spirited and flowing.' Fortunately, Marlowe's reputation, if not enhanced by the posthumous publication of this translation, is in no need of it to complete his fame, and a later writer deems 'it is a spirited translation though the inaccuracies are manifold; in licentiousness, it is a match for the original.'[74] The version was evidently that of a young man, and, even if when written intended for publication, it was kept out of sight in Marlowe's more mature life, and probably was never intended for the publicity it ultimately obtained. It may be asserted, however, that this translation is highly spirited and fluent, and far in advance, as regards poetic power, of almost every, if not all, previous versified English translations from foreign languages. In those days the 'licentiousness' would scarcely cause surprise or invoke literary animadversion.

It has been a matter of much speculation as to how Marlowe was employed after taking his bachelor's degree. It is utterly useless to picture him, as Colonel Cunningham does, trailing a pike in the wars, or, as with equal probability might be suggested, sailing about the Indian seas with his worthy namesake and possible kinsman, Captain Edmund Marlowe, who was so well spoken of by his contemporaries.[75] All such theories are idle imaginings, and there is not an iota of evidence to prove or even suggest that Kit ever left his native land.

That Marlowe was ever an actor, as suggested by a pseudo-antique ballad, is quite as unlikely. The name of probably every grown actor of his epoch has been preserved and printed, and had he ever trod the stage it may be assumed as a certainty that those who sneered at him living, and slandered him dead, would have gleefully referred to the fact. His two scholarships would have provided him with the wherewithal to live whilst he continued in residence at the University, and during the seven years or so that he was on the college books, it is equally certain that in case of need his income could have been supplemented by the Chapter at Canterbury, the members of which would not have hesitated to help a pupil from the King's School needing assistance and showing deserts. If he had still wanted any addition to his slender income, and always admitting that none of his relatives was able or willing to aid him, he could have followed the example of some of his college contemporaries, such as George Peele, and have taught the younger students; but there is little probability that such an addition to his income was sought or needed.

Marlowe's academic studies would necessarily occupy a fair amount of his time during the three years he was expected to remain in residence between the attainment of his B.A. degree and his proceeding in 1587 to the higher distinction of M.A. Before the attainment of this latter degree, which could not have been acquired even in those days without much hard study, Marlowe had undoubtedly devoted some of his time to poesy. He must also have visited and mingled with the literary society of London. Rare as his journeys to the metropolis may have been, and to Canterbury still rarer, there is no doubt that by 1587 the young poet had visited London more than once, and renewed or made acquaintance with several of its leading literati, and must have been introduced into the coteries to which they belonged.

There is no doubt that the Universities, both of them, were at this period hotbeds of seditious doctrines. Freethought was becoming prevalent, especially amongst the educated classes, and therefore particularly in the Universities. As long as such opinions were regarded as mere philosophical problems they were held as harmless, but directly they impugned anything theological or political that was State established, there was no mercy for their holder. To think but not to speak was the only plan of avoiding the axe, the brand, or, at best, years of imprisonment. Thomas Harriott, the great mathematician and astronomer, writing to Kepler, deplores having to live at a period in which it is impossible to express one's views freely. Francis Kett, who left Corpus Christi College in 1580, about the time Kit entered, having acquired some fantastic notions regarding the Trinity,[76] and being evidently insane, was mad enough to state his views publicly. He was arrested, accused of heresy, tried, condemned for his unorthodox doctrine, and burned to death ; a fate shared by many others of that era.

That Marlowe, a man of illimitable imagination and of the clearest intellect, would be bound by the rules and tenets of a creed defined by human law could not be expected. That he eventually condemned and denied the dogmas of contemporary theologians is more than probable, but that he so far committed himself as to put his views into print, otherwise than as the opinions of his dramatic characters—as those of people of a different clime and race—there is no proof. At this period of his career it is scarcely likely that the seeds of freethought, sown by the discussions around him, had as yet germinated deeply in his mind. Poetry more than theology would doubtless sway his thoughts in those days.

Marlowe worked so well that by 1587 he commenced Master of Arts, as shown by the University records : Chrōs. Marley (and so spelt in his *supplicat*), ' *ex coll. corp. chri.*, was admitted *ad incipiendum in artibus.*' Signed by Robert Norgate, Master, and Henry Ruse, Prelector.[77] Judging from his position in the list of honours, Marlowe did well, and in later days would have come out among the Wranglers. It may be safely assumed, however, that by this time he had determined to give up the idea of taking Holy Orders ; and the mental conflict portrayed in *Faustus* may be deemed representative of the young man's thoughts at this *Sturm und Drang* epoch in his career. ' Settle thy studies,' stands for Marlowe's own reflection, 'and begin to sound the depth of that thou wilt profess.' In this self-questioning it is readily comprehended that the young poet, having been

EXTRACT FROM THE GRACE BOOK OF THE UNIVERSITY OF CAMBRIDGE FOR THE YEAR 1587

SHOWING THE M.A.'S FOR THAT YEAR IN THE ORDER OF THEIR SENIORITY. MARLOWE IS FIFTH

PLATE XVI.

kept and educated on a pension provided for clerical education, would deem that in honesty he should, 'having commenced, be a Divine in show'; and yet, after further mental examination, see that he should not, thinking as he thought, pretend to expound the dogmas of that State religion in which he could no longer believe.

What could he do ? What should he be ? What profession or calling could he follow to the satisfaction of his own feelings and in all integrity ? Current Philosophy could not satisfy his aspirations nor Logic his ambition. The discussions of the schools appeared but paltry to a mind 'still climbing after knowledge infinite.' Medicine had no attraction for him :

> 'Couldst thou make men to live eternally,
> Or, being dead, raise them to life again,
> Then this profession were to be esteemed ';

but seeing how poor its proudest triumphs were he bade Physic farewell.

Neither had Jurisprudence any charm for him ; what is it at best but

> ' A petty case of paltry legacies !
> Such is the subject of the Institute
> And universal body of the Law.
> This study fits a mercenary drudge,
> Who aims at nothing but external trash ;
> Too servile and illiberal for me ! '

This being the sum of his reflections his thoughts return to the Church. 'When all is done Divinity is best !' But his mind cannot rest here. How reconcile the teaching of the Scriptures with the illusive doctrines of Christianity ? 'The reward of Sin is death,' and yet 'if we say that we have no sin we deceive ourselves and there's no truth in us. Why then, belike we must sin, and so consequently die! Ay, we must die an everlasting death.' How can such contradictions be reconciled? No more of Divinity!

Marlowe's idea of Holy Orders having been abandoned, and all the professions condemned, the only occupation open to him was literature. He would not, however, attempt to clothe the dry bones of Philosophy with learning ; nor retell the lying legends styled History; nor the still more fabulous myths of Biography; nor disquisitions on classic lore. He would be a poet! Not one who wrote sonnets 'to his mistress's eyebrow,' or indicted ponderous epics, but one who would stir the heart of the nation, rouse the spirit of the people by doing what some of his contemporaries were then attempting to do, but which he could do so much better! He would produce dramas!

> 'O what a world of profit and delight,
>   Of power, of honour, of omnipotence,
>   Is promised to the studious!'

Be an author, a dramatic poet, and have dominion far beyond that of emperors and kings ; have power that 'stretcheth as far as doth the minds of man.' Such evidently were Marlowe's self-communings and such the resolution he must have arrived at. So all thoughts of Holy Orders were abandoned, his dear old college bade good-bye, and Cambridge and her endowments forsaken for the new life.

RICHARD BOYLE, EARL OF CORK

After a portrait at Chatsworth.

PLATE XVII.

CHAPTER III

No promise or hope of preferment would have been needed to draw Marlowe to London, the centre of literary activity as well as of political affairs. That he intended to rely upon his literary abilities for fame and fortune is self-evident. He was not the sort of man likely to look for the help of others to make a career for him, although most of his school and college associates had already migrated to the metropolis, and could prove service-able in time of need, should such ever arise. Amongst old Cambridge companions there was Richard Boyle, who had been destined for the Bar, but who, finding he was unable to support himself at that, had forsaken Jurisprudence, and had, as he records in his *Remembrances,* 'put myself into the service of Sir Roger Manwood, Lord Chief Baron . . . where I served as one of his clerks.'[78]

It was probably through the Boyles, or some of his Canterbury friends, that Marlowe made the acquaintance of Roger Manwood. Like so many of Marlowe's associates, Manwood was of Kentish extraction, having been born at Sandwich, where

his father was in business as a draper, and of
which place his grandfather had been twice mayor,
and, in 1523, its parliamentary representative. Soon
after he had been called to the Bar, Roger Manwood
was appointed Recorder of Sandwich and then elected
to represent that ancient Cinque Port in Parliament.
In 1578 he had been made Lord Chief Baron of the
Exchequer, was knighted, and was in great favour
at Court. Evidently he was a very desirable
acquaintance for a young man having to make his
position in the world, and there is every reason to
believe that he was on friendly terms with the poet.
It is worth notice that in early life the future judge
had displayed his dramatic proclivities by appearing in
the character of the 'Lord Chief Baron,' in the masque
of *Palaphilos*, at the Inner Temple revels of 1561.

When the Lord Chief Baron Manwood died in
December 1592, Marlowe composed the following
epitaph on him :

> 'In obitum honoratissimi Viri, Rogeri Manwood, Militis,
> Quæstorii Reginalis Capitalis Baronis.
>
> *Noctivagi terror, ganeonis triste flagellum,*
> *Et Jovis Alcides, rigido vulturque latroni,*
> *Urna subtegitur.   Scelerum, gaudete, nepotis !*
> *Insons, luctifica sparsis cervice capillis,*
> *Plange ! fori lumen, venerandæ gloria legis,*
> *Occidit : heu, secum effœtas Acherontis ad oras*
> *Multa abiit virtus.   Pro tot virtutibus unt,*
> *Livor, parce viro ; non audacissimus esto*
> *Illius in cineres, cujus tot millia vultus*
> *Mortalium attonuit : sic cum te nuntia Ditis*
> *Vulneret exsanguis, feliciter ossa quiescant,*
> *Famaque marmorei superet monumenta sepulchri !*' [79]

The Manwoods were connected by marriage with the Sidneys, one of whom was at King's School at the same time as Marlowe, and with the Walsinghams, another Kentish family, with whom Kit was, or subsequently became, very intimately acquainted. The poet's associations with other persons of note, or influence, or genius, resident in the metropolis, will be referred to later on.

When he came to London Marlowe doubtless brought some of his manuscripts with him. A favourite work amongst English classical students at that time was the *Helenæ Raptus* of Coluthus. Several Latin editions of it had recently appeared, and, so say the Coxeter MSS., Marlowe translated it into English in 1587. His version is authoritatively stated to have appeared in 1595, but no copy of the work is known to exist. Before he left Cambridge he must have been engaged upon dramatic writing, and when he arrived at the metropolis he doubtless had with him the original draft of *Tamburlaine*. The drama had been completed by 1587, as it was produced upon the stage in that year.[80]

Whatever Marlowe's position or means may hitherto have been, the great success which this drama immediately attained made his fame if not his fortune, and procured him the friendship of several persons of rank and reputation. With the leading literati of the period he naturally became acquainted. George Chapman, the translator of

Homer, became his trusty friend, and to be a friend of Chapman was a good reputation in itself, for he bore an unblemished character amongst his contemporaries. He was described by Wood as of 'reverend aspect and graceful manners, religious and temperate.' Chapman was also on intimate terms with Spenser, Shakespeare, Matthew Roydon, and all the most famed poets of the time; and with the Walsinghams, to whom several of his books were dedicated.[81]

The work that made Marlowe famous, famous 'not for an age but for all time,' was *Tamburlaine*. Although it was produced by 1587, the first known edition of it did not appear in print until 1590. By the latter date, the author of the play was noted and well known to all, but, for a reason doubtless deemed best by the publisher, no author's name was given on the title-page. Richard Jones, who published *Tamburlaine* and many of the earliest known works of various writers of repute, is described by Thomas Lodge as 'a needie pirate'; whilst Nicholas Breton declared he was 'an unfair dealer'; so that Marlowe is scarcely likely to have reaped much benefit from the man's enterprise. The title-page of the first known edition of the work reads as follows:

'*Tamburlaine the Great, who, from a Scythian Shephearde by his rare and woonderfull Conquests, became a most puissant and mightye Monarque. And (for his tyranny and terrour in Warre) was tearmed The Scourge of God. Devided into two Tragicall*

*Discourses, as they were sundrie times shewed upon
Stages in the Citie of London. By the right honor-
able the lord Admyrall, his servauntes. Now first
and newlie published. London. Printed by Richard
Jhones: at the sign of the Rose and Crowne neare
Holborne Bridge. 1590.'*

The 'two Tragicall Discourses' referred not only
to *Tamburlaine* as it originally appeared, but also to
a second play, or sequel, evidently produced in hot
haste by Marlowe in consequence of the great and
immediate popularity of his first production. This
continuation is thus set forth on the half-title of the
second part of the 1590 edition :

' *The Second Part of the bloody Conquest of mighty
Tamburlaine. With his impassionate fury, for the
death of his Lady and love faire Zenocrate: his
fourme of exhortacion and discipline to his three
sons and the maner of his own death.*'

The appearance of *Tamburlaine* created a new era
in and produced a deep and lasting impression on the
literature of England. The blank verse in which
the drama was written, ' Marlowe's mighty line,'
as Ben Jonson described it, created a revolution
in English poetry. Hitherto nothing worthy the
name of blank verse had appeared in the language ;
the unrhymed lines which one or two renovators had
timidly substituted for the prevalent ' jigging veins of
rhyming mother wits ' gave no forecast of the magnificent music, the sonorous sound with which the
advent of this burst of rhymeless rhythm startled

the town. 'At a touch of the master's hand the heavy-gaited verses took symmetry and shape. That the blank verse of *Tamburlaine* left much to be desired in the way of variety is undeniable. Its sonorous music is fitted rather for epic than dramatic purposes. . . . Later, Marlowe learned to breathe sweetness and softness into his "mighty line," to make the measure that had thundered the threats of Tamburlaine falter the sobs of a broken heart.'[82]

This drama of the young poet—he was but three-and-twenty—produces an impression of having been wholly and solely the work of Marlowe, written without the assistance of any collaborateur, and without having been modified by the subsequent insertion of extraneous or added matter. Even if the published copy were pirated, the drama seems entirely by Marlowe, and palpably the product of a young, unrestrained, impetuous genius, with all the glow of youth about it. The reader feels as if in personal contact with the hero, identifying him with the author himself. Tamburlaine is the incarnation of audacious ambition and endowed with invincible faith in himself and in his fortune. Inspired with the conviction that earthly glories are more real than spiritual, earthly pomp more substantial than priestly promise—with what intense scorn does the ever-triumphant Tamburlaine regard conquered kings frantically appealing to their deaf, dumb deities! With what audacity does he question ancient faiths and scoff at time-honoured superstitions! Priests and their prayers had ofttimes been scoffed at, defeated monarchs been derided, but in such cases it had ever been the individual, and not the system, who had been contemned. Now, for the first time, did undaunted genius dare to question the credibility of creeds and the divine right of kings! With ruthless and insolent logic did Tamburlaine expose the imaginary strength of all these spiritual things as compared with the material results of human power!

Judged by any English play previously produced the results were marvellous. Nothing existed, either by predecessor or contemporary, with which it could be compared. Even the mere mechanical skill with which it was constructed was so great an advance upon the work of other men. His contemporaries were still using alliteration, the rusty old weapon bequeathed to them by their forefathers, without regarding its force or fitness, but in Marlowe's hands it became a plastic thing of power and beauty.

Marlowe's conception of his hero, with his infinite ambition, his inordinate lust of dominion, and unbounded belief in his own victorious destiny, was wholly his own. The mere story may have been due to the old chroniclers, to recent English translations from Pedro Mexia and Petrus Perondinus; but neither the Castilian of the one, nor the Latin of the other, gave hints of the character created by Marlowe.

Tamburlaine's tall stature and 'his joints so strongly knit' may have been suggested by one author, or even several; but this marvellous warrior, almost a demi-god, 'threatening the world with high astounding terms'—terms which would be almost ludicrous were they not foreshadowings of such terrible realities —was the conception and design of none but the gentle, kind, youthful Cantab. No one save Marlowe, and he only by the gift of his rare genius, has ever exalted to real grandeur the vulgar lust of earthly power, until it becomes 'like his desire, lift upward and divine.' He sets forth Tamburlaine's aspirations for sovereignty over his fellowmen in these lines :

> 'Nature . . .
> Doth teach us all to have aspiring minds :
> Our souls, whose faculties can comprehend
> The wondrous architecture of the world,
> And measure every wandering planet's course,
> Still climbing after knowledge infinite,
> And always moving as the restless spheres,
> Wills us to wear ourselves, and never rest,
> Until we reach the ripest fruit of all,
> That perfect bliss and sole felicity,
> The sweet fruition of an earthly crown.'

The bathos of the conclusion, even if it be correctly transcribed, and if no connecting lines have fallen out, cannot destroy the grandeur of the poet's aspirations, 'still climbing after knowledge infinite.' That he did intend the splendours of sovereignty to be glorified is confirmed by other passages in his writings; as in the reply of Theridamas to Tambur-

laine's question, ' Is it not passing brave to be a
king ? '—

> ' A god is not so glorious as a king.
> I think the pleasures they enjoy in heaven,
> Cannot compare with kingly joys on earth.—
> To wear a crown, enchased with pearl and gold,
> Whose virtues carry with it life and death ;
> To ask and have ; command and be obeyed ;
> When looks breed love ; with looks to give the prize :
> Such power attractive shines in princes' eyes ! '

And in *Henry the Sixth* he reverts to the felicity
of sovereignty :

> ' How sweet a thing it is to wear a crown,
> Within whose circuit is Elizium,
> And all that poets feign of bliss and joy.'

The involved metaphors of Marlowe's response to
his self-set query, 'What is Beauty?' somewhat shroud,
yet cannot nullify the poetry. It would be difficult,
if not impossible, in the whole range of poetic literature to find a passage so nearly expressing the poet's
aspirations to unburden his longings in words :

> ' If all the pens that ever poets held
> Had fed the feeling of their masters' thoughts,
> And every sweetness that inspired their hearts,
> Their minds, and muses on admirèd themes ;
> If all the heavenly quintessence they still [1]
> From their immortal flowers of poesy,
> Wherein, as in a mirror, we perceive
> The highest reaches of a human wit ;
> If these had made one poem's period,
> And all combined in beauty's worthiness,
> Yet should there hover in their restless heads
> One thought, one grace, one wonder, at the least,
> Which into words no virtue can digest.'

---

[1] Distil.

Corrupt though these lines may be from what he originally wrote, they accord with Marlowe's frequently overwrought endeavours to 'wreak his soul upon expression.'

Tamburlaine's ever-restless striving to do deeds never dared before are but expression of the poet's own aspiration, and serve to make the portrait autobiographical. Is not self-revelation made in such words as these?—

> ' Shall we wish for aught
> The world affords in greatest novelty
> And rest attemptless, faint and destitute ? '

There is little or no plot in *Tamburlaine*. The drama is scarcely more than a series of living pictures, depicting this Scythian peasant overthrowing one mighty monarch after another, and 'scourging kingdoms with his conquering sword.' It does indeed require 'a great and thundering speech,' such as Tamburlaine's, to bring haughty monarchs and martial leaders to the knowledge of their helpless abasement, when they fall into the merciless hands of 'the scourge of God.'

The play of *Tamburlaine* is beset with passages pregnant with beauty and splendour, or typical of the author's overweening self-confidence. This idiosyncrasy becomes truly magnificent in the audacious speeches of the Scythian shepherd.

> ' But since they measure our deserts so mean,
> That in conceit bear empires on our spears,
> Affecting thoughts coequal with the clouds,

he exclaims of his Persian opponents, and to their leader, whom he would win to his cause, he asserts :

> ' I hold the Fates bound fast in iron chains,
> And with my hand turn Fortune's wheel about :
> Sooner shall the sun fall from his sphere,
> Than Tamburlaine be slain or overcome.'

His ambition becomes truly sublime by its intensity ; his grandiloquence is too grand to be bombastic. How lofty and impressive is Marlowe's description of his hero, of this low-born Scythian :

> ' Valiant Tamburlaine, the man of fame . . .
> Of stature tall and straightly fashionèd,
> *Like his desire lift upward and divine.*
> So large of limbs, his joints so strongly knit,
> Such breadth of shoulders as might mainly bear
> Old Atlas' burden . . .
> .   .   .   .
> Pale of complexion, wrought in him with passion,
> Thirsting with sovereignty and love of arms ;
> His lofty brows in folds do figure death,
> And in their smoothness amity and life ;
> About them hangs a knot of amber hair,
> Wrappèd in curls, as fierce Achilles' was,
> On which the breath of Heaven delights to play,
> Making it dance with wanton majesty.
> His arms and fingers, long, and sinewy,
> Betokening valour and excess of strength ;—
> In every part proportioned like the man.'

Unlike Shakespeare, who generally draws his similitudes from homely themes and popular lore, Marlowe's magnificent comparisons are with classic subjects, or, what is so remarkable for the period, with astronomical objects and the processes of Nature, many of them doubtless suggested by conversations

with, and perusal of recent works by, the class of
men he had already made the acquaintance of in
London, and to whom further reference will be made
in the course of this narrative.

A representative passage is :

> ' As when the seaman sees the Hyades
> Gather an army of cimmerian clouds,
> (Auster and Aquilon with wingèd steeds,
> All sweating, tilt about the watery heavens,
> With shivering spears enforcing thunder-claps,
> And from their shields strike flames of lightening)
> All-fearful folds his sails and sounds the main,
> Lifting his prayers to the Heavens for aid
> Against the terror of the winds and waves.'

Lines oft referred to by his contemporaries, descriptive of Tamburlaine's inexorable will, are the
following :

> ' The first day when he pitcheth down his tents,
> White is their hue, and on his silver crest,
> A snowy feather spangled white he wears,
> To signify the mildness of his mind,
> That, satiate with spoil, refuseth blood.
> But when Aurora mounts the second time
> As red as scarlet is his furniture ;
> Then must his kindled wrath be quenched with blood,
> Not sparing any that can manage arms.
> But if these threats move not submission,
> Black are his colours, black (his) pavilion ;
> His spear, his shield, his horse, his armour, plumes,
> And jetty feathers, menace death and hell ;
> Without respect of sex, degree, or age,
> He razeth all his foes with fire and sword.'

In *Tamburlaine*, written with the freshness of
youth, Marlowe not only gives untrammelled scope
to his imagination, but bares his very inmost mind

to our gaze, dauntlessly proclaiming by the mouths of his dramatic puppets his own opinions. He does not dissemble his views on theological matters, or on statecraft, or on rulers. His thoughts are set forth as freely as he would have men's speech to be. Under the guise of a self-seeking despotism, Tamburlaine, as 'The Scourge of God,' is beheld not only overthrowing but exposing the impotence of human creeds and the instability of regal institutions. Ancient monarchies crumble, as fabrics of cards, before the lowly-born peasant-warrior; and the supernatural powers claimed by priests dissolve like clouds before the potence of his material might. These were, indeed, new and dangerous suggestions to make, even by the voices of dramatic characters, in his time and clime. In his fight for freedom of thought, an attempt which his contemporaries failed not to recognise and animadvert upon, Marlowe did not shrink from reference to Christians 'Ringing with joy their superstitious bells,' any more than he did from deriding the powerlessness of 'Mighty Jove and holy Mahomet' to protect their peoples against the ill strokes of Fortune. But Marlowe does not abjure faith in one chief supreme deity—'First mover of that sphere . . . the glorious frame of Heaven!'— although he intimates again and again, through the intervention of his dramatic characters, that to die is not 'perchance to dream,' but to 'slumber eternally'; the freed soul may be 'resolved in liquid air,' and 'I am assured that death ends all.'

This youthful ringleader of free thought, this champion of revolutionary upheaval against countless centuries of mental oppression, not only flings his broken gyves into the face of time-honoured Monarchy and long-revered Belief, but, as becomes a son of the soil, proclaims to down-trodden aspirants :

> 'Your births shall be no blemish to your fame,
>   For virtue is the fount whence honour springs';

and :

> 'I . . .
>   Shall give the world to note for all my birth,
>   That virtue solely is the sum of glory,
>   And fashions men with true nobility!'

Such a man needs no oaths to ratify his word.   He asserts :

> 'My friend, take here my hand,
>   Which is as much as if I swore by Heaven,
>   And called the gods to witness of my vow.'

In his passionate love of beauty, his strenuous striving for freedom of thought, his contempt for worldly aggrandisement, and his lofty conception of personal honour, Marlowe appears to be but little in sympathy with his age and surroundings.   His words and thoughts are so noble, and his sentiments so lofty, that the mind revolts at seeing his name coupled with the debauched and dissolute desperadoes it has been customary to link it with.

Judged by the standards of later times, there is, of course, much in *Tamburlaine* open to criticism and many blemishes to blame.   The bombast with which the play is deemed to be stuffed, the exaggeration

'carried sometimes to the verge of burlesque,' may
be true; but, as Mr. A. H. Bullen acknowledges,
'there is nothing mean or trivial in the invention,'
and that is what was felt at once by Marlowe's contemporaries. 'The young poet,' he adds, 'threw into
his work all the energy of his passionate nature. He
did not pause to polish his lines, to correct and curtail;
but was borne swiftly onward by the wings of his
imagination. The absence of chastening restraint is
felt throughout, and, indeed, the beauty of some of
the most majestic passages is seriously marred by the
introduction of a weak or ill-timed verse.'

Tamburlaine was open to sneers and jeers. Meaner
minds could not rise to Marlowe's height: they
could only see the seamy side of his design. The
language did frequently verge on the bombastic, and,
at times, may have hovered on the boundary-line
between the sublime and the ridiculous; yet, taken
for all in all, presented a nobler, grander, statelier,
and more poetic drama than England had yet seen.
With all its faults, it was, says Dyce, 'undoubtedly
superior to all the English tragedies which preceded
it; superior to them in the effectiveness with which
the events are brought out, in the poetic feeling which
animates the whole, and in the verve and variety of
the versification. . . . Not a few passages might be
gleaned from *Tamburlaine* as grand in thought, as
splendid in imagery, and as happy in expression, as
any which his later works contain,' or, it may be added,
are contained in the works of any other dramatist.

F

A reason why critical opinions coincide so closely with regard to the merits of *Tamburlaine*, as they do also with regard to those of *Edward the Second*— Marlowe's last work—is certainly due to the fact that the text of both dramas is the least corrupt of his plays ; both have been preserved nearly in the condition in which they left their maker's hand, untinkered and unadded-to by the pens of meaner men.

Of course contemporary stage-managers could not afford to ignore 'such conceits as clownage keeps in pay,' and the usual buffooneries of the period had to be foisted in between the acts, either by the players, or by the management. Joseph Hall (Bishop of Exeter) in his satire, *Virgidemiarum*, referring to the absurdity and vulgarity of these distracting interludes, draws particular attention to them in connection with *Tamburlaine*. The author of this drama was, he points out :

> ' One higher pitch'd doth set his soaring thought
> On crownèd kings that Fortune hath low brought :
> On some uprearèd, high-aspiring swaine
> As it might be the Turkish Tamburlaine.
> Then weeneth he this base drink-drownèd spright
> Rapt to the three-fold loft of heaven hight,
> When he conceives upon his faignèd stage
> The stalking steps of his great personage,
> Graced with huf-cap termes and thund'ring threats
> That his poor hearer's hayre quite upright sets ' ;

so, to counteract the terror likely to thrill the audience, and as considerate as Bottom, in the

Midsummer Night's Dream, to propitiate their over-strung feelings :

> ' Now least such frightful showes of Fortune's fall
> And bloudy tyrants' rage should chance apall
> The dead-stroke audience, midst the silent rout
> Comes trampling in a selfe-misformed lout,
> And laughs and grins, and frames his mimick face,
> And justles straight into the prince's place :
> Then dothe the theatre eccho all aloud
> With gladsome noyse of that applauding crowd :
> A goodly hoch-poch when vile russettings
> Are matched with monarchs and with mightie kings.'

These lines were written whilst *Tamburlaine* still held possession of the stage, although its author had already passed away.

That Marlowe had any hand in the rubbish these clowns ranted for the benefit of the groundlings is unconceivable, but that he was compelled to submit to the intervention of their fooling is as equally certain.   With reference to such ' gag,' in the 1592 edition of *Tamburlaine* the printer, Richard Jones, prefixed an address ' To the Gentlemen-Readers and Others that take pleasure in Reading Histories,' in which he, or some one over his signature, says, ' I have purposely omitted and left out some fond and frivolous gestures, digressing and, in my poor opinion, far unmeet for the matter, which I thought might seem more tedious unto the wise than any way else to be regarded, though haply they have been of some vain-conceited fondlings greatly gaped at what time they were shewed upon the stage in their graced deformities : nevertheless now to be mixtured in print with such matter of worth, it would prove a great disgrace to so honourable and stately a history. Great folly were it in me to commend unto your wisdoms either the eloquence of the author that writ them, or the worthiness of the matter itself.'

Ben Jonson, who must have smarted as sorely as any of his contemporaries under such inflictions, thus characterises the audiences of the age : the audiences to which the masterpieces of the time had to be submitted :

> ' The wise and many-headed bench that sits
> Upon the life and death of plays and wits,
> (Composed of gamester, captain, knight, knight's man,
> Lady or pucelle, that wears mask or fan,
> Velvet or taffata cap, ranked in the dark,
> With the shop's foreman, or some such brave spark
> That may judge for his sixpence) had, before
> They saw it half, damned thy whole play, and more ;
> Their motives were, since it had not to do
> With vices, which they looked for, and came to.'[83]

The sensation which the production of *Tamburlaine* made was till then unparalleled. It was a new excitement, arousing admiration from some, but from others nothing save envy, hatred, and malice. The contemporary play-writer, Robert Greene, who belonged to one of the wildest sets of the metropolis, and who, although M.A. of Cambridge and an author of works which might have brought him in sufficient wherewithal to live had he been commonly prudent, was at this time a social outcast, and the veriest booksellers' hack.   This man, apparently out of mere envy of the young dramatist's success, whilst his own plays were being damned, conceived an unquench-able hatred of Marlowe.   There is no evidence whatever that Marlowe had any personal knowledge of Greene, beyond the fact of the latter having, in a most libellous manner, in a posthumous tract styled him a 'quondam acquaintance.'

Greene's Groatsworth of Wit, 'that crazy death-bed wail of a weak and malignant spirit,' that pamphlet, letter, libel, or whatever it may be styled, is generally quoted and referred to as if it might be accepted as positive proof against any one, 'without,' as Richard Simpson says, 'making allowance for the ingrained falsehood of the man.   Greene gives us to understand that he and Marlowe were great friends; yet in ad-dressing Marlowe he makes against him the vilest insinuations, and those which we can now read are little in comparison with those which the manuscript probably contained.'[84]   Chettle, who edited the 'copy' for the printer, subsequently stated that he had no personal knowledge of Marlowe, 'whose learning,' he added, 'I reverence,' and had therefore only obtained his character by hearsay.   He declared that when he copied out Greene's manuscript, he 'stroke out what there in conscience I thought he in some displeasure writ; or had it been true, yet to publish it was in-tollerable.'[85]

Robert Greene, whose character was of the very shadiest hue, out of spite through envy, or from some

real or imaginary grievance, could not refrain from
flinging mud at Marlowe, and, later on, at Shakespeare.   Apparently because the productions of the
younger man's genius had displaced Greene's plays
in popular favour, he pursued Marlowe with innuendo
and slander, year by year, until he himself was carried
off by debauchery and disease.   In an epistle prefixed to his *Perimedes*, published in 1588, Greene
would not forbear from recounting how a play of his
had been scorned because, unlike certain 'gentlemen
poets,' 'I could not make my verses jet upon the
stage in tragical buskins, every word filling the mouth
like a fa-burden of Bow-bells, daring God out of
heaven with that atheist, *Tamburlaine* . . . such mad
and scoffing poets that have poetical spirits, as bred
of Merlin's race, if there be any in England, that set
the end of scholarism in an English blank verse,' and
so on.   Merlin is of course a hit at Marlin, as the
poet's name was frequently written, and as Marlowe
was known among his associates by the nickname
of 'Tamburlaine,' as Shakespeare was subsequently
by that of 'Falstaff,' the mischief to be made by this
spiteful reference can be appreciated.

Greene had another fling at his hated and too
successful contemporary in *Menaphon*, registered in
1589.   After a reference to *Tamburlaine*, to intensify
his sneers he goes out of his way to style the story
of a certain love-passage 'a Canterbury tale,' adding
that it had been told by some 'propheticall full mouth
that as he were a Cobbler's eldest sonne, would by

the laste tell where another's shoe wrings.' In his
Farewell to Folly, in 1591, so lasting was his malice,
Greene again sneers at Marlowe. He tells his
'University Readers,' where he deemed the shaft
would rankle deepest, that copies of his (Greene's)
Mourning Garment had so ready a sale that the
pedlar 'found them too dear for his pack, and was
fain to bargain for the life of *Tamburlaine*, to wrap up
his sweet powders in those unsavoury papers.' 'In
the heyday of Marlowe's success in 1588-1591,' says
Richard Simpson, 'Greene was as jealous of him as
he was of Shakespeare in 1592, and for a similar
reason.'[86]

Later on it will be seen how vile and atrocious a
plot this miserable Greene framed, not only to slur
the fame but even to jeopardise the very life of his
illustrious contemporary. He laid the foundation of
all the scandal and calumny which for more than
three centuries have smirched the fair name and fame
of Marlowe, and gave the cue to every literary hack
who sought for an example amongst the great, to
justify the alleged failings of genius.

Naturally the caterers for public amusement sought
out the new luminary, the author of *Tamburlaine*,
and asked for more light; and Marlowe, incited by
the success of his first drama, set to work upon another drama upon the same subject. The Prologue
states:

> 'The general welcomes *Tamburlaine* received,
> When he arrivèd last upon the stage,
> Hath made our poet pen his Second Part.'

The Second Part of Tamburlaine furnishes proof of the haste and want of revision with which it was given to the world. Still more than the original play is it amissing in plot; although generally more sober and subdued in tone, yet in incident, such as there is, it is less restrained. The introduction of captive kings, harnessed to the chariot of Tamburlaine and dragging their conqueror across the stage, is one of the best known, most parodied, and most frequently adverted to of any scene of the Elizabethan drama. Flourishing his whip above the kings, this mighty warrior exclaims:

> ' Holla, ye pampered jades of Asia!
> What can ye draw but twenty miles a day,
> And have so proud a chariot at your heels,
> And such a coachman as great Tamburlaine!'

Intermixed with the most sacred names of Christianity are those of Mohammedanism, and of the heathen deities of Greek and Latin mythology, in a manner which would appear grotesque or profane to modern spectators. Thus the hero, welcoming his 'loving friends and fellow-kings,' exclaims:

> 'If all the crystal gates of Jove's high court
> Were opened wide, and I might enter in
> To see the state and majesty of Heaven,
> It could not more delight me than your sight.'

And in the lines where the King of Natolia alludes to the gross treachery and perjury of the Christian princes, there is a curious mingling of Christianity and Heathendom:

' Can there be such deceit in Christians,
  Or treason in the fleshly heart of man,
  Whose shape is figure of the highest God !
  Then, if there be a Christ, as Christians say,
  But in their deeds deny him for their Christ,
  If he be son to ever-living Jove,
  And hath the power of his outstretchèd arm ;
  If he be jealous of his name and honour,
  As is our holy prophet, Mahomet ;—

  .   .   .   .

  Open, thou shining veil of Cynthia,
  And make a passage from the empyreal heaven
  That he who sits on high and never sleeps,
  Nor in one place is circumscriptible,
  But everywhere fills every continent
  With strange infusion of his sacred vigour,
  May in his endless power and purity,
  Behold and venge this traitor's perjury !
  Thou Christ, that art esteemed omnipotent,
  If thou wilt prove thyself a perfect God,
  Worthy the worship of all faithful hearts,
  Be now revenged upon this traitor's soul,
  And make the power I have left behind,
  (Too little to defend our guiltless lives),
  Sufficient to discomfort and confound
  The trustless force of those false Christians.'

Of course it is a Mohammedan who is supposed to
be speaking, and the passage does not show Marlowe
at his best.

The drama, if drama it may be styled, is full of
splendid passages, but such descriptions as that
where Tamburlaine describes how he purposes to
make his native city of Sarmarcand famous, and the
life he designs for himself there, however suitable for
a poem, do but delay and deaden the action of a
play :

'Then shall my native city, Sarmarcanda,
And crystal waves of fresh Jaertis' stream,
The pride and beauty of her princely seat,
Be famous through the furthest continents,
For there my palace-royal shall be placed,
Whose shining turrets shall dismay the heavens,
And cast the fame of Ilion's towers to hell.
Thorough the streets with troops of conquered kings,
I 'll ride in golden armour like the sun ;
And in my helm a triple plume shall spring,
Spangled with diamonds, dancing in the air,
To note me emperor of the threefold world,
Like to an almond-tree y-mounted high,[87]
Upon the lofty and celestial mount
Of ever green Selinus quaintly decked
With blooms more white than Erycina's brows,
Whose tender blossoms tremble every one,
At every little breath through heaven is blown.
Then in my coach, like Saturn's royal son,
Mounted his shining chariot gilt with fire,
And drawn with princely eagles through the path
Pavèd with crystal and enchased with stars,
When all the gods stand gazing at his pomp,
So will I ride through Sarmarcanda streets,
Until my soul, dissevered from this flesh,
Shall mount the milk-white way, and meet him there.'

The character most successfully depicted in this play is that of Calyphas, one of the three sons of Tamburlaine, and even in this instance it is somewhat doubtful whether Marlowe is speaking in sympathy with, or in disdain of, the opinions of the unmartial-minded prince.   When aroused by his two warlike brothers to assist against the foe, Calyphas, memories of whose sayings evidently dwelt in Shakespeare's mind when he was creating Falstaff, answers thus :

' *Cal.*   Away ye fools! my father needs not me,
Nor you in faith, but that you will be thought
More childish-valorous than manly-wise.
If half our camp should sit and sleep with me,
My father were enough to scare the foe.
You do dishonour to his majesty,
To think our helps will do him any good.

 .   .   .   .   .   .

I know, sir, what it is to kill a man;
It works remorse of conscience in me;
I take no pleasure to be murderous,
Nor care for blood when wine will quence my thirst.

 .   .   .   .   .   .

Go, go, tall stripling, fight you for us both,
And take my other toward brother here,
For person like to prove a second Mars.
'Twill please my mind as well to hear you both
Have won a heap of honour in the field,
And left your slender carcases behind,
As if I lay with you for company.

 .   .   .   .   .   .

Take you the honour, I will take my ease;
My wisdom shall excuse my cowardice.
I go into the field before I need! . . .
The bullets fly at random where they list;
And should I go and kill a thousand men,
I were as soon rewarded with a shot,
And sooner far than he that never fights;
And should I go and do no harm nor good,
I might have harm, which all the good I have,
Joined with my father's crown, would never cure.'

The ostensible origin of the *Second Part* is Tamburlaine's 'impassionate fury for the death of his Lady and love faire Zenocrate.' That 'great Emperess' is a somewhat colourless lady—for Marlowe had not learned to depict a woman—only at rare intervals displaying any individuality, as when she pleads for her father's life, or for the preservation of her native place, or when she bewails the miserable fate of Bajazeth and his consort. Some of the hero's references to her are full of pathos and beauty, and one is not only noteworthy as a foreshadowing of the ever-famed allusion to the Grecian Helen, but as one out of many proofs that Marlowe did repeat himself, all assertions to the contrary notwithstanding, an important fact when recalled to mind in connection with Shakespearian matters :

> ' Her sacred beauty hath enchanted Heaven ;
> And had she lived before the siege of Troy,
> Helen (whose beauty summoned Greece to arms,
> And drew a thousand ships to Tenedos)
> Had not been named in Homer's Iliads.'

Tamburlaine's most touching and most human reference to his beloved is, when told of her death,

> ' Say no more !
> Though she be dead, yet let me think she lives ! '

Among the autobiographical allusions in this drama none is more noteworthy than the poet's continually acknowledged belief in one omnipotent deity, as if to prove that, wavering or distrustful as might be his opinions about many of the tenets of Christianity, on this point his mind and faith were firm.

The popularity of *Tamburlaine* as a play was largely due to the impersonation of the hero by the famous Edward Alleyn. This much admired actor,

the chief favourite of Elizabethan and Jacobean play-
goers, had commenced his dramatic career when a
boy, probably by impersonating female characters, but
no records of this 'prentice period have been discovered.   Having perfected his genius by experience
he was ripe for a suitable part to play, and the
presentation of Tamburlaine afforded him the requisite opportunity.   His acting of the Scythian
monarch captivated the London audiences and helped
to enhance Marlowe's reputation as well as his own.
The appearance of the rough posters of those days
with the announcement of a play having the name of
either Alleyn as the actor or Marlowe as the author,
was sufficient to attract a large audience.[88]

When Alleyn first appeared in Marlowe's drama
he could not have been more than about one-and-
twenty, he having been born in 1566, and the young
man's handsome presence greatly promoted his
success.   His elocutionary powers must have been
unrivalled, for Thomas Heywood, in his Prologue
to a later play by Marlowe, after referring to the
author as 'the best of poets in that age,' states that
Alleyn

> ' Wan
> The attribute of peerless ; being a man
> Whom we may rank with (doing no one wrong)
> Proteus for shape, and Roscius for a tongue,
> So could he speak, so vary :'

and Ben Jonson, who would not flatter, and whose
own elocutionary attainments were famed, after com-

paring Alleyn, to his favour, with the great actors of
Rome, exclaims:

> ' How can so great example dye in mee,
>   That, Allen, I should pause to publish thee?
>   Who both thy graces in thy selfe hast more
>   Outstript, than they did all that went before;
>   And present worth in all dost so contract,
>   As others speake, but onely thou dost act.
>   Weare this renowne; 'tis just, that who did give
>   So many Poets life, by one should live.' [89]

Not only did Alleyn's personal appearance impress
the spectators, but the costumes provided for him
in *Tamburlaine* were by their gorgeous and costly
character calculated to arouse admiration. In his
Diary, Henslowe, the stage-manager and proprietor,
records how much he paid for Alleyn's crimson velvet
breeches, and how much his copper-laced coat cost,
and what was paid for Tamburlaine's bridle, the
bridle used for the harnessed kings. Other curious
stage properties, of which the purchase is recorded,
in connection with Marlowe's dramas, were a cage for
Bajazeth, the 'cauldron' for the *Jew of Malta*, the
dragon for *Faustus*, as, also, 'the city of Rome' and
the Pope's mitre. Cupid's bow and arrows were
doubtless for *The Tragedy of Dido*, but 'Eve's
bodice,' 'Kent's wooden leg,' the 'tree of golden
apples,' 'a rainbow,' and many other strange articles,
were evidently required for the various works of
other dramatists. [90]

The sums of money expended at that period for
certain articles of attire for the actors seem exhor-

bitant. Nineteen pounds was given for a cloak and seven pounds for a gown ; as much money was given by the company for the gown of the heroine, in the *Woman Killed by Kindness*, as was paid to the author, Ben Jonson, for writing the play. Indeed, Drummond records that Ben Jonson informed him he had never gained two hundred pounds for all the plays he had ever produced ! [91]

It is seen from Henslowe's *Diary* that the highest price he ever gave an author for a play was the eleven pounds he paid Jonson and Dekker for *Page of Plymouth*, a murder-tragedy. It is not therefore surprising that whilst players and theatre proprietors amassed fortunes, the authors of the dramas they grew rich by lived and died in penury. When an author, flushed by the receipt of a few hardly won pounds, arrayed himself in new garments, or indulged in a more expensive meal than usual, his improvidence or gluttony furnished an edifying text for a sermon, or subject for a reproachful pamphlet, whilst the well-clothed actor and well-fed stage-manager obtained unstinted meed of praise and respect for the genius of the one or the industry of the other.

When a play became unusually popular, Henslowe's heart was opened and, over and above what he had already paid the author, he would still further encourage him by a gift or royalty of ten shillings ! This magnificent donation he was never known to exceed ; but on rare occasions, and after a very successful performance, he spent a further 'small sum' among the actors in 'good cheer.' Well might even so famous and popular an author as Marlowe lament that

> 'Learning . . .
> And Poverty should always kiss;
> And to this day is every scholar poor:
> Gross gold from them runs headlong to the boor.

> .   .   .   .   .

> That Midas' brood shall sit in Honour's chair,
> To which the Muses' sons are only heir;

> .   .   .   .   .

> And few great lords in virtuous deeds shall joy
> But be surpris'd with every garish toy,
> And still enrich the lofty servile clown,
> Who with encroaching quite keeps learning down.' [92]

Notwithstanding the immense popularity of his dramas, it is worthy of attention that the lofty spirit of Marlowe would not allow him to stoop, as many of his contemporaries did, to palter with obscene puns or pander to the public taste with double-edged words. The translations of his early life followed the thoughts of their originals, but there is not the slightest evidence that he ever intended them for publicity; whilst his dramatic works, which were expressly prepared for public representation, are free from every taint of vicious suggestion. The printer's address, in the 1592 edition of the *Tragical Discourses*, 'to the Gentlemen-Readers and Others that take pleasure in Reading Histories,' explaining the omission from the book of the clown's vulgar interpolations between the acts, doubtless expressed Marlowe's own views upon the subject. The printer's hope that the *Dis-*

courses 'will be now no less acceptable unto you to read after your serious affairs and studies than they have been lately for many of you to see when the same were shewed in London upon stages,' minus the frivolous fooling and often obscene jesting of professional mountebanks, could not but portray the poet's own feelings on the subject.

After the success of his *Tamburlaine* it may be believed, and certainly hoped, that Marlowe visited his family and friends at Canterbury. Even if his parents found it difficult to forget their disappointed hopes with respect to his anticipated clerical career, they must have felt proud of his dramatic fame. Rumours of the popularity of his plays must have reached home, and the confirmation of any written statements he may have sent them must have been some compensation for their frustrated expectations.

At this time the Marlowe family was leading the even tenor of citizen life : John Marlowe, the poet's father, had taken on various lads as apprentices to his business, and in 1583 had, as has been pointed out, married one of his daughters to a citizen of Canterbury. In 1587, Thomas Arthur, the brother of Catherine Marlowe, Kit's mother, is found settled with his wife, Ursula, and a numerous family in the parish of St. Dunstan, Canterbury, at the church of which parish his youngest son, Daniel, was christened on the 19th of March of that year.

In 1588 the fear of a Spanish invasion was spreading all over the country and, especially in

the southern portion of the kingdom, causing great
agitation amongst the inhabitants. Urgent appeals
were made to the people to assist the state in preparing to resist the anticipated attack. The practice
of archery continued to be maintained as a pastime,
the introduction of firearms, heavy, cumbersome, and
uncertain in aim as they were, not having yet super-
seded the favourite national pursuit. One means of
national defence adopted to repel the expected
invasion was the formation of troops of bowmen or
archers. Citizens and countrymen alike volunteered
for service in these troops, and amongst those who
were enrolled, it is interesting to find, was John
Marlowe, evidently the poet's father. In a manuscript muster-roll of the period the name of the
patriotic freeman figures as that of a bowman. In
one of the burgher manuscript records of this
same time evidence of his credit, if not of his position as a citizen, is furnished by an entry, immediately
following one of the 7th April 1588, respecting a
loan of five pounds being repaid by Henry Carre,
'out of Streeter's legacy, which Marley the shoemaker had and delivered in at Candlemas. No. xxx.
R. Eliz.'

In those days, when no banking arrangements
were in force, it was customary for sums of money
to be placed in the hands of persons of good credit
for safe custody until needed, and the above record
testifies that John Marlowe was regarded as a man
of integrity and substance.

CHARLES HOWARD, LORD HIGH ADMIRAL OF ENGLAND,
EARL OF NOTTINGHAM, ETC.

From a contemporary painting.

PLATE XVIII.

CHAPTER IV

THE DRAMATIST

THE next important item in Marlowe's literary life was the production of *Doctor Faustus.* This drama appears to have been originally put upon the stage by the Lord Admiral's men in 1588, although the earliest known reference to its public appearance is the 30th September 1594, in Henslowe's *Diary*, when a revival of it took place, with most gratifying results for the stage proprietor.

Faustus not only sustained but enhanced the author's reputation. As with the other plays of Marlowe it is intended to depict one prominent trait of a character; as in *Tamburlaine* the poet vehemently strove to express the insatiable longing of a warrior—a man apart from the common herd—for kingly power and despotic dominion over the physical bodies of weaker men, so in *Faustus* his intention is to portray the unquenchable thirst of a student to obtain sway over the minds of his fellow-men by mental or spiritual means. In *Faustus* there is no plot, scarcely a tale to tell, and even more than in *Tamburlaine* is the spectator dependent upon a series of scenes, which in this case show the gradual subjugation of a mighty mind by the power of evil passions. From the very commencement of the tragedy, when the hero weighs and finds wanting to satisfy his inordinate desires all the advantages proffered by the leading professions until the terrific ending, the one leading object he has ever in view is the acquisition of 'mind-conquering learning.' The deity he worships, for its power to rule mankind, is 'scholarism'; the word Marlowe was sneered at by Greene for using to describe scholastic knowledge. To acquire full possession of 'Learning's golden gifts,' Faustus is prepared to risk everything, and thus falls an easy prey to the tempter. 'Had I as many souls as there be stars,' is his assertion, 'I'd give them all' to become potent in magical arts, for then I shall be a very demigod, and

> 'All things that move between the quiet poles
> Shall be at my command : emperors and kings
> Are but obeyèd in their several provinces.
>
> .   .   .   .   .   .
>
> But his dominion that exceeds in this
> Stretcheth as far as doth the mind of man.'

What follows in the drama proves that the play of *Faustus* is, perhaps even without the author's direct intention or conception, no more nor less than an impersonation of CONSCIENCE. Even as good or evil, virtue or vice, was personified in the old mystery plays, so has Marlowe, with all his poetic power and genius, given but a spiritualised embodiment of a moral attribute. From time to time, during the progress of this tragedy, a 'Good Angel' and an 'Evil Angel' enter upon the scene and alternately sway the hero's mind by their counsels. In these suggestive promptings of Conscience, which they typify, the Good spirit always succumbs to the Evil, and has ultimately to leave Faustus to his fate. After their first appearance he soliloquises and ponders over the promise made by his malevolent inspirer to make him lord and commander of the terrestrial and celestial elements:

> 'How am I glutted with conceit of this!
> Shall I make spirits fetch me what I please,
> Resolve me of all ambiguities,
> Perform what desperate enterprise I will?
>
> .   .   .   .   .   .
>
> I'll have them read me strange Philosophy,
> And tell the secrets of all foreign kings;
> I'll have them wall all Germany with brass,
> And make swift Rhine circle fair Wertenberg;
> I'll have them fill the public schools with silk,
> Wherewith the students shall be bravely clad;
> I'll levy soldiers with the coin they bring,
> And chase the Prince of Parma from our land,
> And reign sole king of all our Provinces;
> Yea, stranger engines for the brunt of war
> Than was the fiery keel at Antwerp's bridge,
> I'll make my servile spirits to invent.'

Flushed with these fantastic aspirations, he seeks the assistance of two acquaintances who, as he knows, are already students of necromantic arts, and informs them how dissatisfied he is with all the science of the schools:

> 'Philosophy is odious and obscure,
> Both Law and Physic are for petty wits;
> Divinity is basest of the three,
> Unpleasant, harsh, contemptible, and vile.'

Valdes, one of his visitors, assures him,

> 'Faustus, these books, thy wit, and our experience
> Shall make all nations to canonise us.
> As Indian Moors obey their Spanish Lords,
> So shall the spirits of every element
> Be always serviceable to us three;
> Like lions shall they guard us when we please,
> Like Almain Rutters [1] with their horsemen's staves;
> Or Laplarid giants, trotting by our sides;
> Sometimes like women, or unwedded maids,
> Shadowing more beauty in their airy brows
> Than have the white breasts of the Queen of Love.
> From Venice shall they drag huge argosies,
> And from America the golden fleece
> That yearly stuffs old Philip's treasury;
> If learnèd Faustus will be resolute.'

So determined is Faustus to follow their suggestions and his own desires that he asserts,

> 'Ere I sleep I'll try what I can do:
> This night I'll conjure tho' I die therefore.'

That very night, necromantic conjurations having been carried out, Faustus succeeds in getting Mephistophilis, an evil spirit, to visit him. To this being he explains that he is prepared to abjure the dogmas of the faith he has been educated in provided whilst he lives he may have his wish for supernatural powers gratified. After some discourse with this spirit, Faustus wishes to discuss matters of more moment than 'these vain trifles of men's souls,' and demands, 'What is that Lucifer, thy lord?' whereupon this magnificently suggestive dialogue ensues:

[1] German cavalry.

'MEPH. Arch-regent and commander of all spirits.
FAUST. Was not that Lucifer an Angel once?
MEPH. Yes, Faustus, and most dearly loved of God.
FAUST. How comes it then that he is Prince of Devils?
MEPH. O, by aspiring pride and insolence;
  For which God threw him from the face of Heaven.
FAUST. And what are you that live with Lucifer?
MEPH. Unhappy spirits that fell with Lucifer,
  Conspired against our God with Lucifer,
  And are for ever damned with Lucifer.
FAUST. Where are you damned?
MEPH. In Hell.
FAUST. How comes it then that thou art out of Hell?
MEPH. Why this is Hell, nor am I out of it:
  Think'st thou that I who saw the face of God,
  And tasted the eternal joys of Heaven,
  Am not tormented with ten thousand Hells,
  In being deprived of everlasting bliss?
  O Faustus! leave these frivolous demands,
  Which strike a terror to my fainting soul.'

Even these words, wrung from the tortured spirit, do not deter the headstrong Faustus, who bids Mephistophilis learn manly fortitude from him, 'and scorn those joys thou never shalt possess.' He commands him to bear the tidings to great Lucifer that he, Faustus, is prepared to surrender his soul to him, provided that for four-and-twenty years he may be let to

  'Live in all voluptuousness;
  Having thee ever to attend on me;
  To give me whatsoever I shall ask,
  To tell me whatsoever I demand,
  To slay mine enemies, and aid my friends,
  And always be obedient to my will.'

Scarcely, however, has Faustus bound himself to Lucifer than he dares to reflect, 'the God thou

serv'st is thine own appetite,' and in the midst of
his doubts the Good and Evil Angels again manifest
themselves, alternately swaying his racked thoughts
towards penitence or obduracy by their expostula-
tions. Again and again are the warnings of conscience
vainly poured into the deaf ears and dumb heart of
the lost scholar, until finally, persuaded by the
malicious insinuations of the malignant spirit, the unfortunate man once more succumbs to his evil destiny.
In the whole range of English literature it would
be difficult to parallel the impressive beauty of this
portrayal of the scruples and sophistries of a tortured
but enervated conscience. The lessons of this
'mystery,' so far in power beyond all the tedious
'religious comedies' of his theological predecessors,
strike awe into the minds of the most thoughtless.

In the exercise of his newly acquired powers
Faustus, with self-torturing iteration, now demands
of Mephistophilis, really of 'Conscience grim, that
spectre in my path!'[93] 'tell me where is the
place that men call Hell?' causing his mentor to
ejaculate :

> ' MEPH. Where we are tortured and remain for ever :
>   Hell hath no limits, nor is circumscribed
>   In one self place ; for where we are is Hell,
>   And where Hell is there must we ever be :
>   And, to conclude, when all the world dissolves,
>   And every creature shall be purified,
>   All places shall be Hell that is not Heaven.
> FAUST. Come, I think Hell's a fable.
> MEPH. Ay, think so still, till experience change thy mind.
> FAUST. Why, think'st thou then that Faustus shall be damned ?

MEPH. Ay, of necessity, for here's the scroll
      Wherein thou hast given thy soul to Lucifer.
FAUST. Ay, and body too; but what of that?
      Think'st thou that Faustus is so fond to imagine
      That, after this life, there is any pain?
      Tush; these are trifles, and mere old wives' tales.
MEPH. But, Faustus, I am an instance to prove the contrary,
      For I am damnèd, and am now in Hell.
FAUST. How! now in Hell?
      Nay, an this be Hell, I'll willingly be damned here;
      What? walking, disputing, etc.?'

To occupy the ever restless, wavering mind of Faustus, this attendant spirit conjures up sights interesting even to the scholar's palled and over-wrought mind, so that, as he confesses,

    ' And long ere this I should have slain myself,
      Had not sweet pleasure conquered deep despair.
      Have I not made blind Homer sing to me
      Of Alexander's love and Ænon's death?
      And hath not he that built the walls of Thebes
      With ravishing sound of his melodious harp,
      Made music with my Mephistophilis?'

Amongst other distractions, to ween his mind from impending fate, ' to glut the longings of my heart's desire,' and to suffocate ' these thoughts that do dissuade me from my vow,' once more he craves a sight of Helen of Troy, on her appearance exclaiming, in a passage famous wherever the English literature is studied,

    ' Was this the face that launched a thousand ships
      And burnt the topless towers of Ilium?
      Sweet Helen, make me immortal with a kiss!
      Her lips suck forth my soul; see where it flies!—
      Come, Helen, come, give me my soul again.

Here will I dwell, for Heaven is in these lips,
And all is dross that is not Helena.
I will be Paris, and for love of thee,
Instead of Troy, shall Wertenberg be sacked:
And I will combat with weak Menelaus,
And wear thy colours on my plumèd crest:
Yea, I will wound Achilles in the heel,
And then return to Helen for a kiss.
Oh, thou art fairer than the evening air
Clad in the beauty of a thousand stars;
Brighter art thou than flaming Jupiter
When he appeared to hapless Semele:
More lovely than the monarch of the sky
In wanton Arethusa's azured arms;
And none but thou shalt be my paramour!'

Although to some extent the desires of Faustus appear to be gratified, no real satisfaction ensues, and all his joys prove as deceptive as 'Dead Sea apples.' Gradually his conscience becomes more and more enfeebled, until at last his Evil Angel triumphantly declares, 'Faustus never shall repent.'

And so the end approaches. Some scholars, old friends of Faustus, call on him, only to find him in the greatest mental distress. Asked by one what ails him, he responds, 'Ah, my sweet chamber-fellow, had I lived with thee then had I lived still! but now I die eternally. LOOK! comes he not! comes he not!' What Faustus sees is to them invisible, and what he sees is only in 'his mind's eye,' yet to him is none the less real. Power others cannot see holds down the hands he would uplift in prayer, and when he would implore mercy stays his tongue. The time for repentance is past, and Faustus must now pay the penalty of his iniquity. In vain his companions proffer their aid :

> ' 2ND SCHOL. Oh, what shall we do to save Faustus?
> FAUST. Talk not of me, but save yourselves and depart.
> 3RD SCHOL. God will strengthen me. I will stay with Faustus.
> 1ST SCHOL. Tempt not God, sweet friend; but let us into the
>   next room, and there pray for him.
> FAUST. Ay, pray for me, pray for me!'

The sequel is almost too terrible, too heartrending to read, and what it can have been to see acted on a stage, and by such a man as Alleyn, is beyond conception. Rising fresh from the perusal of the awful final scene it scarcely seems incredible that what old Prynne has recorded should have found believers. He affirms that in Queen Elizabeth's time the visible apparition of the Devil appeared 'on the stage at the Belsavage Playhouse (to the great amazement both of the actors and the spectators) whilst they were there prophanely playing *The History of Faustus*, the truth of which I have heard,' avers the old puritan libeller, 'from many now alive, who well remember it, there being some distracted with that fearefull sight.' [94]

It needed no devil from hell to accentuate the horrors of that play. No finer sermon than Marlowe's *Faustus* was ever preached! No more terrible an exposition was ever offered of the ruin man can bring upon himself by permitting his grosser passions to overpower him. With the victim's frightful end before us, so impassioned and yet seeming so true to nature—could nature be so tried—that we would wish to exclude it from our minds; with his agonising cry ringing in our heads; his last despairing shriek echoing in our hearts, we close the book reverently, joining in the solemn monody of Chorus:

> 'Cut is the branch that might have grown full straight,
> And burnèd is Apollo's laurel bough.'

It is most unfortunate that this splendid apotheosis of Conscience has only been preserved in a disfigured and dislocated condition. 'Fond and frivolous' scenes, and the 'conceits of clownage' were foisted in between the sublime phantasies of the poet, to gain plaudits from the groundlings. This grand conception of genius can now only be beheld bedecked with the tawdry habiliments in which hack hirelings of the period attired it. Lines and passages have been left out, and miserable comicalities inserted, so that what has been left for posterity to judge by is but the mutilated torso of a stupendous broken colossus, overgrown by a network of poisonous weed and hideous fungus. Every one of critical capacity must long for, were it possible, the disentanglement of Marlowe's text from these degrading interpolations.

With reference to the introduction of these buffooneries into the midst of such solemn business as *Faustus* contains, one of the latest of Marlowe's editors points out that he 'could not don alternately the buskin and the sock. His fiery spirit walked always on the heights; no ripple of laughter reached him as he scaled the "high pyramides" of tragic art.

But while the poet was pursuing his airy path, the actors at the Curtain theatre had to look after their own interests.   They knew that though they should speak with the tongues of angels, yet the audience would turn a deaf ear unless some comic business were provided.   Accordingly they employed some hack writer, or perhaps a member of their own company, to furnish what was required.   How execrably he performed his task is only too plain.'[95]

Towards the close of 1588 an incident occurred in Marlowe's career, the cause of which cannot be thoroughly explained, although the following details may suggest a plausible reason for it.   As is so well known, the civic authorities of London disapproved of all theatrical entertainments within the metropolis, and during the reign of Elizabeth continually promulgated severe edicts against any such performances taking place within the city boundaries.   This was not altogether due to the puritan element in the corporation, although that had no little to do with the evil repute stage-acting bore among sober-minded citizens, as to the idea that such pernicious enticements allured and led into all kinds of vicious company their apprentices and the youthful members of their households.

Mr. William Prynne's work, *The Player's Scourge or Actor's Tragedie*, is believed to have had not only readers but admirers among the more industrious and godly-minded members of the city companies, and many of them were believers in the author's theory that popular stage-plays were 'the very Pompes of the Divell,' and that the 'profession of Play-poets, of Stage-players; together with the penning, acting, and frequenting of Stage-playes are unlawfull, infamous, and misbeseeming Christians'; are, indeed, as unlawful as 'Dancing, Dicing, Health-drinking,' and such other disgusting proceedings. This being the confirmed opinion of many of the leading citizens, it is not surprising to find that the civic authorities took very stringent measures to prevent their city being contaminated by the presence of actors within its precincts.

In consequence of certain players about this period having been accused of referring to 'matters of Divinity and State, without judgment or decorum,' and contrary to the Queen's commandment that neither 'matters of religion nor of the governaunce of the estate of the commonweale shalbe handled or treated,' Edward Tylney, Master of the Revels, wrote to Lord Burleigh, 'that he utterly mislikes all plays within the city.' Thereupon Lord Burleigh informed the Lord Mayor of Mr. Tylney's displeasure with the companies of players in the service of the Lord Admiral and of Lord Strange, and enjoined him to 'stay them,' which his civic lordship gladly availed himself of the long-desired opportunity to do. He 'sent for both companies and gave them strict charge to forbear playing till further orders. The Lord Admiral's players obeyed; but the Lord Strange's, in a contemptuous manner, went to the Cross Keyes' (in Gracechurch Street) 'and played that afternoon.   Upon which the Mayor committed two of them to the Compter, and prohibited all playing for the future, till the' (Lord) 'Treasurer's pleasure was further known.'[96]

This proceeding on the part of the Lord Mayor shows what power the city authorities exercised within their own jurisdiction, and should throw some light upon an affair in which Marlowe himself bore a principal part.   Meanwhile, in explanation if not in extenuation of the autocratic method exercised by those in authority of dealing with both authors and actors of dramas in those days, it should be pointed out what power, for good or evil, was then exercised by the Stage.   At that time the Stage, to a great extent, possessed the influence which in a later age passed to the Press.   Having no daily journals or other accessible means of rapid and general communication on topics of common interest, the public looked to and found what it wanted in the Stage.   The play supplied references to the political, religious, and social events of the day. Writers and players found their profit in responding to the popular feeling of their audience, and although many times fine and imprisonment rewarded their attempt to meddle with matters of state, they persisted in their efforts.   'Statesmen wanted the Stage to be a mere amusement,' said Richard Simpson, 'to beguile the attention of the hearers from graver matters; the English stage-poets felt they had a higher mission . . . they preached a varied body of philosophy, such as no other pulpit ever equalled.'

In 1591 Sir John Harrington said, with reference to *The Play of the Cards*, 'when some advised it be forbidden, because it was too plain : " They which do that they should not, should hear that they would not." ' Few men in authority had opinions coinciding with Sir John, and nearly all the dramatists, not excluding Shakespeare, had to cut and mutilate and modify their productions to satisfy the requirements of state or civic officials. No man was so bold in his utterances nor so regardless of danger in those days as was Marlowe, and even he was compelled to submit to the power of might.

It is a fair commentary on the light in which the citizens regarded the influence and teaching of the dramatists to cite what Stowe, in his *Survey of London*, records with respect to the corporation's action, some few years earlier than the incident about to be referred to with respect to Marlowe. It being believed that young people, especially the children of well-to-do tradesfolks, were 'inveigled and allured' to listen in playhouses where they heard 'publicly uttered popular and seditious matters, unchaste, uncomely, and unshamfaced speeches,' it was determined to put a stop to such horrors. An Act was accordingly passed by the Common Council wherein it was ordained 'that no play should be acted till first perused and allowed by the Lord Mayor and Court of Aldermen ; with many other restrictions.

. . . But these orders were not so well observed as they should be ; the lewd matters of plays encreased, and they were thought dangerous to religion, the state, honesty of manners, and also for infection in that time of sickness. Wherfore they were afterwards for some time totally suppressed.

'But upon application to the Queen and the Councel they were again tolerated, under the following restrictions : that no plays be acted on Sundays at all, nor on any other holidays till after eveningprayer. That no playing be in the dark, nor continue any such time, but as any of the auditors may return to their dwellings in London before sunset, or at least before it be dark. That the Queen's players only be tolerated, and of them their number and certain names to be notified in the Lord Treasurer's letters to the Lord Mayor, and to the Justices of Middlesex and Surrey. And those her players not to divide themselves in several companies. And that for breaking any of these orders, their toleration cease. But all these prescriptions were not sufficient to keep them within due bounds, but their plays so abusive oftentimes of virtue, or particular persons, gave great offence, and occasioned many disturbances, whence they were now and then stopped and prohibited.'[97]

In view of these various enactments, and many others of a similar character, it is not difficult to comprehend that Marlowe became liable, by the infringement of one of these civic laws, for all kinds

H

of pains and penalties.   He may have rendered himself suspected on account of the language of his *dramatis personæ*, or he may have attempted to uphold the right of the actors to perform, and have even incited them to do so, in spite of the Lord Mayor's attempt to stay them.   Be the cause whatever it may have been, the result was that Marlowe, who was now writing for Lord Strange's company, had to go before the Recorder, and enter into recognisances to appear personally at the next Sessions at Newgate.   The following is a translation of the official record of these proceedings, according to the legal Latin of the Middlesex Session Roll.

'Middlesex Sessions.

'*Memoranda.*

'That this first day of October in the thirty-first year of the reign of our sovereign Lady Queen Elizabeth, Richard Kytchine, of Clifforde Inn, gentleman, and Humphry Rowland, of East Smithfield, in the aforesaid county, horner, appeared before William Fletewode, Sergeant at Law and Recorder of the City of London, one of the Justices of the Queen, in the aforesaid county, to assign and to become surety for Christopher Marley of London, gentleman, each in the sum of twenty pounds, and the said Christopher Marley, entered into recognisances, under a penalty of forty pounds to be levied on his goods, chattels. lands, and tenements, to appear personally at the next Sessions at Newgate, to answer

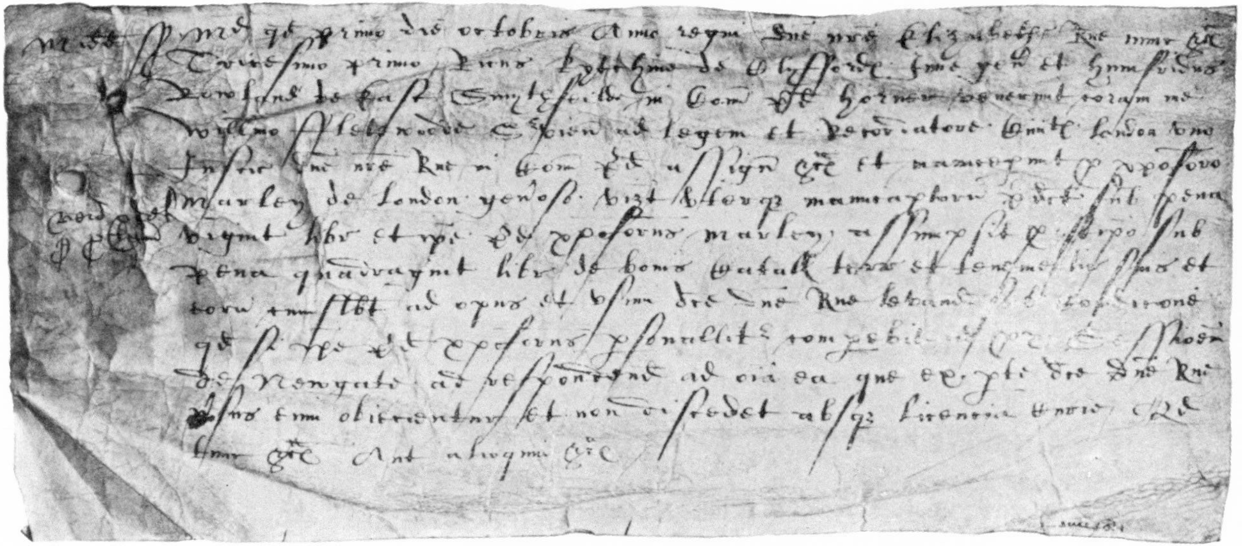

'RECOGNIZANCE, 31 ELIZABETH', AT MIDDLESEX SESSIONS, OCTOBER 1589

PLATE XIX

to all that is alleged against him on the part of our
sovereign Lady, the Queen, and not to depart without the license of the Court.

‘G. D. ROLL.—3rd October, 31st Elizabeth.’[98]

It is very tantalising that the Roll contains nothing
further, and that nothing more respecting the case can
be discovered. The record neither furnishes Marlowe’s address, which might have thrown some light
upon his position and style of living, nor, what is
still more vexatious, does it specify the offence with
which he was charged. That he was allowed out
on bail shows that he was not charged with anything very heinous, although, as the amount of his
bail was not inconsiderable, it is clear that the offence
was not a petty one, such as common assault, riotous
behaviour, or the like. The fact that the case was
to be tried at Newgate Sessions proves that the
alleged offence had been committed in the city of
London, and there is, therefore, every reason to
believe that it arose out of dramatic affairs.

As the indictment was endorsed G. D. (Gaol
Delivery), it is considered that the charge was one
of a felonious nature, such as would be deemed any
infringement of the Queen’s proclamation of 1559,
in which ‘the Queen’s Majesty doth straightly forbid
all maner Interludes to be playde eyther openly or
privateley, except the same be notified before hande
and licensed within any citie or towne corporate by
the Maior or other chiefe officers of the same . . .

and if anye shal attempt to the contrary : her majestie giveth all maner of officers that have authoritie to see common peace kept in commaundment to arrest and enprison the parties so offendinge, for the space of fourtene dayes or more, as cause shal be nede. And furder also untill good assurance may be founde and gyven, that they shalbe of good behaviour and no more to offende in the likes.' [99]

This proclamation does not appear to have been repealed or modified during Elizabeth's reign, and would fully account for Marlowe's appearance at Clerkenwell and remand to Newgate, the records of which place are supposed to have been destroyed during the Gordon Riots. [100]

It is self-evident that if there had been any reasonable prospect of Marlowe being proved guilty of seditious utterances, atheistic doctrines, or any other equally serious criminal charge, such as specified by the Recorder, Sergeant Fleetwood, in his work on *The Office of a Justice of Peace*, the poet would not have been let off on bail, as they would have been Star Chamber matters, and further inquiry into his conduct would have been recorded. That the accused was considered good for forty pounds seems to imply that Christopher Marlowe, gentleman, was thought to be a person of substance at that time.

Some further information about the two persons whose recognisances were taken jointly with Marlowe's would be interesting ; who they were and what were their connections with the poet. Richard

Kytchin, whose name was not a common one, doubtless belonged to a family which at that period
furnished several members to the legal profession.
There was a Richard Kytchin, or Kitchin, M.A.,
who was Fellow of Corpus Christi College, Cambridge, in 1548, and it might have been he who
came to the rescue, in 1583, of the brilliant young
Arts Master of his college, or, what is still more
probable, it was a son of this veteran Cantab. There
was, also, a John Kytchin, author of a work on
Jurisdictions, which was highly popular and frequently reprinted in the sixteenth century, and he,
doubtless, was a kinsman of the Kytchin in question.

Humphrey Rowlands, or Rowland, although apparently a trader, may have had some connection
with literature, and it is not improbable was a relative of Samuel Rowlands, the well-known dramatic
writer. This author was a contemporary of Marlowe, and in his popular play of *The Knave of Cards*
thus alludes to one of his works :

> ' The gull gets on a surplice,
>   With a cross upon his breast ;
>   Like Alleyn playing *Faustus*,
>   In that manner was he dressed.'

In the history of the Horner's Company it is stated
that the trade of this company declined when the use
of horn for lanterns—such lanterns as are reminiscent of Dogberry and Verges—was abandoned.
The Horner Company appears to be a thing of the
past, although in Queen Elizabeth's time a wealthy

and influential community. This worshipful company was formerly much celebrated for a burlesque procession it made annually from Deptford to Greenwich, in which each person wore some ornament of horn upon his head. This festival was supposed to have originated in a compulsory grant wrung from King John when he was detected in an adventure of gallantry at Eltham.[101]

Marlowe's next drama was *The Jew of Malta.* Stephen Gosson, an old scholar of the King's School at Canterbury, in his work entitled *The Schoole of Abuse*, published in 1579, and, in somewhat contradictory terms, called 'a pleasant invective against Poets, Pipers, Plaiers, Jesters, and such like Caterpillers of a Commonwealth,' expressly exempts from his otherwise almost universal denunciation of dramatic writings a play called *The Jew.* Nothing is known of this play, but the early date of the reference to it precludes it from any possibility of having been Marlowe's. This being so it has been assumed that it furnished the groundwork for the later *Jew of Malta*, but as no copy of this earlier piece has come to light the suggestion, as mere unsupported supposition, may be neglected.

Although the earliest known edition of Marlowe's *Jew of Malta* is that of 1633, the play itself was produced on the stage about the early part of 1589. The drama was brought out by Lord Strange's players, for whom Marlowe was still writing, and who continued to act at the Cross-Keys, notwithstanding the incessant opposition of the corporation. As the introductory lines contain a reference to the death of the Duke of Guise, who was assassinated in 1588, the drama could not have been written earlier than that year, unless the allusion was a later interpolation, which is not improbable, seeing how corrupt the text is.

In *The Jew of Malta* Marlowe sought once more to depict the attempt of a strong mind to domineer over his fellowmen. As Tamburlaine attempted to gain his ends by force of arms, as Faustus did by means of ' Learning's golden gifts,' so did Barabbas seek supremacy by the power of wealth. In this Jew the greed for riches is sublimated and even ennobled; his longing for inexhaustible wealth is not the vulgar avarice of a Shylock, heaping up riches for riches' sake, but an intense lust for gold as a means for the acquisition of power, and as a tangible evidence of his supremacy over the rabble. The grandeur of his passion for wealth, his grandiose efforts to heap up 'infinite riches in a little room,' exhalt Barabbas to heroic proportions, so that Shylock is a pigmy in comparison. The treatment the Maltese Jew receives excites our pity ; the magnitude of his crimes—of his revenge—almost compels our admiration.

If the conception of this drama be not so original as that of *Faustus*, the execution of it, at least so far as the two first acts are concerned, is more artistic. The hand of a mature workman is now apparent, and

the glow of youth which permeated every fibre of
Tamburlaine is now seen restrained, the weird aspirations of a *Faustus* subdued and replaced by the
practical knowledge of a man of the world.   The two
first acts of this drama are regarded by Hallam as
' more vigorously conceived, both as to character and
to circumstance, than any other Elizabethan play, except those of Shakespeare ' ; [102] and it must be averred
that not only is Shakespeare's indebtedness to it
strongly marked, but that instances can be cited to
show that he did not always improve what he
adapted from his contemporary.

Yet *The Jew of Malta* is regarded as the most
unequal of Marlowe's known plays.   ' The masterful
grasp that marks the opening scene was a new thing
in English tragedy,' is the opinion of his latest editor.
' Language so strong, so terse, so dramatic, had
never been heard before on the English stage.   In
the two first acts there is not a trace of juvenility ;
all is conceived largely and worked out in firm, bold
strokes.' [103]   How it came about that the firm hand
was fettered and the potent stroke grew feeble may
not be known, although it is easy to imagine.   In all
probability the success of his previous productions
had been so phenomenal that he was urged to further
efforts ; his brain, weary and exhausted by the
demands made upon it, could not continue to en-
gender masterpieces to order, so that the work he
had started upon so grandly was scamped.   Instead
of carving out a peerless statue for the admiration of

posterity, he has left nothing more than a partially hewn bust; yet the fact must not be overlooked that the work has evidently been tampered with by hack revisers.

It is the opinion of a perplexed commentator that in the last three acts of *The Jew of Malta*, 'vigorous drawing is exchanged for caricature; for a sinister lifelike figure we have a grotesque stage-villain,' but this seems going further than facts justify. Great as the falling-off in characterisation may be, it must not be overlooked that Barabbas has had terrible provocation, and that if he were transformed to a demon, with a ghoulish monomania for murder, the transformation is due to the unbearable wrongs which had been inflicted upon him.

Haste in execution has decidedly injured the play; but although Marlowe may not be 'quite guiltless of the extravagance and buffoonery of the last three acts of *The Jew of Malta*,' it is possible that some later interpolations may have been made to suit popular taste, and that despite the fiendish ferocity which the hero ultimately displays, he is after all the most natural and lifelike of his author's creations. Barabbas is no shadowy prototype of Shylock, but a being of flesh and blood and dowered with the passions of humanity. Like his Venetian brother, notwithstanding his overweening ambition, he does not disdain to stoop to conquer, for 'we Jews,' he explains,

'We Jews can fawn like spaniels when we please:
And when we grin we bite, yet are our looks

As innocent and harmless as a lamb's.
I learned in Florence how to kiss my hand,
Heave up my shoulders when they call me dog,
And duck as low as any barefoot friar ;
Hoping to see them starve upon a stall,
Or else be gathered for in our synagogue,
That, when the offering basin comes to me,
Even for charity I may spit into 't.'

The superlatively rich Jew of Malta, although de-
frauded like his successor of Venice, is of a hardier
and more vigorous mind than Shylock.   With a few
subtle touches the strength of his character is displayed ; when, for instance, finding himself bereft of
all his beloved treasure, instead of giving way to
despair, or succumbing to self-murder, to

' Vanish o'er the earth in air
And leave no memory that e'er I was,'

he sets to work to reap riches anew, and to plot dire
vengeance on his cruel foes.

The Jew of Malta possesses a nearer approach to
a plot than either of its predecessors from Marlowe's
pen ; and yet the story is made up of nothing more
than the schemes of Barabbas to counteract his
Christian adversaries and revenge himself upon them
for their cruel and unjust treatment.   The opening
scene depicts the Jew seated in his counting-house.
In a masterly monologue he describes his untold
wealth, and after referring with scorn to the petty
coins, the 'paltry silverlings,' he has just been paid
by the men who bought his 'Spanish oils and wines
of Greece,' he continues :

'Well fare the Arabians, who so richly pay
  The things they traffic for with wedge of gold,
  Whereof a man may easily in a day
  Tell that which may maintain him all his life.
  The needy groom that never fingered groat,
  Would make a miracle of thus much coin.
  Give me the merchants of the Indian mines,
  That trade in metal of the purest mould;
  The wealthy Moor, that in the eastern rocks
  Without control can pick his riches up,
  And in his house heap pearls like pebble stones,
  Receive them free, and sell them by the weight;
  Bags of fiery opals, sapphires, amethysts,
  Jacinths, hard topaz, grass-green emeralds,
  Beauteous rubies, sparkling diamonds,
  And seld-seen costly stones of so great price,
  As one of them indifferently rated,
  And of a carat of this quantity,
  May serve in peril of calamity,
  To ransom great kings from captivity.
  This is the ware wherein consists my wealth;
  And thus methinks should men of judgment frame
  Their means of traffic from the vulgar trade,
  And as their wealth increaseth, so inclose
  Infinite riches in a little room.'

Merchants visit him, approaching the wealthy Jew
as senators would a mighty potentate, and give him
news of his vessels in various parts of the world.
Confident in the power of his measureless property,
Barabbas thus royally soliloquises:

'Thus trowls our fortune in by land and sea,
  And thus are we on every side enriched:
  These are the blessings promised to the Jews,
  And herein was old Abram's happiness:
  What more may heaven do for earthly man
  Than thus to pour out plenty in their laps,
  Ripping the bowels of the earth for them,

Making the sea(s) their servants, and the winds
To drive their substance with successful blasts?
Who hateth me but for my happiness?
Or who is honoured now but for his wealth?
Rather had I, a Jew, be hated thus,
Than pitied in a Christian poverty:
For I can see no fruits in all their faith,
But malice, falsehood, and excessive pride,
Which, methinks, fits not their profession.
Haply some hapless man hath conscience,
And for his conscience lives in beggary.
They say we are a scattered nation:
I cannot tell, but we have scrambled up
More wealth by far than those that brag of faith.'

But misfortune is in the wind : the Turks send a
fleet to enforce payment of the tribute long overdue
to them by the Maltese. At the intercession of the
Christian governor, the Turks, with unwonted generosity, grant a reprieve of a month and sail away.
The only method of raising the heavy sum required
appears to be to squeeze it out of the Jews. The
leading men of the Hebrew race are summoned
before the governor, and told that each one, to make
up the ten years' tribute, will have to pay one half of
his estate. The penalty for refusal is either to become a Christian, or the absolute loss of the whole of
his property. All save Barabbas agree to resign half
their fortunes, but he, for his momentary refusal, is
adjudged to have the whole of his wealth confiscated
to the State. His remonstrances and pleadings are
met by scriptural allusions, to which he responds :

'What, bring you scripture to confirm your wrongs?
Preach me not out of my possessions.

Some Jews are wicked, as all Christians are:
But say the tribe that I descended of
Were all in general cast away for sin,
Shall I be tried by their transgressions?
The man that dealeth righteously shall live:
And which of you can charge me otherwise?'

His words are wasted. Upon hearing it decreed that his money, his ships, his lands, and all his possessions are to be seized, and his mansion converted into a nunnery, the Jew asks if it is intended to bereave him of his life. 'To stain our hands with blood,' the governor declares, 'is far from us and our profession,' to which Barabbas answers:

'Why, I esteem the injury far less
To take the lives of miserable men
Than be the causes of their misery.
You have my wealth, the labour of my life,
The comfort of mine age, my children's hope,
And therefore ne'er distinguish of the wrong.'

All is useless. His residence is seized accordingly and turned into a nunnery. Then the difficulty of Barabbas is how to recover and secretly remove the enormous treasure in coin and jewels hidden therein. His daughter Abigail has been ejected from their home, but Barabbas instructs her to return to it and offer herself to the abbess as a nun, hoping by the girl's means to recover his wealth. As he tells Abigail, 'Religion hides many mischiefs from suspicion.' Thus instigated, the girl solicits admission to the new-made nunnery, is admitted, and duly received into the sisterhood.

At night Barabbas watches outside his former

abode, and whilst he waits in hopes of regaining his
coveted wealth his daughter appears. Seeing her,
the Jew exclaims :

> ' But stay, what star shines yonder in the east ?
> The loadstar of my life, if Abigail ' ;

and Abigail it proves to be. She has discovered and
throws down to him bag after bag of his beloved
wealth, which he seizes and speedily conveys to a
place of safety.

Subsequently Abigail leaves the nunnery and
returns to her father, who is now meditating deep
vengeance for the wrongs he has suffered. Two
Christians, one of whom is the governor's son,
are suitors for the Jew's fair daughter ; she favours
one, but holds the other in dislike. At her father's
command she is forced to feign affection for both,
and is betrothed to both of them. Barabbas finds
means to excite the jealousy of the two young
men ; they quarrel, fight, and kill each other. Upon
learning the facts, the unfortunate Abigail flies from
her cruel father, re-enters the nunnery, and becomes
a Christian in reality. When news of this reaches
the ears of Barabbas his love for his only child is
turned to hate, and by help of his slave Ithamore
he poisons her and all the nuns. Before her death
Abigail, under the seal of confession, informs a friar
how her father has brought about the death of her
two lovers. The man at once sees an opportunity of
making money out of the secret.

In company with a colleague the friar calls on the

Jew and attempts to frighten him out of a portion of his wealth. Again aided by the slave, Barabbas murders the would-be blackmailer, and following the lines of a very ancient story—a story derived from oriental sources, but very popular all over Europe in the middle ages—makes the other friar fancy that he has killed his companion. He is given into custody, sentenced, and executed as the murderer. Ithamore, the Jew's slave, being enticed by a courtesan into her house, causes the arrest of Barabbas and the revelation of his villainies. Whilst in the company of Bellamira, Ithamore breaks into song, singing this variant of Marlowe's well-known lyric, 'Come live with me and be my Love':

> 'We will leave this paltry land,
> And sail from hence to Greece, to lovely Greece.
> I'll be thy Jason, thou my golden fleece;
> Where painted carpets o'er the meads are hurled,
> And Bacchus' vineyards overspread the world;
> Where woods and forests go in goodly green,
> I'll be Adonis, thou shalt be Love's Queen.
> The meads, the orchards, and the primrose lanes,
> Instead of sedge and reed, bear sugar-canes:
> Thou in those groves, by Dis above,
> Shalt live with me and be my love.'

Despite the probably intentional grotesque associations of 'primrose lanes' and 'sugar-canes,' and the invocation 'by Dis,' there is a sweetness about the lines due as much to sound as sense. There is no need to pursue the story. Remembering the age in which *The Jew of Malta* was written, it will be conceded that it is unparalleled amongst contem-

porary works for audacity of speech.   It is difficult
to gauge the temerity of a man who, whilst the fire
had scarcely ceased smouldering which had consumed
his fellow-collegian, Kett, for questioning the verity
of the Trinity, could proclaim,

> ' I count Religion but a childish toy,
> And hold there is no sin but ignorance ' ;

or who, in those days when to question, even in
thought, ' the divine right of kings,' was an un-
pardonable crime, should put into the mouth of one
of his players the words,

> ' Many will talk of title to a crown :
> What right had Cæsar to the empery ?
> Might first made kings, and laws were then most sure
> When like the Draco's they were writ in blood.'

There is little wonder that a man who would address
the public of those days in such words had to suffer
compulsory introduction to the City Recorder.

By this time Marlowe had not only made the
acquaintance of many persons distinguished in
literature and politics, and acquired the friendship
of the best of them, but, what many will deem even
more valuable for him, he had gained a reputation
for the success of his dramas.   Men like Henslowe,
knowing nothing of poetry, of genius, or of real
worth, were sharp enough to discern and make use
of the successful talent displayed by young or
needy authors.   No one could equal the young man
from Warwickshire, William Shakespeare, in patch-
ing up and revising old plays, but he had not yet had

WILLIAM SHAKESPEARE

After the engraving by Martin Droeshout.

PLATE XX.

the experience and success of his famous contemporary and friend, Christopher Marlowe, in the production of a drama wholly and solely his own.

At this time there were various old dramas which had had their quantum of popularity but no longer possessed sufficient novelty, or were not well enough up to date, to attract fresh audiences. To remedy this the few shrewd theatrical proprietors of the period sought the aid of new men to remodel the old stock : to revise the dramas they had purchased from the needy authors, but which had outlived their power of attraction. Shakespeare happened to be willing and able for the work. Either at the suggestion of these employers, or prompted by his own shrewdness, he set to work on a few of these once popular pieces; availed himself of the plots generally, and of their most effective incidents, and, by his unrivalled skill in gauging the dramatic suitability of their situations, combined with his wonderful insight into character, succeeded in transmuting the tedious old plays into intensely interesting dramas, the base metal into gold : out of the discarded material he built up imperishable monuments of art.

Doubtless urged more by necessity than inclination, Marlowe had been forced into following a similar method; he also seems to have worked at the reconstruction or revision of some of the old dramas. The lesson gained by experience in such work would

I

have a sobering effect upon the rashness and un-
restraint of youth, although it was calculated to
impair the workman's originality and damp down the
fire of poesy glowing within.

One of the plays Marlowe appears to have been
thus engaged upon was an ancient favourite, *The
Troublesome Raigne of John, King of England*, and
it is singular that a subject so seemingly unattractive
should have exercised such fascination for the public.
The reign of King John had been a favourite theme
with the dramatists from the earliest days; even
John Bale (Bishop of Ossory), who lived in the first
half of the sixteenth century, and deluged the country
with a flood of so-called 'sacred' plays, wrote one
on King John, which he had printed abroad in
1538. The bishop is said to have adapted it from
a still older play on the same subject. That *The
Troublesome Raigne* owed anything to Bale's play
is improbable, but, whatever its origin, it was
eminently successful in stirring up audiences and
exciting their passions against the promoters of the
threatened Armada. Its popularity did not wane
even when the newly revised and much modified
edition of it by Shakespeare and a coadjutor was
put upon the stage. The old drama still kept some
hold on the public long after its rival had appeared,
and even maintained possession of the boards well
into the seventeenth century.

Who was the author of *The Troublesome Raigne*,
and who co-operated with Shakespeare in his re-

vision of it? Was Robert Greene the original producer, and whence did he filch it? The general opinion is that Greene was the part-author of the older play, and that it was the work, or one of the works, he referred to in his attack on Shakespeare, when he accused him of bedecking himself with the plumage of others.[104] Much of the old play, however, is too vigorous, too manly, and too straightforward to have been the composition of Greene, so that if he had anything to do with the work it must have been as a partner with a better man, but who that man was is too speculative a subject to hazard a suggestion about.

That the greatly revised and much improved version of *King John* by Shakespeare contained some of Marlowe's work no one thoroughly acquainted with his mannerisms can doubt, but the suggestion that he wrote the whole of it is preposterous. No character of the Shakespearian drama shows the imprint of its creator more decidedly, although in his youthful style, than does the Bastard. ' Sir Richard Plantagenet ' is typically Shakespearian in every muscle of him.

Another drama, or rather a dramatic trilogy, which bears still more marked impression of Marlowe's work is that now known as *Henry the Sixth*. As with *King John*, this dramatic series is founded upon the productions of some anonymous predecessor or predecessors, and some writers contend that this play is also one of those which Greene referred to in connection with stolen plumes, and which a certain unidentified 'R. B. Gent.' alluded to in a pamphlet entitled *Greene's Funeralls* :

> 'Nay more, the men that so eclipst his fame,
>   Purloynde his Plumes, can they deny the same?'

Greene's invective appears to be unmistakably directed at Shakespeare, when he sneers, in his *Groatsworth*, at 'an upstart crow beautified with our feathers, that, with his *Tygres heart wrapt in a players hyde*, supposes he is as well able to bombast out a blanke verse as the best of you ; and, beeing an absolute Johannes-fac-totum, is in his owne conceyt the onely Shake-scene in a countrey.' These allusions, quite in Greene's usual malicious style of innuendo, are too transparent to be mistaken. The quotation is but slightly parodied from a line in the *True Tragedie of Richard, Duke of York*, the play on which the second and third parts of the drama now known as *Henry the Sixth* are founded ; the 'Shake-scene' is self-evident, and the *fac-totum* refers to Shakespeare's general theatrical utility.

Henslowe, in his famous, ill-spelt *Diary*, refers to a play entitled *Henry the Sixth*, as being first acted at his theatre on the 3rd March 1592, and this is the piece Thomas Nashe thus refers to in his *Pierce Pennilesse* of that year: 'How would it have joy'd brave Talbot (the terror of the French) to thinke that after he had lyne two hundred yeare in his tombe, he should triumphe againe on the stage, and have his bones new embalmed with the teares of ten thousand spectators at least, (at severall times), who, in the tragedian that represents his person, imagine they behold him fresh bleeding.' [105]

This *First Part of King Henry the Sixth*, whenever it may have originally appeared, and by whomsoever written, is very unequal, and furnishes but slight evidence of containing much of the handiwork of the two men, Marlowe and Shakespeare, who are now believed to have jointly remodelled it. The workers warmed, apparently, as they progressed, and towards its conclusion display more mastery over their materials. The three parts into which *Henry the Sixth* is divided are replete with passages taken from, or reminiscent of, Marlowe's earlier dramas, and it is the theory of those who will not forgo their belief in Shakespeare's sole authorship of these plays, that from his having acted in Marlowe's dramas, and having studied them sympathetically, he unconsciously, although continually, made repeated references to and quotations from them! Is it possible that Shakespeare, knowing Marlowe's writings so intimately as he did, could embody whole lines of them unconsciously? Shakespeare either knowingly plagiarised, or Marlowe himself set them in the places where they are now found. The latter proposition is not only more agreeable to believe, but it is in every respect more probable. The statement that Marlowe never repeated himself is incorrect: like many great writers he frequently revised the wording of his ideas, as innumerable instances might be cited from his works to prove : several of them have already been referred to in these pages.

Students of Marlowe's style cannot fail to detect plenteous evidence of its presence in *Henry the Sixth.* It is impossible to ignore his massive rhythm and his mighty line in that drama. His masterly method of alliterating sound, unparalleled for three centuries, reveals the author. His dexterous introduction of similar sounding *syllables* in any part of a word, rolling successively through a verse, like wave following wave upon the rising beach; the dragging in of classical allusions irrespective of their appropriateness; as, also, other signs of his less artistic mannerisms, are equally apparent. Beyond all cavil or dispute, Marlowe's handiwork is as clearly discernible in *Henry the Sixth*, as is Shakespeare's; and this drama, or trilogy of dramas, should bear their names jointly on the title-page.

What a feeling of wondering admiration is aroused at the thought of these two mighty minds working at the same drama! And perhaps together! One conjuring up visions of unrealisable aspirations, and the other realising and immortalising characters of fiction as well as of fact. Never in the history of the world's literature could so noble a pair have partnered, and in such glorious work. The very thought of it is a poem! The creators of Faustus and of Hamlet sitting face to face as they wrought out their conceptions! Exhausting worlds and then creating new! The poet of *Hero and Leander* exchanging divinest thoughts with the creator of *Romeo and Juliet*! The wit-combats at 'The Mermaid' fade into insignificance compared with this!

From time to time in *Henry the Sixth* the two poets seem to be seen, face to face, speaking through their *dramatis personæ*. Shakespeare appears as Winchester, the haughty conservative prelate, whilst Marlowe assumes the *rôle* of Gloucester, the people's beloved Lord Protector. Cannot the voices of the two poets be heard in this dialogue?—

'WIN. Com'st thou with deep premeditated lines,
  With written pamphlets studiously devised?
  Humphrey of Gloster, if thou canst accuse,
  Or aught intend'st to lay unto my charge,
  Do it without invention, suddenly;
  As I with sudden and extemporal speech
  Purpose to answer what thou canst object.
GLO. Presumptuous priest! This place commands my patience,
  Or thou should'st find thou hast dishonour'd me.
  Think not, although in writing I preferr'd
  The manner of thy vile outrageous crimes,
  That therefore I have forged, or am not able
  Verbatim to rehearse the method of my pen:
  No, prelate; such is thy audacious wickedness,
  Thy lewd, pestiferous, and dissentious pranks,
  As very infants prattle of thy pride.
  Thou art a most pernicious usurer;
  Froward by nature, enemy to peace;
  Lascivious, wanton, more than well beseems
  A man of thy profession and degree;
  And for thy treachery, what's more manifest,—
  In that thou laid'st a trap to take my life,
  As well at London Bridge, as at the Tower?
  Besides, I fear me, if thy thoughts were sifted,

The king, thy sovereign, is not quite exempt
From envious malice of thy swelling heart.

WIN. Gloster, I do defy thee.—Lords, vouchsafe
To give me hearing what I shall reply.
If I were covetous, ambitious, or perverse,
As he will have me, how am I so poor?
Or how haps it, I seek not to advance
Or raise myself, but keep my wonted calling?
And for dissension, who preferreth peace
More than I do, except I be provok'd?
No, my good lords, it is not that offends;
It is not that, that hath incens'd the duke:
It is, because no one should sway but he;
No one but he should be about the king;
And that engenders thunder in his breast,
And makes him roar these accusations forth.
But he shall know I am as good—

GLO.   As good!
Thou bastard of my grandfather!

WIN. Ay, lordly sir; for what are you, I pray,
But one imperious in another's throne?

GLO. Am I not Protector, saucy priest?

WIN. And am I not a prelate of the church?

GLO. Yes, as an outlaw in a castle keeps
And useth it to patronage his theft.

WIN. Unreverent Gloster!'

The personal characteristics of the two young
poets, Marlowe and Shakespeare, are set forth in
the discourses of their puppets. Gloucester is full
of pity for the poor and oppressed, and is scornful
of priestly claims; Winchester upholds the rights of
princes and the pomp and circumstance of rank.
The one, so alien to his exalted position, is full
of free thought and radical theory; the other courtly
and tenacious of the power incidental to his position.
It is characteristic of Marlowe, when writing in the

earlier period of this drama, to be a defender of 'the Maid of Orleans,' *la Pucelle*. Alas, that other hands had to work out her degradation!

In this *Henry the Sixth* it is interesting to note that Kentish men, quite ignored in Shakespeare's other plays, are, from time to time, spoken of with admiration and respect. Shakespeare's workmanship, his early workmanship, before he had learned to keep control over his pen, and restraint upon the idiosyncrasies of his youth, may be readily detected by well-marked characteristics : by his word-quibbles, his puns, his conceits, his proverbial philosophy, his constant flood of similes, and, in fine, by his complete subjugation to the 'euphuisms' of the time. Eventually Shakespeare shook himself free of this fashionable foible, only to fall under the influence of Marlowe ; this latter submission to the style of the brother bard, of whom for a time he was a most devoted follower, took place during that early portion of his career whilst he was engaged in the reconstruction or revision of the early historical or chronicle plays. Eventually the tables were turned, and Marlowe, from being the admired master, became in his last completed drama, *Edward the Second*, the admiring comrade.

How strongly Marlowe subjugated his mind and style to Shakespeare's is shown in *Edward the Second*, wherein he is seen restraining and curbing his glowing and impetuous language ; and, in place of impassioned soliloquies, uttered in and out of season by all sorts and conditions of men, he makes his several dramatic personages utter words more suited to their separate and respective characters and conditions. In *Henry the Sixth*, Marlowe's puppets are merely pegs on which to hang his own thoughts and theories: Gloucester, not only a royal prince next in rank to the king, but, as Lord Protector, legally and practically ruler of the realm, is made to utter all kinds of radical expressions and free thought speeches, not only out of character with his exalted position, but far in advance of the age he lived in.

Unlike Shakespeare's characters, whose talk generally accords with their rank and condition, Marlowe's personages all speak in the same poetic, often farfetched, strain. How incongruous it sounds to hear the crafty, villainous Richard, afterwards the third of that name, discourse like a lovelorn lad, even in the heat of battle, and, when he should be con cerned about his father's fate, in such a style as this :

> ' See how the morning opes her golden gates,
> And takes her farewell of the glorious sun !
> How well resembles it the prime of youth,
> Trimm'd like a younker, prancing to his love ! '

Little less out of place is Edward the Fourth's address to Queen Margaret :

> ' Helen of Greece was fairer far than thou,
> Although thy husband may be Menelaus ;
> And ne'er was Agamemnon's brother wrong'd
> By that false woman, as this king by thee.

MICHAEL DRAYTON

From an old engraving.

PLATE XXI.

His father revell'd in the heart of France,
And tam'd the king, and made the dauphin stoop;
And, had he match'd according to his state,
He might have kept that glory to this day;
But when he took a beggar to his bed,
And grac'd thy poor sire with his bridal-day,
Even then that sunshine brew'd a shower for him,
That wash'd his father's fortunes forth of France,
And heap'd sedition on his crown at home.
For what hath broach'd this tumult but thy pride?
Had'st thou been meek, our title still had slept,
And we, in pity of the gentle king,
Had slipp'd our claim until another age.'

If that be not Marlowe's work, it only proves how closely Shakespeare followed in his footsteps.

Reverting to the more personal or external story of Marlowe's career, it is now necessary to refer in the first place to the class of men with whom he was really associated, as contrasted with those he is generally supposed to have reckoned on his list of friends, and who are assumed to have been his intimate acquaintances. The latter class includes Robert Greene, the quality of whose friendship has already been exposed; George Peele and Thomas Nashe, neither of whom claimed a personal knowledge of Marlowe; and Thomas Kyd, the evidence of whose intimacy with him is of an apocryphal character.

Amongst the known friends and associates of the poet at this period were, in addition to Chapman, apparently Shakespeare, Spenser, and Michael Drayton; the last described by his contemporary, Francis Meres, as 'among scholars, soldiers, poets, and all

sorts of people, is held for a man of virtuous disposition, honest conversation, and well-governed
carriage, which is almost miraculous among good
wits in these declining and corrupt times.' [106]   Drayton's lines on Marlowe, although evidently suggested
by Shakespeare's in the *Midsummer Night's Dream*,
show how deeply and reverently he regarded one no
longer able to appreciate or repay his homage.

Conspicuous in the circle of Marlowe's friends
were the Walsinghams of Scadbury, Chislehurst, in
Kent. Both the father and the son, brother and
nephew respectively of the queen's friend and faithful
adviser, Sir Francis Walsingham, are seen to have
been on the most intimate terms with the poet.
Edward Blount, the publisher, when alluding to the
friendship of the Kentish knight for Marlowe, reminds
Sir Thomas that he had bestowed many kind favours
upon the poet, having appreciated 'the worth which
you found in him with good countenance and liberal
affection.' [107]   It must be recalled to mind that, besides
being a generous friend to the best literary men of
his time, Sir Thomas Walsingham was well known
for his exemplary life and untarnished reputation;
from all doubtful adventures or dissolute companions
he had ever kept severely aloof.

With Sir Roger Manwood, Chief Baron of the
Exchequer, member of a Kentish family, having a
country residence at St. Stephens, Canterbury,
Marlowe appears to have had a personal acquaintance, otherwise his epitaph on the knight could

SIR WALTER RALEIGH

PLATE XXII.

scarcely have been worded in the way it was. Many also of his schoolfellows from King's and his fellow-students from Corpus Christi College had migrated to London and were making positions for themselves, and as they were generally of a literary or scholastic turn, some of them were certain to have come into contact with the now famous poet, whose mien and manner must have made him a welcome guest in many circles.

Probably the friend whose society and character exercised the greatest influence upon Marlowe was Sir Walter Raleigh. With one exception the Devonshire knight was the most remarkable Englishman of his time; certainly the most noteworthy of Elizabeth's court. Sir Robert Naunton, who must have known Raleigh personally, in *Fragmenta Regalia*, sums up his account of Sir Walter thus: 'He had, in the outward man, a good presence, in a handsome and well-compacted person; a strong natural wit, and a better judgment, with a bold and plausible tongue, whereby he could set out his parts to the best advantage; and these he had by the adjuncts of some general learning, which by diligence he enforced to a great augmentation and perfection, for he was an indefatigable reader, by sea and land, and *one of the best observers both of men and of the times.*' [108] Queen Elizabeth, notwithstanding her vanity, was a shrewd observer of men also, and she, Naunton adds, took Raleigh for an oracle.

Many of the best literary, scientific, and political

men of the times regarded Raleigh as their leader in
thought and deed. His experience, varied knowledge, and subtle reasoning, rendered him, for good
or ill, the kind of being who, if any, could influence
such a genius as was Marlowe; whilst even the
flattery of his addressing the younger man a poem in
answer to his popular pastoral song, 'The Passionate
Shepherd to his Love,' could not have been read
without some pleasure on Marlowe's part.

The famous club at the 'Mermaid,' celebrated for
' wit-combats' between Shakespeare and Ben Jonson,
as related by Fuller, and charmingly commemo-
rated for its pleasures in the lines of Beaumont, was
founded by Raleigh, who was of a social nature, and
loved to gather round him all that was best and
most original in society. He held evening recep-
tions, doubtless the first man in London who did so,
and collected about him a coterie of eminent people.
That Marlowe was one of these there seems little
reason to doubt. The earliest references to the
poet not only allude to his friendship with Raleigh,
but even assert that he read a paper on the Trinity
before Sir Walter Raleigh and his brother Carew
and others at the knight's house.

The distinguished company which met at Raleigh's
house their contemporaries considered, if they did
not style, atheists, although more modern nicety of
tongue would refer to them as 'Free-thinkers.' It
included some of the most remarkable Englishmen
of that time. One of them was Edward Vere,

HENRY PERCY, EARL OF NORTHUMBERLAND

From a painting by Vandyke.

PLATE XXIII.

Earl of Oxford, a member of one of the most ancient families of his country, and of whom, although he has been slandered by others, it was said, 'it may be a question whether the nobility of his house, or the honour of his achievements, might most commend him'; Henry Percy, Earl of Northumberland, whose own talent and goodness in encouraging talent in others were only rivalled by his misfortunes, was yet another and most frequent guest; as were also Matthew Royden, the poet, Walter Warner and Robert Hughes, the mathematicians, and still greater and more remarkable, England's eminent mathematician and, until Isaac Newton, her greatest astronomer, Thomas Harriott.

Little as the name of Harriott is known to the public of these days, his learning, his scientific discoveries, and his inventions place him in the very first rank of England's notable sons. His reputation has been obscured, and his very name forgotten among the mob of England's illustrious men, but research is bringing his deeds and discoveries to light ; a preliminary, if not an exhaustive biography of him by a New Englander has recently been published,[109] and the time must be near at hand when his name will be lauded and his doings deemed pre-eminent amongst those of the Elizabethan era. His tomb in the centre of the Bank of England, in the very heart of the city of London, will, for his sake, be ofttimes visited as a 'Mecca of the mind.' For nearly forty years Harriott was the friend of Raleigh, standing by him until his untimely end. He had represented the knight's interests on his voyage to America in 1585 (whither it now seems proved Raleigh himself never went), and on his return published a very re-markable *Report of Virginia* ; remarkable for the comprehensive and foreseeing views it contains with regard to the future of America, and as ' one of the earliest examples of a statistical survey on a large scale.' [110]

Harriott not only foresaw many of the later dis-coveries in physics and astronomy, but by means of the telescope—the honour of inventing which machine he divides with Galileo—he also made many important discoveries, such as, amongst others, of the spots on the sun, the satellites of Jupiter, and the horns of Venus. He was one of the most illustrious mathematicians not only of his own but of all times ; ' it is believed that in logical analysis, in philosophy, and in many other departments of science, few in his days were his equals, whilst in pure mathematics none was his superior.' Hallam points out that Harriott, 'destined to make the last great discovery in the pure science of algebra . . . arrived at a complete theory of the genesis of equations, which Cardan and Victè had but partially conceived.' [111] Anthony à Wood designated Harriott 'the Universal Philosopher.' That he should be regarded by the people of his times as a magician is not wonderful, but that his blameless life and devoted attachment and gratitude to Sir Walter Raleigh should be made

GEORGE CHAPMAN

From the portrait in his translation of 'The Works of Homer,' 1616.

PLATE XXIV.

use of by Chief Justice Popham to insult the latter
on his trial, by accusing him from the bench of having
been 'bedevilled by Hariot,' shows that Jeffreys was
not the only judge deserving to be castigated as
'infamous.' [112]

When no longer able to help and enjoy the
continual companionship of Harriott, Raleigh introduced him to Henry Percy, Earl of Northumberland,
and that enlightened nobleman, as long as he lived,
provided Harriott with a pension of eighty pounds
a year and a home at Sion House. When both
Percy and Raleigh were imprisoned in the Tower of
London as state prisoners, only Harriott was permitted to visit and hold almost unrestricted inter-
course with the two so-called 'traitors.' [113]

Another lifelong friend of Harriott was Robert
Hues or Hughes, also a distinguished mathematician
of his time, a fellow-collegian of his at Oxford, and
also, as he, a friend and partaker of the bounty of
Henry Percy. In his translation of Homer, Chapman refers to Hughes as 'another right learned,
honest, and entirely loved friend of mine,' and
thus expresses his indebtedness to Harriott, whose
knowledge of Greek appears to have been profound :
' No conference had (I) with any one living in all the
novelties I presume I have found. Only some one
or two places I have shewed to my worthy and most
learned friend, Mr. Harriott, for his censure how
much mine own weighed : whose judgement and
knowledge in all kinds, I know to be incomparable

K

and bottomlesse; yea, to be admired as much, as his most blamelesse life, and the right sacred expence of his time, is to be honoured and reverenced.'[114] Other friends and companions of Harriott, according to the accounts of the time, were Ben Jonson, the poet Hoskins, Broughton, Dr. Burrill, Rev. Gilbert Hawthorne, and others more or less noted.

Such was the class of men that Marlowe would be wont to meet at Sir Walter Raleigh's, and discuss with him and his brother Carew philosophical, physical, and literary subjects 'of a nice and delicate nature,' as a contemporary records.[115] Of course the meetings of these noblemen and gentlemen could not occur without the slander and animadversion of society. The state feared these 'free-thinkers.' The populace regarded them as assembled for awful and unlawful purposes, whilst contemporaries libelled and vilified them. Writing to Kepler, Harriott, as has already been noted, deplored that 'it was impossible to express one's view freely' in public, and others had to utter similar complaints. Amongst those who calumniated and invented absurd fictions about this galaxy of notable persons was a Father Parsons. In his little book, *Responsio ad Elizabetha Edictum*, issued in 1592, he refers to 'Sir Walter Raleigh's school of atheism . . . as of the diligence used to get young gentlemen to his school, wherein both Moses and our Saviour, the Old and New Testament, are jested at, the scholars taught among other things to spell God backwards.'[116]

After this testimony of a contemporary it is not
surprising to find later gossip-mongers, such as
superstitious Aubrey and credulous Anthony à Wood,
having their little legends to tell, and to learn that
'Harriott was unsound in religious principles and
matters of belief; that he was in fact not only a
deist himself, but that he exerted a baleful influence
over Raleigh and his *History* (*of the World*), as well
as over the Earl of Northumberland.' Raleigh, it
may be pointed out, was nine years older than
Harriott, who was born in 1560, and Henry Percy
was his senior by some years. À Wood's account
of Harriott is that, 'notwithstanding his great skill
in mathematics, he had strange thoughts of the
Scriptures and always undervalued the old story of
the Creation of the World, and could never believe
that trite position, *ex nihilo nihil fit*. He made a
Philosophical Theology wherein he cast off the Old
Testament, so that consequently the New would
have no foundation.'[117] Old Anthony would be
surprised could he see how many persons of 'great
skill' nowadays dare to 'undervalue the old story'
and discredit the 'trite position.'

These were the men that Marlowe associated with,
for his association with them cannot now be gain-
said or doubted. Of all his various contemporaries,
if none exercised such a deep dramatic influence
upon him as Shakespeare, certainly the most per-
manent impression generally was that of Raleigh.
Historic record and literary tradition point to their

companionship, and the manner in which their speculative theories and logical conclusions coincide testify to their long and strong intimacy of thought. If Raleigh and Chapman were his intimate friends, it is scarcely possible to doubt that other members of their circle shared his acquaintance. They and other learned men of the time, men whose opinions and conversation were an education to know, were his associates. This being the case, how is it possible to believe that Marlowe could for long, if indeed ever, have been on intimate terms with the dissolute vagabond Greene, and a partaker of the debauchery of his reprobate comrades.

From his first mention of Marlowe until his last posthumous squirm, Greene never ceased sneering at his popular rival. During his lifetime the man dared only utter sneers and snarls, but when dying he strove, by a legacy of libel, to make such allusions to Marlowe's religious and political creed as would for ever crush the too successful dramatist and not improbably cause him to end his career at the stake.[118] Such malignity might be deemed unique amid the blackest records of human infamy had not Isaac D'Israeli shown a parallel.[119]

No one personally acquainted with Marlowe has left any testimony that he was known to Greene save by name. When Greene, exhausted by evil living, expired in 1592, he left an unpublished pamphlet bearing the title, or, at any rate, subsequently issued as, *Greene's Groatsworth of Wit bought*

with a Million of Repentance. This quintessence of
envy, hatred, and malice, doubtless left with some
bookseller as security for a small advance of ready
money, with instructions not to publish it until after
the writer's decease, was ultimately put into the
hands of Henry Chettle, a useful man of all-literary
work, to edit. According to Chettle's own apologetic
account, given when brought to book by Shakespeare
and Marlowe both, for the false statements and vile
innuendoes the tract contained, he had 'only in the
copy this share; it was il written, as sometimes
Greene's hand was none of the best; licensed it
must be, ere it could bee printed, which could never
be if it might not be read : to be briefe, I writ it over
and, as near as I could, followed the copy, onely in
that letter I put something out, but in the whole
booke not a worde in ; for I protest it was all
Greene's, not mine, nor Maister Nashes, as some
unjustly have affirmed.'

In addition to this explanation Chettle, referring
to the aspersions on Marlowe, 'whose learning,' he
remarks, 'I reverence, and at the perusing of
Greene's book, strooke out what there in conscience
I thought he in some displeasure writ or, had it been
true, yet to publish it was intollerable, him I would
wish to use me no worse than I deserve.'[120]

That what was struck out must have been intoler-
able may be believed when what Chettle allowed to
appear is read. This so-called 'Groatsworth of
Wit' begins by the awful indictment, evidently of

Marlowe, 'Wonder not (for with thee will I first be-
ginne), thou famous gracer of tragedians, that Greene,
who hath said with thee, like the foole in his heart,
"There is no God," should now give glorye unto his
greatnesse, for penetrating is his power, his hand
lyes heavy upon me, he hath spoken unto me with
a voyce of thunder and I have felt he is a God that
can punish enemies. Why should thy excellent wit,
his gift, be so blinded that thou shouldest give no
glorie to the giver? Is it pestilent Machiavellian
policie that thou hast studied? O peevish follie!
what are his rules but meere confused mockeries,
able to extirpate in small time the generation of
mankinde? for if *sic volo, sic iubeo*, holde in those that
are able to commaund, and if it be lawfull, *fas et nefas*,
to doo anything that is beneficiall, onely tyrants
should possesse the earth, and they, striving to
exceed in tiranny, should ech to other be a slaughter-
man, till, the mightyest outliving all, one stroke were
left for Death, that in one age man's life should end.
The brocher of this dyabolicall atheisme is dead, and
in his life had never the felicitie he aymed at, but,
as he beganne in craft, lived in feare and ended
in despaire. *Quam inscrutabilia sunt Dei judicia!*
This murderer of many brethren had his conscience
seared like Cayne, this betrayer of him that gave
his life for him inherited the portion of Judas; this
apostate perished as ill as Julian: and wilt thou, my
friend, be his disciple? Look unto mee, by him
perswaded to that libertie, and thou shalt finde it

an infernall bondage. I know the least of my
demerits merit this miserable death; but wilfull
striving against knowne truth exceedeth all the
terrors of my soul. Deferre not (with mee) till this
last point of extremitie; for little knowest thou how
in the end thou shalt be visited.'[121]

Any one conversant with the conditions of state
policy of that period can readily comprehend the
danger this awfully worded indictment against 'my
friend' would put Marlowe in; Burleigh and his
servitors would not care to investigate the motives of
the dying wretch who, had he really wished to do a
farewell kindness to the man he had continuously
insulted for so many years past, would have sent
his advice to him privately, instead of having the
arraignment of his assumed 'atheism'—then a capital
offence—proclaimed to the public.

On Greene's references to Shakespeare and other
contemporaries there is no need to dwell. Shakespeare it is seen was able to obtain an apology from
Chettle. Nashe, incensed at having had his name
coupled with the libel, immediately issued a denial of
his having had anything to do with it. 'I am adver-
tised,' he stated, 'that a scald triviall lying pamphlet,
called *Greene's Groatsworth of Wit*, is given out to
be of my doing. God never have care of my soule,
but utterly renounce me, if the least word or sillible
in it proceeded from my pen, or if I were any way
privie to the writing or printing of it.'[122]

With this indignant denial may be dismissed

Greene's posthumous attack upon the reputation of the two men who had succeeded so grandly in the field where he had failed.   Commentators upon Greene's writings have avoided allusion to the habit he had of foisting filthy, coarse, and vulgar words into his publications, and do not often point out that Greene's character is in no way a savoury subject; his utter absence of all feelings of honour; his many known deeds of dishonesty; his mean, shabby actions to obtain money for the moment's demands; his attempt to divert attention from his own paltry plagiarisms of Marlowe's plays by accusing Shakespeare of similar thefts; and, above all, his many years of ceaseless attacks upon the fame of, and attempts to bring into contempt, this popular contemporary, whom he at the same time insulted by pretensions of being his 'friend'—all combine to render his memory a blot on the literary history of his time.[123]

Among other reputed associates of Marlowe was Thomas Nashe, the most vitriolic satirist of his own if not of all times.   He may not have been the most desirable of acquaintances, any more than would be George Peele, if any faith may be placed in the popular stories told of him, yet neither of them, as far as proven statements go, appears to have committed any mean, cowardly, or malicious acts. There is no proof, and no contemporary evidence, that either of them was personally known to Marlowe, or that the poet condescended to take part in any of their squabbles and paper warfare, beyond Nashe's allegation that Marlowe had said of Richard Harvey, that 'he was an ass, good for nothing but to preach of the Iron Age.'[124]

That Gabriel, Richard Harvey's brother, abused Marlowe after the poet's death counts for nothing, as it was that unscrupulous calumniator's wont to libel those no longer able to defend themselves. That Nashe ever slandered the dead man seems scarcely possible, seeing that in his published reply to Harvey's vituperations he declared, 'I never abused Marlowe in my life.' He could scarcely have ventured upon such a statement, or have referred to Harvey's libels against Marlowe, if his own hand had really been fouled with calumniative ink.

Of Thomas Kyd, another dramatic contemporary, presumedly personally acquainted with Marlowe, the story is mysterious. It is a moot point whether Kyd was one, and if so, which one, of the 'quondam acquaintances' referred to by Greene, 'that spend their wits in making plays.' The man's reference to Shakespeare as 'an upstart crow, beautified with our feathers,' who 'supposes he is as well able to bombast out a blank verse as the best of you and, being an absolute Johannes factotum is, in his own conceit, the only Shakescene in a country,' was well calculated to touch home with Kyd.[125] Although the early drama of *Hamlet*, which has been ascribed to Kyd, subsequently provided Shakespeare with the ground-work of his masterpiece, is not supposed to have been then before the public, but it is almost certain that its author had had a hand in some of the plays which had already served 'the young man from Warwickshire' as the bases of his popular pieces.

Kyd's great dramatic success, *The Spanish Tragedy*, had fairly taken the town by storm : it is stuffed almost as full of horrors as is *Titus Andronicus*, and at the climax as huge a heap of dead *dramatis personæ* cumbers the stage as in the final scene of *Hamlet* itself; but in those days the public loved to sup its fill of horror. There is every probability that Nashe alluded to *The Spanish Tragedy* as early as 1589,[126] and Ben Jonson couples it with *Titus Andronicus* in a manner that implies that the same year was about the heyday of the popularity of both.[127] The production of the early version of the *Andronicus*, in which Kyd is generally presumed to have had a hand, is assigned to April 1592, and not too late, therefore, to have been mentioned in the *Groatsworth* by Greene, as he did not die until the September of that year.

Kyd was a hack-writer who turned his hand to anything likely to pay. Despite the great popularity of his *Tragedy*, it cannot be said to display any signs of literary genius. The man himself was of a morose, gloomy temperament, and does not appear to have had any friends amongst the authors of his period, although their references to his successful drama are very numerous.[128] The alleged intimacy of Marlowe with this Kyd shall be referred to later on, but for the present it is desirable to return to the story of the poet's own literary labours.

Edward the Second, the last of Marlowe's complete dramatic works, was not entered upon the Stationers' Books until July 6, 1593, but there is good reason to believe that it had been written, if not produced upon the stage, quite as early as 1591. Even as Shakespeare's earliest dramas show the pervading influence of Marlowe, so did Marlowe's latest work, *Edward the Second*, testify to the all-powerful influence which Shakespeare had now acquired over him. 'The very structure of *Edward the Second*,' says Richard Simpson, 'seems to bear witness to *the counsel and aid of Shakespeare*';[129] and indeed it is difficult to resist the belief that some of Shakespeare's own work is present in the play. The general restraint and suppression of the author's own personality, the absence of that intense poetic fire which in Marlowe's previous plays glowed through and through the lines, and the clearer individuality of the separate characters, manifest a thorough change from all Marlowe's previous writings. The critics have, generally, admired this departure from his earlier style, and deem that Marlowe was on the road to rival Shakespeare at his best; but admirers of Marlowe's former works, with their limitless ambition, and their irrepressible youthful energy, for ever striving and struggling after the unattainable, must feel their admiration calmed and subdued by this latest work. The desirable power of depicting character is in it, but the poet's fervour has vanished. *Edward the Second* may have received its author's latest corrections, and may embody his most matured thoughts, but only occasionally does it burn with the wonted 'fine frenzy.' It is apparently 'the most elaborate of his works,' and the published form is doubtless of 'a text free from any serious corruption,'[130] but the poesy and passion which vivified 'Marlowe's mighty line' is no longer there.

Edward the Second was the first 'historical' play in the language deserving the name, and with that fact to guide the reader it is difficult to gauge the real influence of Shakespeare upon its production, and even to doubt whether after all it was not due to its appearance that Shakespeare devoted himself to kindred themes. It is customary to compare Marlowe's play with Shakespeare's *Richard the Second*, the motive of the two plays being very similar, and the preference is generally given to the former. A great modern poet, whose unerring acumen in regard to poetic matters is universally acknowledged, deems that there is more discrimination of character in the earlier drama, and that the figures are more lifelike, and stand out more clearly as individual personalities.[131] Charles Lamb's remark is so well known that it hardly bears repetition, that 'the reluctant pangs of abdicating royalty in Edward furnished hints which Shakespeare scarce improved in his *Richard the Second*, and the death scene of Marlowe's king moves pity and terror beyond any scene, ancient or modern, with which I am acquainted.'[132]

Drawing attention to the individuals in this drama, one of Marlowe's latest editors points out that 'the character of the gay, frank, fearless, shameless favourite Piers Gaveston is admirably drawn. Even in the presence of death, with the wolfish eyes of the grim nobles bent on him from every side, he loses nothing of his old jauntiness. Marlowe has thoroughly realised this character, and portrayed it in every detail with consummate ability. Hardly less successful is the character of young Spenser, the insolent compound of recklessness and craft, posing as the saviour of society while he stealthily pursues his own selfish projects. . . . Edward, with all his weakness, is not all ignoble. In all literature there are few finer touches than when, after recounting his fearful suffering and privations in the dungeon, he gathers his breath for one last kingly utterance :

> " Tell Isabel, the queen, I looked not thus
> When for her sake I ran at tilt in France,
> And there unhorsed the Duke of Cleremont."

What heart-breaking pathos in those lines! For a moment, as his thoughts travel back across the years, he forgets the squalor of his dungeon and rides blithely beneath the beaming eyes of his lady.' [133]

The play is not beset with so many detachable gems as are its author's earlier works, but still poetic lines and characteristic utterances are not infrequent. Passages and allusions are cited from it to confirm the suggestion that Marlowe had been a

soldier, but there is not the slightest evidence or
probability that such ever was his occupation. The
discharged soldier's exclamation, in the first scene :

> ' Farewell, and perish by a soldier's hand,
> That would'st reward them with an hospital,'

sounds like a bid for the groundlings' applause, the
doleful condition of thousands of discharged warriors
being at that epoch the burning question of the day.
Another attempt to please the public, hitherto so
alien to Marlowe's disposition, is Edward's speech,
when threatened by the archbishop with excommuni-
cation unless he banish his favourite :

> ' Why should a king be subject to a priest?
> Proud Rome ! that hatchest such imperial grooms,
> For these thy superstitious taper-lights
> Wherewith thy anti-Christian churches blaze,
> I 'll fire thy crazèd buildings, and enforce
> The papal towers to kiss the lowly ground !
> With slaughtered priests make Tiber's channel swell,
> And banks raised higher with their sepulchres !'

The applause which greeted this girding at papal
pretensions seems to reach our ears as we read.
Such deference to public feeling was unwonted with
Marlowe, and unless the passages were interpolated,
or suggested to him by a shrewd observer, would
seem to imply that the poet had begun to learn that to
live the public's maw must from time to time be suitably
fed. Marlowe's reflections in this drama are sometimes so Shakespearian in tone and temper, that one
is frequently prompted to think he must have been
dipping his pen into the inkhorn of ' the young man

from Warwickshire.' There is the ring of Shakespeare's voice in these words of fiery young Mortimer, the prototype of the still more fiery Hotspur :

> ' I scorn, that one so basely born
> Should by his sovereign's favour grow so pert,
> And riot it with the treasure of the realm.
> While soldiers mutiny for want of pay,
> He wears a lord's revenue on his back,
> And Midas-like, he jets it in the court,
> With base outlandish cullions at his heels,
> Whose proud fantastic liveries make such show,
> As if that Proteus, god of shapes, appeared.
> I have not seen a dapper Jack so brisk ;
> He wears a short Italian hooded cloak,
> Larded with pearl, and, in his Tuscan cap,
> A jewel of more value than the crown.
> While others walk below, the king and he
> From out a window laugh at such as we,
> And flout our train, and jest at our attire.'

And again, in the advice of the crafty younger Spenser to Baldock, tutor of the king's niece :

> ' Then, Baldock, you must cast the scholar off,
> And learn to court it like a gentleman.
> 'Tis not a black coat and a little band,
> A velvet caped cloak, faced before with serge,
> And smelling to a nosegay all the day,
> Or holding of a napkin in your hand,
> Or saying a long grace at a table's end,
> Or making low legs to a nobleman,
> Or looking downward with your eyelids close,
> And saying, "Truly, an't may please your honour,"
> Can get you any favour with great men.
> You must be proud, bold, pleasant, resolute,
> And now and then stab, as occasion serves.'

All this is quite foreign to Marlowe's customary spiritual tone, which dealt only with mental problems, leaving to his famous friend the task of holding the mirror up to outward and visible show.   Does not the sign-manual of Shakespeare appear in such similes as these :

> ' The shepherd nipt with biting winter's rage
>   Frolics not more to see the painted spring,
>   Than I do to behold your majesty.'

Yet the accustomed poetic phase is found strongly pervading other passages, as when, for example, Gaveston pictures the allurements he will provide to charm his royal master :

> ' I must have wanton poets, pleasant wits,
>   Musicians, that with touching of a string
>   May draw the pliant king which way I please.
>   Music and poetry is his delight;
>   Therefore I'll have Italian masks by night,
>   Sweet speeches, comedies, and pleasing shows;
>   And in the day, when he shall walk abroad,
>   Like silvian nymphs my pages shall be clad;
>   My men, like satyrs grazing on the lawns,
>   Shall with their goat-feet dance the antic hay.[1]
>   Sometime a lovely boy in Dian's shape,
>   With hair that gilds the water as it glides,
>   Crownets of pearl about his naked arms,
>   And in his sportful hands an olive-tree,
>
>   .   .   .   .
>
>   Shall bathe him in a spring; and then hard by,
>   One like Actæon peeping through the grove,
>   Shall by the angry goddess be transformed,
>   And running in the likeness of an hart
>   By yelping hounds pulled down, and seem to die;—
>   Such things as these best please his majesty.'

The departure to death of the flippant young Mortimer, who 'as a traveller goes to discover countries yet unknown,' may be characteristic of the

---

[1] An ancient pastoral dance.

individual, but scarcely coincides with the opinion
Marlowe expresses, not only elsewhere but even in
this play, as when he puts into the mouth of Edward
when taken off by his captors :

> 'Of this I am assured,
> That death ends all.'

Marlowe's next dramatic venture, if indeed *The
Massacre of Paris* be by Marlowe, is by a general
consensus of opinion deemed the weakest and least
attractive of the works ascribed to him.   That he did
write some portions of this play does not seem open
to doubt, but whether he left the manuscript in a
fragmentary condition, and some weaker hand hastily
patched it together, or whether only an imperfect,
grossly corrupted copy of it is all that has been preserved—and there is strong evidence to support this
latter view—cannot be ascertained.   Another theory,
also with its probabilities, is that a manager induced
the popular poet to revise the nebulous production of
some underling, and that Marlowe, after devoting a
certain amount of labour to the task, abandoned it
in disgust, or was prevented from completing it by
his premature death.   Some of the soliloquies by the
Guise have a touch of the master's hand, as have also
some characteristic allusions, as that to 'Religion! Fie,
I am ashamed . . . to think a word of such a simple
sound, of so great matter should be made the ground,'
bear the imprint of his stylus.   Also :

> 'A royal seat, a sceptre, and a crown ;
> That those which do behold, they may become
> As men that stand and gaze against the sun.'

L

The exclamation of Ramus, the logician, when threatened with death by murderers on St. Bartholomew's night, unless he give them gold, is very characteristic: 'Alas, I am a scholar! how should I have gold?'

All in all, however, *The Massacre of Paris* displays few of Marlowe's idiosyncrasies, and as already suggested, is the poorest of the works attributed to him with any shadow of authority.

Another drama in which the poet was concerned is the tragedy of *Dido, Queene of Carthage.* This work, although left in a very imperfect condition, contains many traces of Marlowe's poetic magic. Nominally it was completed by Thomas Nashe, and albeit it is difficult to declare what portions are due to that 'biting satirist,' it is by no means impossible to assign to Marlowe much that is certainly his. His alliterative skill is much displayed, making it probable that *Dido* was an unfinished early effort.[133a] Typical of his younger days are the lines in which Æneas tells his adventures:

'With twice twelve Phrygian ships I ploughed the deep,
  And made that way my mother Venus led;
  But of them all scarce seven do anchor safe,
  And they so wrecked and weltered by the waves,
  As every tide tilts 'twixt their open sides;
  And all of them, unburdened of their load,
  Are ballassèd with billows' watery weight,
  But hapless I, God wot, poor and unknown,
  Do trace these Libyan deserts, all despised,
  Exiled forth Europe and wide Asia both,
  And have not any coverture but heaven.'

Or in Jupiter's address to Ganymede :

> ' Vulcan shall dance to make thee laughing-sport,
> And my nine daughters sing when thou art sad ;
> From Juno's bird I 'll pluck her spotted pride,
> To make thee fans wherewith to cool thy face ;
> And Venus' swans shall shed their silver down,
> To sweeten out the slumbers of thy bed ;
> Hermes no more shall show the world his wings,
> If that thy fancy in his feathers dwell.'

Some of the very lengthy speeches of Æneas furnish proofs of a similar parentage ; take this :

> ' Neoptolemus,
> Setting his spear upon the ground, leapt forth,
> And, after him, a thousand Grecians more,
> In whose stern faces shined the quenchless fire
> That after burnt the pride of Asia.'

Or these words of Venus to Juno :

> ' We two, as friends, one fortune will divide :
> Cupid shall lay his arrows in thy lap,
> And to a sceptre change his golden shafts ;
> Fancy and modesty shall live as mates,
> And thy fair peacocks by my pigeons perch.'

But innumerable passages, quite as representative, might be quoted in demonstration of the master's presence. Who can doubt the authorship of this speech by Dido ?—

> ' Speaks not Æneas like a conqueror ?
> O blessèd tempests that did drive him in !
> O happy sand that made him run aground !
> Henceforth you shall be (of) our Charthage gods.
> Ay, but it may be, he will leave my love,
> And seek a foreign land called Italy :
> O, that I had a charm to keep the winds
> Within the closure of a golden ball ;

Or that the Tyrrhene sea were in my arms,
That he might suffer shipwreck on my breast!

.   .   .   .

What if I sink his ships?   O, he will frown !

.   .   .   .

Armies of foes resolved to win this town,
Or impious traitors vowed to have my life,
Affright me not; only Æneas' frown
Is that which terrifies poor Dido's heart;
Not bloody spears, appearing in the air,
Presage the downfall of my empery,
Nor blazing comets threaten Dido's death;
It is Æneas' frown that ends my days.
If he forsake me not, I never die;
For in his looks I see eternity,
And he'll make me immortal with a kiss.'

It will be seen here, as in so many other lines of
Marlowe, that he repeats some of his best known
phrases : apparently such lines and thoughts, though
published later, are of his younger and less mature
days.   But it is needless to continue quotations when
the reason for citing them has already been attained.

Titus Andronicus is a play frequently ascribed to
Marlowe, although it is always included in the works
of Shakespeare.   Shakespeare's right to it is founded
on the fact that it was published as his in the first
folio, the 1623, edition of his works, and that Meres
mentioned it as Shakespeare's in his *Palladis Tamia*
in 1598.   The 1623 folio was evidently hastily and
carelessly edited, and must not be too rigidly believed
in, whilst the volume by Francis Meres is so fanciful,
so reliant upon rumour and wildly imaginative, that
none of its assertions, unless corroborated by unim-

peachable authority, may be accepted. No one thoroughly acquainted with the styles of Marlowe and Shakespeare dares ascribe *Titus Andronicus* to either, and yet there are lines and even lengthy speeches, the origin of which might be ascribed to both. There is the Shakespearian ring in those words of Demetrius :

> ' She is a woman, therefore may be wooed ;[134]
> She is a woman, therefore may be won,'

and in Aaron's statement that

> ' The emperor's court is like the house of Fame,
> The palace full of tongues, of eyes, of ears,'

and so forth, and there are also traces of Marlowe's work in this most repulsive of all plays, but it is needless to particularise them. '

The Taming of the Shrew is yet another drama in which Marlowe is frequently alleged to have had a hand. It is certainly full of Marloweisms, but there is no proof that their author implanted them there, or that they came there by lawful heritage. In 1594, the same year that a *Tytus Andronicus* was entered on the Stationers' Registers, was printed *The Taming of a Shrew*, and this latter play Shakespeare revised, in his masterly manner, and reproduced as *The Taming of the Shrew*. Although Shakespeare recast and largely rewrote the play, he adhered so closely to the original, doubtless in consequence of its popularity, that in later times there would have been no difficulty in obtaining an injunction to restrain the production of his revised edition of the work. There was nothing illegal in the transaction then : plays were considered common property, and if one obtained popularity it was by no means unusual for an enterprising manager to secure the services of an experienced playwriter to make an adaptation of it for his company.   No one suffered, unless it was the original writer, and his sufferings concerned no one but himself.   Sometimes, indeed, in self-protection or from sheer necessity, the author appears to have made the adaptation himself, without the intervention of any middleman.

Mighty as was the genius of Shakespeare, it is a patent fact that he was, above all, a shrewd man of business, and that as soon as he beheld a work popular, or that had been popular, and that was capable of being made still more so, he took it in hand and transmuted it into an everlasting thing of beauty. *The Taming of a Shrew* was evidently one of these manipulated productions.   Its anonymous author, probably an actor, had embellished his play with many imperfectly remembered or watered-down passages from the popular plays of *Faustus* and *Tamburlaine*, and therefore had no real grounds for complaint against a third person who might make use of the characters, or the plot, or the words, all of them having done service once or twice already. But Marlowe, it is pretty well evident, had nothing to do with this play of *The Shrew*, any more than he had to do with various others fathered upon him after his death.

A noteworthy point about Marlowe's completed dramas deserves recognition, as it is a sure manifestation of the highest genius, and that is the overwhelming grandeur and strength of their terminations. Conclusive proof of a dramatist's poverty of thought is afforded by a clumsy, supernatural *finale*. In *Edward the Second*, the interest and tragic power intensify as the climax is neared, whilst in *Faustus* the spectator breathlessly beholds inexorable fate gradually envelop the powerless victim and drag him down to relentless doom.

In the final scene, Marlowe's stage is not heaped up with a hecatomb of dead bodies, nor does he produce a *deus ex machina* to extricate his personages from their complicated difficulties. The agony of destiny and death is upon them, but though horror upon horror's head accumulates, the grandeur intensifies with the gloom, and the ending, though terrible, is felt to be unavoidable.

CHAPTER V

As a dramatic writer second to one only of his contemporaries, as a lyrical poet Marlowe was chief of
his clime and time. His death song of *Hero and
Leander*, professedly a paraphrase from the Greek of
the somewhat mythical Musæus, is the truest, purest,
most beautiful poem of its age, rich as it was in
lyrical poetry. It is unknown at what period of
Marlowe's career the work was begun, and it is only
known that it was left unfinished; but that it was the
product of his latest life all things seem to testify.
There is a finish and a dexterity in the manipulation
of the rhyme, rhythm, and language, that no tyro
could have attained. The poem is a fragment, incomplete in many respects, but, for all that, is full
evidence in itself that its author was an experienced
'maker,' a man whose skill had only been acquired
by long practice.

Hero and Leander was entered on the Stationers'
Books on September 28, 1593, but, owing to some
inexplicable cause, was not published until 1598. On
its first appearance the posthumously published poem
was dedicated by Edward Blunt, the publisher, to

214

Sir Thomas Walsingham, Marlowe's trusty friend, in the following terms :

'To the Right-Worshipful Sir Thomas Walsingham, Knight.

'Sir, we think not ourselves discharged of the duty we owe to our friend when we have brought the breathless body to the earth : for albeit the eye there taketh his ever-farewell of that beloved object, yet the impression of the man that hath been dear unto us, living an after-life in our memory, there putteth us in mind of farther obsequies due unto the deceased; and namely of the performance of whatsoever we may judge shall make to his living credit and to the effecting of his determinations prevented by the stroke of death. By these meditations (as by an intellectual will) I suppose myself executor to the unhappily deceased author of this poem; upon whom knowing that in his lifetime you bestowed many kind favours, entertaining parts of reckoning and worth which you found in him with good countenance and liberal affection, I cannot but see so far into the will of him dead, that whatsoever issue of his brain should chance to come abroad, that the first breath it should take might be the gentle air of your liking; for, since his self had been accustomed thereunto it would prove more agreeable and thriving to his right children, than any other foster countenance whatsoever. At this time seeing that this unfinished tragedy happens under my hands to be imprinted; of a double duty, the one to yourself, the other to the deceased, I present the same to your most favourable allowance, offering my utmost self now and ever to be ready at your worship's disposing :

'Edward Blunt.'

This lovely fragment of *Hero and Leander* has done more to create and enhance Marlowe's reputation among poets and lovers of choice poetry, and to endear him to his readers, than have all the manifold beauties of his magnificent dramas. Its sensuousness, never deteriorating into sensuality, portraying as it so vividly does the true purity of nature and

the warmth of passion proper to and inherent in
youth, leaves an unforgetable fragrance in the
memory.   The keynote of beauty is struck at the
beginning.   Tenderly, but firmly, the outlines of
Hero's supernatural loveliness are depicted :

> ' Some say for her, the fairest, Cupid pined,
> And, looking in her face, was strooken blind ';

whilst fate-forestalled Leander had

> ' A pleasant-smiling cheek, a speaking eye,'

and every grace that youth could have :

> ' The men of wealthy Sestos every year
> For his sake whom their goddess held so dear,
> Rose-cheeked Adonis, kept a solemn feast :
> Thither resorted many a wandering guest
> To meet their loves : such as had none at all
> Came lovers home from this great festival.'

Of course the twain were doomed to meet :

> ' On this feast-day—O cursèd day and hour !—
> Went Hero thorough Sestos, from her tower
> To Venus' temple, where unhappily,
> As after chanced, they did each other spy.'

To meet, to see, and so to love, was inevitable, for,
as their minstrel sings,

> ' It lies not in our power to love or hate,
> For will in us is overruled by fate.
> When two are stript long ere the course begin,
> We wish that one should lose, the other win ;
>
> .   .   .   .   .   .
>
> The reason no man knows, let it suffice,
> What we behold is censured by our eyes.
> Where both deliberate, the love is slight :
> Who ever loved, that loved not at first sight ? '

And then Leander pleaded to her in his simple, boyish way, but with the eloquence love taught him ; although Hero sought, yet half-heartedly, to put him off,

> ' Hero's looks yielded, but her words made war :
> Women are won when they begin to jar.'

Marlowe now interposes, as incidental to his story, a sweet little pastoral tale of a love adventure of Hermes : of how one day the much-bewinged deity

> 'Spied a country maid,
> Whose careless hair, instead of pearl t'adorn it,
> Glistered with dew, as one that seemed to scorn it ;
> Her breath as fragrant as the morning rose ;
> Her mind as pure, and her tongue untaught to glose :
> Yet proud she was (for lofty Pride that dwells
> In towered courts, is oft in shepherds' cells),
> And too-too well the fair vermilion knew
> And silver tincture of her cheeks that drew
> The love of every swain.'

Leaving this interlude and returning to the lovers, on whose behalf the god of Love himself now intervened, and so exerted his power that

> ' Sad Hero, with love unacquainted,
> Viewing Leander's face, fell down and fainted.
> He kissed her, and breathed life into her lips ;
> Wherewith, as one displeased, away she trips.'

But her flight was only feigned ; for, 'having a thousand tongues to lure him and but one to bid him go,' they dallied the daylight out together.

> ' And now Leander, fearing to be missed,
> Embraced her suddenly, took leave, and kissed :
> Long was he taking leave, and loath to go,
> And kissed again, as lovers use to do.

> Sad Hero wrung him by the hand, and wept,
> Saying, "Let your vows and promises be kept":
> Then standing at the door, she turned about,
> As loath to see Leander going out.'

Although the lovers had plighted their troth in the cloudy night, the news was speedily bruited abroad,

> 'For incorporeal Fame,
> Whose weight consists in nothing but her name,
> Is swifter than the wind';

and every one knew what had happened.

> 'Therefore even as an index to a book,
> So to his mind was young Leander's look.
>
> .   .   .   .   .   .
>
> Leander's father knew where he had been,
> And for the same mildly rebuked his son,
> Thinking to quench the sparkles new-begun.
> But love, resisted once, grows passionate,
> And nothing more than counsel lovers hate;
>
> .   .   .   .   .   .
>
> The more he is restrained, the worse he fares:
> What is it now but mad Leander dares?'

Spurred on by his insatiate passion, the headstrong youth determines to swim the Hellespont to Hero's distant tower.   After strange adventures, cold, wet, and weary, he reached at last the haven of his hopes,

> 'And knocked and called: at which celestial noise
> The longing heart of Hero much more joys
> Than nymphs and shepherds when the timbrel rings.
> Or crookèd dolphin when the sailor sings.
> She stayed not for her robes, but straight arose,
> And, drunk with gladness, to the door she goes;
> Where seeing a naked man, she screeched for fear
> (Such sights as this to tender maids are rare),
> And ran into the dark herself to hide
> (Rich jewels in the dark are soonest spied).

Unto her was he led, or rather drawn,
By those white limbs which sparkled through the lawn.

.   .   .   .

Treason was in her thought,
And cunningly to yield herself she sought,
Seeming not won, yet won she was at length :
In such wars women use but half their strength.'

And so in nuptial bliss the night was passed, and
when the midnight hours had sped,

' Thus near the bed she blushing stood upright,
And from her countenance behold ye might
A kind of twilight break, which through the air,
As from an orient cloud, glimpsed here and there;
And round about the chamber this false morn
Brought forth the day before the day was born.'

And thus this lovely poem was left, as far as
Marlowe was concerned, an 'unfinished tragedy.'

Had *Hero and Leander* remained, as its author
left it, unfinished, it had been well; but, as it would
appear, in compliance with some suggested dying
wish of Marlowe, his friend Chapman proceeded to
complete the idyll. The second edition of the poem,
with George Chapman's continuation appended to it,
appeared in 1598, the same year in which the first
edition of Marlowe's portion appeared. Chapman was
a man of considerable, albeit unequal, power, and of
great command of language; but was totally unlike
his dead friend in poetic fire. His long-drawn sequel
has much retarded the popularity and weakened the
effect of Marlowe's masterpiece. The fall from
Marlowe and Youth and Beauty to Chapman and
Ceremony is too disillusive. Let the reader close

the book where Marlowe breaks off, with the roseate flush of his imagination still flooding the page, his warm passion still palpitating through the rustling leaves, and the music of his verse still lingering in the air, 'like the sweet South, that breathes upon a bank of violets.'

There is another, a very short *Fragment*, assigned to Marlowe, in 1600, on the authority of the editor of *England's Parnassus*, in which anthology it appeared. The lines, 'I walked along a stream for pureness rare,' may be an extract from a charming poem, but in themselves the verses scarcely seem to call for the admiring comments they have lately received.[135] It would not be surprising to discover that this fragment, fathered on Marlowe after his decease, whilst his name was one to conjure by, owes its origin to Michael Drayton. The author of *The Barons Wars*, first published in 1596 as *Mortimeriados*, may for some good reason, or even inadvertently, have omitted the lines from his printed poem; they certainly read like an extract from that portion of his work describing Queen Isabel's chamber in 'The Tower of Mortimer.' In those days so many poems were passed about from hand to hand in manuscript that when they were eventually printed, generally by piratical publishers, they were frequently ascribed to the wrong person. *The Passionate Pilgrime* is a noted case; some lines of *Tamburlaine* are seen to have reappeared in Spenser's *Faery Queen*; whilst innumerable extracts from Marlowe's poems and dramas are found embedded in the works of Shakespeare and others of his contemporaries.

The pretty pastoral song entitled 'The Passionate Shepherd to his Love,' is the most known of all Marlowe's poetic labours, and, together with Sir Walter Raleigh's rejoinder, 'The Nymph's Reply,' has been included in nearly every English anthology of choice lyrical verse during the last three centuries. It was first published in 1599, minus the fourth and sixth stanzas, in *The Passionate Pilgrim*, a small collection of poems by various writers, but all ascribed by W. Jaggard, the publisher, to William Shakespeare. This collection, issued as 'by Shakespeare,' not only contained pieces by Marlowe and Raleigh, but also by Bartholomew Griffin, Richard Barnfield, and, when reprinted in 1612, by Thomas Heywood. Through this reprint of the piracy is known the fact that not only Heywood, but also Shakespeare, was indignant at the fraud, and compelled Jaggard, who may not have been entirely to blame, to withdraw the reputed author's name from the title-page. The publisher was not altogether without excuse for ascribing Marlowe's song to Shakespeare, seeing that it had been largely quoted from in *The Merry Wives of Windsor*, and, as was usual with Shakespeare and some of his contemporaries, without any reference to its authorship.

'Come live with me and be my love' was reprinted, with variations and additions, in *England's*

Helicon, another Elizabethan anthology, in 1600, and eventually, with other variations, in Walton's *Complete Angler* in 1655. In both these works it was assigned to Marlowe, and was accompanied by Raleigh's 'Nymph's Reply.' Quite recently a manuscript Commonplace Book of the sixteenth century has come to light, and amongst its contents is a version of Marlowe's song, differing from any other known one, and of Raleigh's 'Reply,' also with variations. Apparently all these various versions were quoted from memory, and as the 'Thornborough' manuscript is probably the oldest, and contemporaneous with Marlowe, whom the writer may very likely have met at the Earl of Pembroke's, it is now quoted *verbatim* : [136]

> ' Come lyve wth mee and bee my love
> And wee will all the pleasures prove
> that vallyes groves and woodes or feildes
> and craggie Rockes or mountaines yeildes
>
> Where wee will sitt upon the Rockes
> and see the sheppardes feede theire flockes
> by shallowe Ryvers to whose falles
> melodious birdes sings madrygalles
>
> Where wee make a bedd of Roses
> and thowsande other fragrant poses
> a capp of flowers and a kirtle
> imbrodred all wth leaves of myrtle
>
> A belt of strawe with Ivie budes
> wth corrall ¹ claspes and ¹ (amber?) studes
> if theise delightes thy mynde may move
> then lyve wth mee and bee my love

---

¹ Words erased in the Thornborough Manuscript—'amber' and 'bud.'

WILLIAM HERBERT, EARL OF PEMBROKE

From a painting by Vandyke.

PLATE XXV.

A goune made of the finest woolle
which from our little lambs wee pull
faire lined slippers for the coulde
with buckels of the pureste goulde

Thy dyshes shal be filde with meate
suche as the gods doe use to eate
shall one and everye table bee
preparde eache daye for thee and mee

The shepparde swaines shall daunce and singe
for thy delyght eache faire mornningne
if theise delights thy mynde may move
then lyve wth mee and bee my love'

Some errors of transcription or memory may be
due to Thornborough, but the making substantives
in the plural agree with verbs in the singular, as
in the fourth and eighth lines, was customary with
writers of the period. As the Commonplace Book
version of Raleigh's lines also differs in various
respects from the printed forms, it should be given
likewise. It reads thus :

' RESPONSE

' If all the world were love and younge
and truthe in everye shepparde tonge
theise prettie pleasures myghte mee move
to lyve withe thee and bee thy love

The flowers fade and wanton feildes
to waywarde winter reckninge yeildes
a hony tonge and a harte of galle
your fancies springe but sorrowes falle

Tyme dryves the flockes from feilde to folde
when ryvers rage and rockes growe colde
then philomela becomethe dombe
the reste complaines of cares to come

M

Thy gowne thy capp thy bedd of Roses
thy shooes thy kirtle and thy poses
soone vades soone witherethe soone forgotten
in follye ripe in reason rotten

What should wee talke of dainties then
of better meate then serveth men
all this is vaine eates (cates ?) serveth (?) goode
that God dothe blesse and sende for foode

If age coulde taste and love could breede
had age no date nor love noe neede
theise prettie pleasures myght mee move
to lyve with mee (*sic*) and bee my (*sic*) love

　　　　　finis'

It will be seen that Lord Pembroke's chaplain,
Thornborough, must have written down Sir Walter's
'Response' even more hurriedly, or more carelessly,
than he did Marlowe's song.

'A Dialogue in Verse,' and certain other pieces
of a commonplace or vulgar character, have been
ascribed to Marlowe, but it is scarcely worth while
repudiating their pretended paternity. The ascrip-
tion of the first-named fragment, given to the public
by the late J. P. Collier, is doubtless due to the
forger who tried to palm off, amongst many other
mischievous counterfeits, the notorious 'Atheist's
Tragedy,' a pseudo-antique ballad, containing various
pretended incidents in Marlowe's life.

Upwards of half a century ago reference was made
to the alleged existence of a quantity of verse presumedly by Marlowe, but it cannot be learned that
any investigation was made at the time with regard

to the supposed discovery, and now all research has failed to obtain any evidence upon the subject.[137] In 1850 the following particulars were published in *Notes and Queries* over the signature '*m*.':—

'MARLOWE'S AUTOGRAPH. *Seager, a Painter.*—In a MS. which has lately been placed in my hands, containing a copy of Henry Howard's translation of the last instructions given by the Emperor Charles V. to his son Philip, transcribed by Paul Thompson, about the end of the 16th century, are prefixed some poems in a different handwriting. The first of these is an eclogue, entitled *Amor Constans*, in which the dialogue is carried on by "Dickye" and "Bonnybootes," and begins thus: "For shame, man, wilt thou never leave this sorrow?" At the end is the signature, "Infortunatus, Ch. M." Following this eclogue are sixteen sonnets, signed also "Ch. M.," in two of which the author alludes to a portrait-painter named *Seager*. One of these sonnets commences thus:

> '"Whilst thou in breathinge cullers, crimson, white,
>   Drew'st these bright eyes, whose language sayth to me,
>   Loe! the right waye to heaven, love, stoode by thee
> Seager! fayne to be drawne in cullers brighte," etc.'

'I should be glad to receive any information,' continues this correspondent, 'respecting this painter, as also any hints as to the name of the poet Ch. M.

'May I add, also, another query? Is any authentic writing or signature of Christopher Marlowe known to exist?'

It is singular that no response appears to have
been made to these inquiries; and the communication
seems to have been left to pass unnoted into ob-
livion. That Marlowe wrote the twaddle cited is
utterly improbable, but whether the lines were forged
in the sixteenth or nineteenth century does not appear difficult of solution: they have a remarkably
modern air, yet are evidently the work of a man
acquainted with the Elizabethan period. No trace
can be found of 'Paul Thompson,' not even in the
original manuscript of Henry Howard's translation
in the British Museum, Cottonian Collection. There
were two Seagers, brothers, well-known portrait-
painters of the Shakespearian period, who are frequently referred to in contemporary works. No
sonnet by Marlowe has ever been identified, but it
is not improbable that some of those which pass
under the name of Shakespeare are by him. Who
'Bonnyboots' was is still a matter of speculation,
but numerous madrigals and songs, including some
set to music by Thomas Morley, the well-known
Elizabethan composer, have this unknown personage
for their hero.[138]

In 1600 a line-for-line translation of Lucan's *First
Book* was issued, with Marlowe's name as author
upon the title-page. The Introduction, written in
a sarcastic vein, and professedly by Thomas Thorpe,
the piratical publisher of Shakespeare's *Sonnets*, is
dedicated to Edward Blunt, the publisher who spoke
of Marlowe after his decease in such friendly and

eulogistic terms. If this version of Lucan were really by Marlowe, it was not only a posthumous publication, but had evidently never received the translator's final supervision ; although it is considered as equal to the original, it was a wasted labour for such a poet as was the author of *Hero and Leander* to have undertaken.

CHAPTER VI

LIFE'S LAST YEARS

ONCE more reverting to the personal history of Marlowe, it becomes necessary to investigate the recently promulgated account of his association with the author of that once famous drama, *The Spanish Tragedy*. The story of Kyd's alleged intimacy with Marlowe is founded upon the contents of certain manuscripts preserved in the British Museum. These documents should be examined in a critical, if not a sceptical, spirit. They form a portion of the celebrated collection made by Robert Harley, Earl of Oxford, and left by him to the nation. These manuscripts are more noted than known, and probably the authenticity of none of them has as yet been impugned. The question must now be asked, Are some of them of any more historical value than the notorious literary forgeries put forth by Ireland, Collier, and others of their sort? Such evidence as can be adduced in answer to the query will be furnished further on. (*Vide* Appendix B.)

Amongst these documents are many which Lord Oxford purchased from the well-known antiquary and nonjuror, Thomas Baker, a Fellow of St.

John's College, Cambridge, who lived in the reigns
of James the Second and William and Mary.   Baker
is asserted to have obtained possession of the official,
the State papers of Sir Thomas Puckering, Lord
Keeper to Queen Elizabeth.   How he managed to
obtain such papers and how he subsequently disposed of the bulk of them has never been explained.
An alleged portion of them are those now in question.
Originals or copies, the authenticity of some of them
is presumed to deeply affect the life-story and reputation of Christopher Marlowe.   Those purporting to refer to Marlowe's acquaintance with Thomas
Kyd, the writer, shall be commented upon now ;
others, relating to the infamous ' Baines Libel,'
later on.   All of these manuscripts are always spoken
of as *original* genuine documents of the period in
which the poet lived, even by those writers who
question the truth of the statements ascribed to
Baines, although Baker himself asserts that they
were ' copies ' of the originals made in his own handwriting.[139]

According to one of these manuscripts, a *facsimile*
of which has recently been published, Marlowe was
intimately acquainted with Kyd about 1591.   Following the story suggested by this document, a letter
supposed to have been written by Kyd to Sir John
Puckering, in the summer of 1593, the writer refers
to ' some occasion of our ' (Marlowe and Kyd)
' writing in one chamber two years since,' at which
suggested period, it should be recalled to mind,

Marlowe was at the zenith of his popularity, and his position and prospects were apparently very prosperous : his dramatic writings were in request, and his income should have been sufficient for his needs. He was associating with men of rank and wealth, men able and willing to have assisted him, were it needed, by money and influence, and when it is not improbable that he had a share in some of the theatrical ventures of the time.

On the other hand, Kyd appears to have been hard put to to live, and is seen to have been turning his pen at that very period to any hack work, however derogatory, in order to obtain subsistence. Yet, strange to relate, Kyd, according to this recently-discovered letter from him to Puckering, was then, and had been for some time, in the service of a highly respected and honoured but unnamed nobleman.[140]

Apparently this nobleman, who is represented by the letter to be a devout, or, at any rate, punctiliously careful citizen, was the one man in London ignorant of the fact that his trusted dependant, the sharer in the 'devyne praiers used duelie in his L'ps house,' was none other than the notorious writer of 'catchpenny,' tracts about 'secret murthers,' and the poisoning of citizens, concerning which the whole city must have been chattering. This 'penny-a-liner' is the man who is represented as speaking of Marlowe with contemptuous scorn, and as denying that he 'shold love or be familer frend with one so irreligious,' and 'besides he was intemperate and of a cruel hart, the verie contraries to which my greatest enemies will saie by me.'

This personage, this Kyd, of whom nothing kind has ever been recorded, after having thus stigmatised the man known during his life to his literary contemporaries as 'kind Kit Marlowe,' proceeds to remark that it is not 'to be numbered amongst the best conditions of men to tax or upbraid the dead,' then displays his charitable disposition by utterly uncalled-for reference to rumours, well knowing that such accusations often brought men to the stake, that the noble-hearted Harriott, the learned Warner, the poet Royden, and some stationers in St. Paul's Churchyard, 'whom I in no sort can accuse nor will excuse,' were apparently atheists. If this letter be the genuine composition of Thomas Kyd, and, for the sake of human nature it is to be hoped that it is not, there is no term too ignominious to designate him by.

'My first acquaintance with this Marlowe' is the somewhat involved statement in the letter ascribed to Kyd, 'rose upon his bearing name to serve my Lord, although his' (unnamed) 'Lordship never knewe his service, but in writing for his plaiers, ffor never cold my L. endure his name or sight, when he had heard of his conditions.' The names of the noblemen who could have employed the players who acted Marlowe's tragedies, were Lord Strange, afterwards Earl of Derby, the Earl of Pembroke, and Charles Howard, the Lord High Admiral, and none of these noblemen are known to have had anything to do with Kyd or his plays, and certainly in none of them can be discovered the ultra devout lordship who equally patronised prayers and players and obtained plays from an author he could not endure the name or sight of.

Although this letter is undated, it was, as already stated, assumed to have been written in the summer of 1593, some time after June 1st; this, however, is the merest conjecture, as there is no clue whatever to the date of its composition. In it Kyd is represented as referring to his arrest on the suspicion of being the author of, or concerned in the production of, a 'libell that concerned the State,' and as having his room ransacked for incriminating matter. What was discovered amongst his papers is supposed to have given rise to his having been further suspected of atheism. How readily the designation of atheist was bestowed at this time by one man upon another whose political, even as well as religious, opinions differed from his own, has been referred to already; but when this accusation involved a charge against a person of disbelieving in religion as established by law, or by the queen's authority, the charge was regarded as most heinous, and, if proved, was punishable by death.

In the letter in question Kyd is thus made to explain how suspicion arose of his orthodoxy being tainted: 'When I was first suspected for that libell that concerned the state, amongst those waste and

idle papers (which I carde not for) and which un-
askt I did deliver up, were founde some fragments
of a disputation, toching that opinion, affirmed
by Marlowe to be his, and shufled with some of
myne (unknown to me) by some occasion of our
wrytinge in one chamber twoe yeares synce.'

These fragments (preserved in the Harleian
MSS.) are endorsed on the back, '12 May 1593,
vile hereticall Conceiptes denyinge the deity of
Jhesus Christe oʳ Savior fownd emongst the papers
of Thos. Kydd prisoner'; they contain nothing of
an atheistic nature, but are really an exposition of
deism or unitarianism, supported by the quotation
of various biblical texts.   The whole matter is
summed up by the writer's opinion, 'I call that
true religion which instructeth mans minde with
right faith and worthy opinion of God. And I call
that right faith which doth creddit and beleve that
of God which the scriptures do testify not in a
few places.' Words certainly not sufficient to sub-
stantiate a charge of atheism nowadays, but much
too free and independent for that time ; for even less
men were consigned to a terrible death.

Time need not be expended in criticising these
fragments, as, although they may not have propounded anything that Marlowe, who was alive
at the date when they were 'found,' would have
disapproved of, neither their composition nor calligraphy is his.   The letter ascribed to Kyd contains
several Latin quotations written in an *italicised* hand-

writing differing from the rest of the document; and this italicised script is apparently that of the writer of the fragments, as a comparison will prove to any unprejudiced person. The last fragment was apparently signed, but, either by accident or intention, the signature has been torn off, or perhaps worn off, and only the first letter of it, either K or R, now remains. So Marlowe may be acquitted of the authorship of the theological disputation.

This letter is evidently intended to be read as having been written after Marlowe's death, and to inform the Lord Keeper of circumstances about the poet with which he was unacquainted, yet it is a strange fact that in the middle of May, although the writer of the letter was ignorant of it, Marlowe was charged with or accused of a state offence, for which he was ordered to put in an appearance before the 'Star Chamber,' as the room wherein the Privy Council held its sittings was designated. It is impossible that the charge against Marlowe could have resulted from this letter to Puckering, because, as is seen, *the letter was confessedly written after the poet's death*, and yet is presumed to introduce the name of Marlowe to the Lord Keeper for the first time.

Among the Acts of the Privy Council is a record that on the 18th May 1593, those present in the Star Chamber being the Archbishop of Canterbury, the Lord Keeper, the Lord Treasurer, Lord Derby, the Lord Chamberlain, Lord Buckhurst, Sir John Wolley, and Sir John Fortescue, a warrant was issued to

Henry Maunder, one of the messengers of Her Majesty's Chamber, 'to repair to the house of Mr. Thomas Walsingham, in Kent, or to any other place where he shall understand Christofer Marlow to be remaining, and by virtue thereof to apprehend and bring him to Court in his company.' [141]

Unfortunately, no documents can be discovered to show why Marlowe's presence was required by the Privy Council. The existing records of that all-powerful State body show that as at that time no crime, or alleged crime, was too considerable to escape its adjudication, so likewise was no offence too trivial for it to take cognisance of. No person, however powerful, or of any importance whatever, appears to have been able to avoid a visit to the much-dreaded office. Noblemen, knights, gentlemen, ladies, high sheriffs, learned professors, heads of colleges, all were summoned or arrested. Some were ordered into custody, and some punished, but the majority of them appear to have been severely admonished only : let off with a caution as to their future behaviour.

Woe betide those who neglected or refused to obey the order to appear ! They it was who were punished. There were instances, however, when excuses for non-attendance were accepted. At the very period when Marlowe was wanted, Mr. John Hall, gentleman, from Southampton, on his appearance excused the non-attendance of his sister, Mrs. Anne Rolles, who had also been summoned, on the very pertinent reason that she 'was not well at ease, and thereby (though she was in town) not in case to repair hitherto.' The plea seems to have been accepted on the understanding that on her recovering her ease Mrs. Rolles should attend on their Lordships.[142]

Only on the 23rd of the month preceding Marlowe's appearance, Dr. William Coale, president of Corpus Christi College, Oxford, who had been similarly sent for by their Lordships, entered an appearance, and was instructed in a similar way as was the poet, not to depart without special licence from Her Majesty's Privy Council.[143]

Mr. Thomas Walsingham, to whose house the Privy Council's messenger was to repair, was first cousin to Sir Francis Walsingham, the queen's secretary, and was father to Marlowe's friend, Sir Thomas Walsingham. Mr. Walsingham had an estate at Scadbury, Chislehurst, and the poet was doubtless visiting there at the time, probably to be away from the plague which was then desolating London.

The rector of Scadbury at this period was none other than the Rev. Richard Harvey, astrologer, almanac-maker, and, above all, brother of Gabriel Harvey, Thomas Nashe's bitter antagonist.[144] If Marlowe's arrest had been publicly effected at Scadbury, it has been surmised that it would have afforded peculiar gratification to the Harvey family, who held his name in detestation for his supposed approval of the satirist Nashe's onslaughts. Gabriel, writhing under Marlowe's silent contempt of him and his clique, was fond of venting his spite upon the poet by styling him or by comparing him with a peacock.

If Marlowe surrendered at the Walsingham's country-house, the affair was conducted so quietly that even the ferret instincts of Gabriel never enabled him to learn anything of the circumstance. The Privy Council records show that on the 20th of May, two days after the issue of the Star Chamber warrant, 'Christofer Marley of London, gentleman, being sent for by warrant from their Lordships, hath entered his appearance accordingly for his indemnity herein, and is commanded to give his daily attendance on their Lordships until he shall be licensed to the contrary.' [145]

This concluding injunction, as shown above, was a common one with their Lordships, when satisfied that the person's promise might be relied on, and that the case admitted of such leniency. Had the alleged crime been anything so heinous as that affirmed by Kyd, in the letter referred to, there would have been a very slender chance of Marlowe ever having been released from the clutches of their Lordships. The Privy Council's decision was really tantamount to letting the accused off on his own personal security, and would only have been adopted in cases where there was not sufficient cause to justify his detention. Either there was not enough evidence against him, or the offence with which he was charged was not of sufficient importance to justify his committal to the

custody of the officers of the Council.   Marlowe was,
doubtless, personally known to Lord Derby and others
of the Council present, but no personal knowledge
or friendly interest would have permitted any leniency
towards him had he been even suspected of atheism,
or even have proved to have been a recusant, against
which class of offenders much severity just then was
being shown.

What Marlowe's offence was is still an enigma.
Had he offended by speaking about religious or State
matters personally or through his dramatic personages?   The most likely cause of his arrest or
summons was that he had been carrying on, or aiding
and abetting others to, dramatic entertainments in
defiance of the Privy Council's order of the 6th of
that very month of May, as he had probably done
in 1588 of the Corporation's edict, that during the
continuance of the plague no plays or interludes
should be held in the city of London, 'for the avoiding of the assembling and the concourse of people
in any usual place appointed near the said city and
liberties thereof.' [146]

At that time there appears to have been several
arrests made of persons connected with these forbidden theatricals.   Edward Alleyn, the actor, who
was touring in the provinces, wrote on the 2nd of
May, from Chelmsford, to his wife in London, with
reference to a rumour which had reached him of her
being concerned in some infringement of the Order
against dramatic entertainments in the metropolis

during the plague : 'They say, that you weare by my lorde maiors officer mād to rid in a cart, you and alle your felowes (actors) which I ame sory to hear.' [147]

Doubtless Marlowe, if not a shareholder in one of the licensed companies, had at any rate, with his usual disdain of authority, upheld the players in their attempt to disregard the recent injunction to deprive them for the time being of their only means of obtaining a livelihood ; or he had done, or had permitted to be done, or had assisted in doing, something contrary to the Order of the Privy Council, even as Mrs. Alleyn was supposed to have done against the civic edict.

Whatever Marlowe's offence, his appearance 'accordingly for his indemnity,' was evidently considered satisfactory, and their Lordships allowed him to be released. Free from the environs of the Privy Council, it was necessary to get out of plague-stricken London with all speed, as the terrible pest was carrying off victims by thousands. There was an universal exodus of all persons able to escape, yet for dramatic purposes, it would probably be desirable for Marlowe to be within easy access of the metropolis ; accordingly, he seems to have gone to Deptford, where Anthony Marlowe, apparently a relative of his, resided.

Anthony was a man of considerable mercantile importance, and as representative of the all-powerful Muscovy Company, contractor to the Government for very large quantities of Admiralty stores. [148] He was married to Elizabeth, daughter of William Gonston, Treasurer of Marine Causes, and was included in the latest visitation amongst those gentlemen entitled to bear arms. As there are good reasons for considering that Anthony Marlowe was interested in and sympathised with dramatic matters, he could not but receive his famous kinsman hospitably.

Lying off Deptford was a vessel nicknamed after the famous sailor, Drake, who had circumnavigated the world in it, *The Golden Hind.* It was strongly built and, in those days, considered a very large ship. A foreigner who visited it about that time records it as looking 'exceeding fit to undertake so protracted and dangerous a voyage' as Francis Drake had made in it. 'The cabins and armouries,' continues this traveller, who was secretary to the Duke of Wirtemberg, 'are in fine order, as in a well-built castle; in the middle, where the largest cannon are placed, it is eighteen good paces wide; what its length must be in proportion may be easily judged.' [149]

This grand old vessel was an object of wonder and curiosity, and large numbers of people came from afar to inspect it. Amongst others, Queen Elizabeth herself paid a visit to it, and being magnificently entertained by 'that old pirate, Francis Drake,' knighted him before her departure, much to the surprise and disgust of certain sober-minded folk.

After the royal visit, *The Golden Hind* became a popular place of resort for holiday folks of various ranks. The cabin was converted into a banqueting-

EXTRACT FROM BURIAL REGISTER OF ST. NICHOLAS CHURCH, DEPTFORD

'Christopher Marlowe, slain by ffrancis Archer, sepultus 1. of June.'

PLATE XXVI.

room, or saloon for refreshments, for the numerous visitors who came daily to the dockyard to see the first English ship that had sailed round the globe. Ben Jonson, Chapman, and Marston, in their play of *Eastward Hoe!* make one of their characters say, 'We'll have our provided supper brought aboard Sir Francis Drake's ship, that hath compassed the world, where with full cups and banquets we will do sacrifice for a prosperous voyage.'[150]

According to a long-lived local tradition, it was on one fatal day at the end of May 1593, Marlowe accompanied some companions in a visit to the famous old vessel.[151] What followed is a matter of conjecture only, without a single iota of contemporary evidence to elucidate the mystery. All that is known with certainty is that the poet, either accidentally or intentionally, was fatally wounded by some person named Francis Archer. Of the various varying accounts of the poet's death, the most probable one is that alluded to by William Vaughan, in 1599, wherein, after saying that the tragedy took place at Deptford, he states that Marlowe, intending to stab with his 'ponyard' a man who 'had invited him thither to a feast, and was then playing at tables' (*i.e.* draughts), was himself so severely wounded by his opponent's dagger that 'hee shortly after dyed.'

The earliest writers to refer to Marlowe's death, although none of them appears to have had trust-worthy accounts of it, speak of him as having received 'all the help surgery could afford,' and, therefore, as not having died from his wound at once. In the duel, riot, fight, accident, assassination, or whatever it may have been, the poet was not apparently killed immediately. He may have lingered for two or three days. The only meaning which can be assigned to Chapman's words, in the 'Address' prefixed to his continuation of *Hero and Leander*, as to Marlowe's 'late desires' that he (Chapman) should complete the poem, is that Marlowe must have spoken about it when he knew that he was dying.

An inquest and a coroner's verdict must have followed the death, but no record of the case can now be traced. On the 1st day of June 1593 all that was mortal of the poet was buried in the churchyard of St. Nicholas, Deptford, near Greenwich.

One of the brightest intellects of the age was suddenly annihilated; one of the country's purest poetic geniuses was snatched from life just as his powers were ripening to fulfilment. Prognostication in the presence of fact is purposeless, yet it is difficult to avoid thinking with what glorious masterpieces might the world have been dowered had Shakespeare's only compeer at thirty have survived to the fifty years which Shakespeare lived to; if only some further fulfilment had been granted to Marlowe's

'Yearning in desire
To follow Knowledge like a sinking star
Beyond the utmost bound of human thought.'

CHURCH OF ST. NICHOLAS, DEPTFORD, BEFORE RESTORATION

PLATE XXVI.

APPENDIX A

Post Mortem. I.

1593. The first of Marlowe's contemporaries known to have mentioned his death was George Peele. His poem in *Honour of the Garter* is dated the 26th of June. It was written to commemorate the investure with that decoration of certain worthies, including Henry Percy, Earl of Northumberland. After addressing that nobleman as 'The Muse's love, patron, and favorite,' because 'other patrons have poor poets none,' now that 'liberal Sidney' and 'virtuous Walsingham are fled to heaven,' Peele continues:

> 'And after thee
> Why hie they not, unhappy in thine end,
> Marley, the Muses' darling, for thy verse,
> Fit to write passions for the souls below,
> If any wretched souls in passion speak.'

Nashe (who subsequently, in reply to one of Gabriel Harvey's attacks, denied that he had ever abused Marlowe), in the Epistle prefixed to his *Christ's Tears Over Jerusalem*, published in 1593, sorrowfully exclaims, 'Poore deceased Kit Marlowe!' and in other works spoke of him admiringly.

Shakespeare is supposed to have written *A Midsummer Night's Dream* in 1593 or 4, and there evidently recalled to his 'mind's eye' his partner in dramatic lore, when he thus apostrophises that dead friend and fellow-worker as the poet whose fiery zeal and lofty ideals brooked no restraint or remonstrance:

> 'The lunatic, the lover, and the poet,
> Are of imagination all compact:
> One sees more devils than vast hell can hold—

> That is the madman.   The lover, all as frantic,
> Sees Helen's beauty in a brow of Egypt.
> The poet's eye, in a fine frenzy rolling,
> Doth glance from heaven to earth, from earth to heaven :
> And, as imagination bodies forth
> The forms of things unknown, the poet's pen
> Turns them to shapes, and gives to airy nothing
> A local habitation and a name.'[152]

No more appropriate and appreciative allusion to Marlowe was ever or could ever have been uttered than those lines by Shakespeare, who again, in *As You Like It*, gently refers to his deceased friend, in quoting a line from *Hero and Leander* :

> ' Dead Shepherd, now I find thy saw of might,
> Who ever loved, that loved not at first sight ?'[153]

George Chapman, however unequal to wage rivalry with Marlowe, still a man of genius, in 1598 published a continuation of his friend's *Hero and Leander*.   In dedicating the composition to Lady Walsingham, wife of Sir Thomas, referred to as 'my honoured best friend,' Chapman apologises for putting his signature to a subject 'On which more worthinesse of soul hath been shewed, and weight of divine wit,' and in his work expresses the hope that he may

> ' Find th' eternal clime
> Of his free soul whose living subject stood
> Up to the chin in the Pierian flood.'[154]

In the same year a youthful poetling, not possessing the divine fire himself, although able to appreciate it in others, also had the temerity to publish a continuation of the dead shepherd's death-song.   The verses and the very name of Henry Petowe had perished had they not been combined in typifying the reverential feelings of even the veriest versifiers of the age towards the idol of their worship.   One short extract will suffice :

> ' Marlo admired, whose honney-flowing vaine
> No English writer can as yet attaine ;
> Whose name in Fame's immortall treasurie
> Truth shall record to endles memorie ;

Marlo, late mortall, now framed all divine,
What soule more happy than that soule of thine?
Live still in heaven thy soule, thy fame on earth !
Thou dead, of Marlos Hero findes a dearth.

.   .   .   .

Oh, had that king of poets breathèd longer,
Then had faire beautie's fort been much more stronger !
His goulden pen had closed her so about
No bastard æglet's quill, the world throughout,
Had been of force to marre what he had made.

.   .   .   .

What mortall soule with Marlo might contend,
That could 'gainst reason force him stoope or bend?
Whose silver-charming toung moved such delight,
That men would shun their sleepe in still darke night
To meditate upon his goulden lynes.'[155]

The *Chorus Vatum* grew stronger and brighter, even Ben
Jonson being heard to say that Marlowe's 'mighty lines
were examples fitter for admiration than for parallel.'[156]
The admiring utterances of Marlowe's contemporaries, the
men who knew him, admired him, and were never known
to whisper a syllable against the character of 'kind Kit
Marlowe,' may fitly finish with the lines of Michael Drayton,
in his Epistle to Henry Reynold's *Of Poets and Poetry*.
They are evidently reminiscent of the above-quoted verses
of Shakespeare, and show that Drayton knew to whom the
words referred :

'Next Marlowe, bathèd in the Thespian springs,
Had in him those brave translunary things
That the first poets had ; his raptures were
All ayre and fire, which made his verses cleare ;
For that fine madness still he did retaine,
Which rightly should possesse a poet's braine.'[157]

Post Mortem. II.

But others than those who *knew*, loved, and reverenced
the deceased poet, could now have their say. Gabriel
Harvey, 'sonne to the halter maker,' as Nashe spitefully
styled the ropemaker's offspring, does not appear to have had

any real reason for venting his venom on 'kind Kit Marlowe,' unless that saying Nashe fathered on him was the poet's, that Richard Harvey, Gabriel's brother, 'was an asse, good for nothing but to preach of the Iron Age.' This Gabriel was an unscrupulous calumniator of the dead. He gathered garbage from every dust-heap with which to disfigure the graves of the defenceless dead. He had not dared to splutter much about Marlowe living, beyond comparing him with a peacock, but for him deceased he prepared his customary obituary. He was the first to gloat over the poet's loss. In some cryptic verse he vindictively refers to 'Tamburlaine's' death from the plague, evidently deeming 'the hawty man' had been carried off by the prevailing epidemic. His marvellous epistle, the *Newe Letter of Notable Contents*, is dated September 1593.

No further unfriendly allusion to Marlowe is discoverable until 1597, four years after his death. In that year Thomas Beard, one of the so-called Puritans, issued a farrago of everything unsavoury that he could scrape together, his compilation being, as he says in his Epistle Dedicatory, 'partly translated out of the French, and partly collected by mine owne industrie out of many authors,' and not, therefore, from his own knowledge. This he issued to the world as *The Theatre of God's Judgements*. Not only is the volume one of the filthiest of the evil-minded school to which it owes its origin, but its superstitious stories are utterly inane. Amongst its examples of God's judgments against atheists is one of a man, who having sold his soul to Satan for a cup of wine, Satan flies off with his bargain in full view of the surrounding company. Other equally edifying tales are told, especially of the wearers of the Papal tiara, several of whom, besides having committed unnameable misdeeds, were, according to Beard, reputed to have been punished for atheistic utterances. Another example, Rabelais, is stated to have been deprived of his senses, so that he might die a brutish death; various poets, for their folly in writing verses, perished miserably, whilst lastly Marlowe served his turn to adorn a tale. Beard's story is:

'Marlin, by profession a scholler . . . but by practise a playmaker and a poet of scurrilitie, who by giving too large a swing to his owne wit, and suffering his lust to have the full reines, fell (not without just desert) to that outrage and extremitie, that he denied God and his sonne Christ, and not onely in word blasphemed the Trinitie, but also (as it is credibly reported) wrote bookes against it, affirming our Saviour to be but a deceiver, and Moses to be but a conjurer and seducer of the people, and the holy Bible to bee but vaine and idle stories, and all religion but a device of policie. But see what a hooke the Lord put in the nostrils of this barking dogge!

'It so fell out, that in London streets, as he purposed to stab one whome hee ought (owed) a grudge unto with his dagger, the other party perceiving so avoided the stroke, that withall catching hold of his wrest, he stabbed his owne dagger into his owne head, in such sort that notwithstanding all the meanes of surgerie that could be wrought, he shortly after died thereof; the manner of his death being so terrible (for hee even cursed and blasphemed to his last gaspe, and together with his breath an oath flew out of his mouth), that it was not only a manifest signe of God's judgement, but also an horrible and fearefull terror to all that beheld him. But herein did the justice of God most notably appeare, in that hee compelled his owne hand, which had written those blasphemies, to bee the instrument to punish him, and that in his braine which had devised the same.' [158]

Even this account, circumstantial as if taken down by an eye-witness, does not persuade the impartial mind from preferring the evidence of the church register: from believing that Marlowe instead of dying by his own hand was slain by Francis Archer. It may be mentioned that when a second edition of Beard's bestial book was published fifteen years later, the words 'London streets' were omitted.

In 1598 was issued another 'hotchpotch' of various marvels of all kinds, relating to celebrated persons and collected from 'authors both sacred and profane, out of which these similitudes are for the most part gathered.' This book, *Palladis Tamia*: *Wits Treasury*, is by a certain 'Francis Meres, M.A. of both Universities.' Fluellin did not devise further fetched coincidences to prove the similarity between Monmouth and Macedon, than did this Meres to prove likenesses between famous English and celebrated Latin authors. When he could not discover any possible resemblance he appears to have invented one. Whilst giving Thomas Beard as his authority for the legend about Marlowe, he could not forego the opportunity of adapting it to his own purposes by adding the necessary embellishment. His revised account runs thus:

'So our tragical poet, Marlow, for his Epicurisme and Atheisme had a tragicall death; you may read of this Marlow more at large in *The Theatre of Gods Judgements*, in the 25th chapter entreating of Epicures and Atheists.

'As the poet Lycophron was shot to death by a certain rival of his, so Christofer Marlow was stabd to death by a bawdy servingman, a rival of his in his lewde love." The invention of "a rival in his lewde love" was absolutely requisite to prove the resemblance between the two tragedies: that the authority quoted did not mention the fact was of no consequence to the fantastic Francis Meres.[159]

The next godly man to push onwards the snowball of slander was William Vaughan, who, in his *Golden Grove*, dated 1699, enlarged upon the favourite subject of atheists. Leo the Tenth, one of his examples, was punished for public confession of infidelity by dying in a fit of laughter; in another case an unnamed Italian warrior, for a similar offence, was the first slain in a battle; whilst Marlowe, 'by profession a playmaker,' was the next warning instance. This example, 'as it is reported, about 14 years ago (*i.e.* 1585) wrote a Booke against the Trinitie; but see the effects of Gods justice. It so hapened that at Detford, a little village about three miles from London, as he meant to stab with his ponyard one named Ingram (*sic*) that had invited him thither to a feast, and was then playing at tables (*i.e.* draughts), hee quickly perceiving it, so avoyded the thrust that withal drawing out his dagger for his defence, hee stabd this Marlow into the eye, in such sort, that his braines comming out at the daggers point, hee shortly after dyed. Thus did God, the true executioner of divine justice, worke the ende of impious Atheists.'[160]

Vaughan, it will be noticed, has really got hold of the name of the place where the catastrophe occurred, and, amid other modifications, furnishes the name, but of course incorrectly, of the slayer. By this time the story of Marlowe's miserable end had been told so often, always with variations and additions, that by its constant repetition it obtained general credence, and was adopted as a record of fact. 'To repeat a story after another is not to confirm it,' is Gifford's expostulation when clearing Ben Jonson's memory from calumny, but still such slanders are continually heard, and as recklessly retold. Versifiers and others affect to believe in everything evil suggested about Marlowe as steadfastly as did Othello in Desdemona's falseness. The anonymous author of *The Return from Parnassus* (a versified drama published in 1606, but written a few years earlier), who, besides manifesting his dislike to university authors generally, had evidently read some of the libels, is supposed to fully confirm the lies of the godly about our poet (whom he did not scruple to plagiarise without the slightest acknowledgment or reference) by these lines :

'Marlowe was happy in his buskin Muse,—
Alas, unhappy in his life and end !
Pity it is, that wit so ill should dwell,
Wit lent from heaven, but vices sent from hell.'[161]

After that nothing more is to be said, so it is needless to continue the catalogue. The longer the date from the poet's days, the less likely were the libels upon his character to be refuted. It has been seen that his contemporaries, the men who really knew Marlowe and consorted with him, Drayton, Chapman, Shakespeare, the magnificent concourse of immortals, uttered nothing but admiring and reverential words of him, and that not one of them spoke a disparaging syllable over the dead poet's grave. The letter imputed to Kyd, even could its authenticity be proved, is tainted testimony, and would not influence any legal tribunal.

No trust can be placed in the posthumous rabid ravings of either Beard or Vaughan, or the fantastic fooleries of Francis Meres, nor of their copyists. All impartial people will be prepared to agree with Dr. Grosart in entirely doubting the traditional 'tragic end'; for, as he points out, 'with one possessed of so strenuous a nostril for scenting out such carrion gossip as Gabriel Harvey, ignorant of that "tragic end," one may well question if ever it were true.'

There was no contemporary statement of the poet's death, except the Deptford register, and that simple record may as well refer to one slain accidentally by relative or friend, as to one purposely killed by a foe.

APPENDIX B

The Baines Libel

Reference has been made in this work to various MSS. of the Harleian Collection in the British Museum. A large portion of this Collection was purchased by Robert Harley, Earl of Oxford, from the well-known nonjuror, Thomas Baker, a fellow of St. John's College, Cambridge. These MSS., which are bound in several large volumes, consist of many documents of surpassing literary and political interest, documents which Baker declared in his will were '*of my own handwriting*,' having been copied from originals, none of which originals are now known to be in existence. A further fifteen of these folio volumes were devised to St. John's College, Cambridge, and the MSS. in them are likewise averred by Baker, to be 'all in my writing.' When Bennet, the editor of Ascham's English works, complained that these documents 'are unskilfully transcribed,' Masters, in explanation, pointed out that this is due to 'their being *copied* from the Original according to the old way of spelling.'[162]

Surely this is sufficient evidence to prove that the MSS. in question are not original, but only copies by Baker. Having disposed of their originality, the next thing is to examine their authenticity: are they really copies of veritable old documents, or are they merely forgeries such as Collier, Ireland, and many others, have foisted on the literary world? If one MS. prove fictitious, the whole collection must be regarded with strong suspicion.

Baker is known to have been an indefatigable collector of antiquities; saturated with literary lore, especially of the Elizabethan period, and always able and willing to supply

historical students with just such items of information as
they needed.   Many of his lucky discoveries have been
embodied in standard works, and may, in these days, be
capable of corroboration, but whence Baker obtained them
is a mystery.   As is also what became of the results of his
many years of seclusive study ; of the wonderful works he
was to produce, but which he died without accomplishing.
Does not the wording of his will provide the key to the
enigma?   The MSS. Baker bequeathed to St. John's College,
Cambridge, have been carefully catalogued : they make
a marvellous collection.   Many of them are by persons
as unknown to history as Chatterton's 'Rowley'; several
furnish particulars of celebrities nowhere else recorded ;
whilst others are unknown pieces by known persons.
There is something strange or unique about most of them.
Occasionally it is noted of a manuscript that 'Baker thinks'
it is in such a person's own writing, although later on, in his
will, he declared the whole contents of these large folio
volumes are 'all in my own hand.' [163]

It has already been remarked in connection with Kyd's
alleged intimacy with Marlowe that Baker is said to have
asserted he had obtained possession of some of Sir John
Puckering's official papers.   Besides the Kyd documents
already referred to, these Puckering papers include two
manuscripts still more strongly affecting the memory of
Marlowe : one, first published by Ritson, the bibliographer,
in his *Observations on Wharton's History of English Poetry*,
and the other recently embodied by Professor F. S. Boas
in the Introduction to his volume of the *Works of Thomas
Kyd*.   If genuine, these two documents are of intense
interest, but if forgeries, they inflict cruel wrong on the
memory of an already much maligned poet.

Many circumstances cast doubt upon the authenticity of
these two documents, even if Baker's own testamentary
declaration be disregarded.   The first and, until Professor
Boas's recent publication, the only one generally known
of these two manuscripts, appears to be the rough and
original draft of the more carefully drawn document

recently published. This original draft has been known and commented upon by numerous writers since it was first unearthed by Ritson.[164] It is styled 'A NOTE,' and is headed as 'Contayninge the opinion of one Christofer Marly, concernynge his damnable opinions and judgment of relygion and scorne of Gods worde.'

This *Note* has been referred to by some authors as being the production of an enemy of the poet, and its charges against him as being unworthy of credit, seeing that whilst some are ludicrously improbable, others are in direct conflict with his known words and opinions; but no one apparently has regarded the *Note* as a forgery and of a much more recent date than the Elizabethan epoch. The authenticity of the document is made suspectable by many circumstances. Many noteworthy alterations and cancellations have been made in the wording of this draft, and especially in the heading; the original heading has been struck through, and the following words substituted for it: '*A Note delivered on Whitsun eve last of the most horreble blasphemes uttereyd by Christofer Marly who within* 111 *dayes after came to a soden and fearfull end of his life.*'

A very remarkable item to be regarded in this *Note* is that as a matter of fact Marlowe was dead and buried before Whitsun eve! Whitsun eve, 1593, occurred on the second of June, and the poet was buried in the churchyard of St. Nicholas, Deptford, on the first of that month! On the face of it it would appear as if the forger had forgotten the leap-years, even as he who forged the letter from Peele to Marlowe, in the Lansdowne Collection, misdated it two years after the poet's death!

The body of this first draft of the *Note* imports that it is an affidavit by 'Richard Bome,' but the signature is 'Rychard Baine.' The diversity of spelling at that period was phenomenal, but the orthography of this *Note* is as suspiciously pseudo-antique as is that of many of the ballads in Percy's *Reliques*. Professor F. S. Boas has brought to light amongst the Harleian MSS., 'bought from Mr. Baker,' another and apparently an amended copy of the *Note*, although he regards it as the original of the Baines Libel. It is a little better devised, as if written more leisurely than the other; it introduces the name of Sir Walter Raleigh as the patron of Harriott, and gives the name in the body of the *Note*, as well as for the signature, most distinctly as ' Richard Baines.'

This so-called *Note* ascribes all kinds of criminal offences, both civil and theological, to Marlowe ; and that it may be seen of what nature its contents are, it is now reprinted, as far as is legally permissible :

' That the Indians and many Authors of Antiquitei have assuredly written of above 16 thowsande yeers agone, wher Adam is proved to have leyved within 6 thowsande yeers.

' He affirmeth That Moyses was but a Juggler, and that one Heriots can do more then hee.

' That Moyses made the Jewes to travell fortie yeers in the wildernes (which jorny might have ben don in lesse then one yeer) er they came to the promised lande, to the intente that those who were privei to most of his subtileteis might perish and so an everlastinge supersticion remayne in the hartes of the people.

' That the firste beginnynge of Religion was only to keep men in awe.

' That it was an easye matter for Moyses, beinge brought up in all the artes of the Egiptians, to abuse the Jewes, being a rude and grosse people.

' That Christ was . . .

' That he was the sonne of a carpenter, and that, yf the Jewes amonge whome he was borne did crucifye him, thei best knew him and whence he came.

' That Christ deserved better to dye than Barrabas, and that the Jewes made a good choyce, though Barrabas were both a theife and a murtherer.

' That yf ther be any God or good Religion, then it is in the Papistes, because the service of God is performed with more ceremonyes, as elevacion of the masse, organs, singinge, men, *shaven crownes*, etc. That all protestantes ar hipocriticall Asses.

'That, yf he wer put to write a new religion, he wolde undertake both a more excellent and more admirable methode, and that all the new testament is filthely written.

'That the Women of Samaria wer . . .

'That St. John the Evangelist was . . .

'*That all thei that love not tobacco and . . . are fooles.*

'That all the Appostells wer fishermen and base fellowes, neither of witt nor worth, that Pawle only had witt, that he was a timerous fellow in biddinge men to be subject to magistrates against his conscience.

'*That he had as good right to coyne as the Queen of Englande, and that he was acquainted with one Poole, a prisoner in newgate, whoe hath great skill in mixture of metalls, and havinge learned such thinges of him, he ment, through help of a cunnynge stamp-maker, to coyne french crownes, pistolettes, and englishe shillinges.*

'That, yf Christ had instituted the Sacramentes with more cerymonyall reverence, it would have ben had in more admiracion, that it wolde have ben much better beinge administered . . .

.   .   .   .

'That one Richard Cholmelei hath confessed that he was perswaded by Marloes reason to become an Athieste.

'*Theis thinges, with many other, shall by good and honest men be proved to be his opinions and common speeches, and that this Marloe doth not only holde them himself, but almost in every company he commeth, perswadeth men to Athiesme willinge them not to be afrayed of bugbeares and hobgoblins and utterly scornynge both God and his ministers, as I Richard Bome will justify bothe by my othe and the testimony of many honest men, and almost all men with whome he hath conversed any tyme will testefy the same, and, as I thincke, all men in christianitei ought to endevor that the mouth of so dangerous a member may be stopped.*

'*He sayeth moreover that he hath coated a number of contrarieties out of the scriptures, which he hath geeven to some great men, who in convenient tyme shalbe named. When*

O

theis thinges shalbe called in question, the witnesses shalbe produced.   'RYCHARD BAINE.'

(Endorsed.)
   'Copye of Marloes blasphemyes
      as sent to her H(ighness?).'

The words printed in italics have been scored through in this manuscript.

As nothing in connection with this *Note* happened it was necessary, if any use were made of it, by sale or gift, to explain the reason, and therefore the 'soden and fearfull end of his life' was endorsed on the draft.[164a]

The two other remarkable documents bearing upon the subject of Marlowe's life and opinions are among the manuscripts in the Harleian Collection 'purchased from Mr. Baker.' Both the letter purporting to have been written to Sir John Puckering by Thomas Kyd (although the signature to it is unlike the authentic signature by him in Lambeth Palace Library) and the theological treatise have already been commented upon, and the reader who is unable to compare these manuscripts with one another, or with genuine documents of the period, must judge by these comments. It may be stated that the watermarks in the paper of all four of these documents bear a suspicious family resemblance to each other, a fact which corroborates Baker's declaration that they are all in his own handwriting, and indicates they are all on paper belonging to one individual.

It may be justly asked, If these are copies, what has become of the originals from which they were copied; and what caused the discrepancies between the two copies of the *Note*? If the *Note* be really a genuine state document, why was a variant of it made, and why is neither copy dated, nor attested, nor witnessed, nor addressed to any one, nor has, apparently, been executed in the presence of any experienced legal functionary; nor furnishes the year of the queen's reign, as all official documents would do; nor why 'her H' (if *Highness* be intended) is used for the sovereign, seeing that since Henry VIII. had replaced the former title by ' Majesty ' the latter had been always used, at least officially ; nor why a contemporary did not know when Whitsun took place ; nor why the spelling is occasionally modern ; nor how many other suspicious particulars can be explained? It is singular that Kyd should be so careful to relate all the various circumstances of his own case in writing to the Lord Keeper, who must have been fully conversant with them already ; but it is a pity, if the letter be genuine, that he so carefully avoided naming the nobleman for whom he and Marlowe had worked and whose sympathy on his behalf he now wished Puckering to arouse. The most extraordinary thing of all this is that none of the persons referred to by Kyd's letter appears to have been punished or even tried for these allegations.

The more the matter is investigated, the more improbable does the indictment appear : with all the facts, as now set forth before us, can any credence be given (not to the statements of the Baines Libel, for they have all along been regarded as palpably false and absurd) to the belief that these documents were written by the persons alleged and at the period stated?

APPENDIX C

The Marlowe Family

An account of how the poet's relatives fared after his death will not prove uninteresting. The well-preserved records of Canterbury show what happened to them. Mary, the first of the children born to John and Catherine Marlowe, died in 1568. There does not appear to be any further trace of Joan after her marriage to John Moore, in 1585, and she, doubtless, predeceased her parents, as her mother left John Moore 40s. by her will, as well as a wardrobe or press. Apparently, Christopher was the last living son, but his decease in 1593 did not leave his parents childless, as they still had three daughters surviving; all three of whom were married. Dorothy, the youngest, born in 1573, was married in 1594 to Thomas Cradwell, or Graddell, vintner, and freeman of Canterbury; Anne was married the same year to John Crawford, shoemaker, and freeman of the same city; and Margaret to —— Jorden or Jurden.[165]

1593 was not only a fatal year for the Marlowes, but for Canterbury, and, indeed, for all England. Upwards of twenty thousand people perished of the plague in England alone, and one of the places most sorely tried was Canterbury. On the 17th August of that year Thomas Arthur, householder, Marlowe's maternal uncle, was carried off by the pestilence; on the 29th of the same month his daughter Joan was buried; on the 6th September Elizabeth, another daughter, followed; his son William was interred the next day; Ursula, his wife, was buried by her husband in St. Dunstan's churchyard on the 13th of the same month, and on the following day their youngest child, little Daniel, was buried—all victims of the plague, and all within less time than a month. Of all the Arthurs only Dorothy was left, she surviving until August 1597.[166]

When dying, this last survivor of the unfortunate Arthur family made the following disposition of such property as she possessed:

'THE WILL NUNCUPATIVE OF DOROTHIE ARTHURE of the Parish of Saint Mary Bredman in the Cittie of Canterbury, viz. The said Dorothie uppon the one and twenteth daye of August in the yere of O^r Lord God one thowsand fyve hundred nyntie and seaven lying sick in the house of John Marley of the said Prsh but of pfect mynde and remembrance Catherine Marley her Aunte did aske her what shee woulde gyve unto her Aunte Barton meaning the wife of Solomon Barton of Canterbury who was Aunte unto the said Dorothie by the Mothers syde as the said Catherine Marley was by the Fathers syde and the said Dorothie said shee would gyve her nothinge nor would not have her sent for to come to her. Then being demaunded by the said Catherine Marley who should have all her goods yf it should please God to call her the said Dorothie said that shee gave all that shee had unto her said Aunte Catherine Marley. The woords were uttered and spoken in the p̄sence of Margaret Crosse the Wyffe of Nicholas Crosse and Margaret Coxe the Wyffe of John Coxe. Witnesses the mark of Margaret Crosse the mark of Margaret Coxe.

'Proved in the Archdeacons Court of Canterbury 27th August 1597.[167]

'$A\frac{50}{361}$.'

As is seen by the above will, John Marlowe had left the parish of St. George the Martyr, and by 1597 was living in the parish of St. Mary Bredman, where he was Parish Clerk. He still carried on his trade of shoemaker, and continued to receive apprentices, as is shown by the accounts of the Chamberlain of the city. He had also taken up with another and, probably, somewhat lucrative occupation. He frequently acted as bondsman or security for married couples at the different churches of the diocese. According to Mr. J. Cowper, in his *Canterbury Marriage Licenses*, certain persons 'were always on hand and ready to give a bond for £40, £100, or £200, according to the period; and that they had degraded what was intended to be a security into a trade.' It is to be assumed that John Marlowe was a responsible person and that his bond was held as good security. His name appears as bondsman over and over again between the years 1588 and 1604.[168]

John Marlowe's last appearance as a security was on the 11th August 1604, at the church of St. Mary Bredman; a few months later and he was dead. His will was very short and definite; it reads as follows:

'IN THE NAME OF GOD AMEN. 1604 (*i.e.* 1605 N.S.) the xxiii[rd] daye of January I John Marlowe beinge sicke of bodye but thankes be to Allmighty God of good and p̄fect remembraunce doe make constitute and ordeyne this my last Will and Testament in manner and forme followinge. First I give and commend my soule into the hands of Allmighty God my Maker and Redeemer and my bodye to be buryed in the Churchyarde of the Pr̄she of St. George w^thin Canterbury as touchinge my temporall goods my debts and funeralls discharged and paid I geve and bequeath wholly to my Wyfe Katheryne whome I make my sole Executrix. In witness whereof I John Marlowe have to this my last Will and Testament set to my hande and seale the daye and yeare above written the marke of John Marlowe in the presence of us whose names are hereunder named. James Bissell the writer hereof Vincent Huffam Thomas Plesington.

'Proved in the Archdeacons Court of Canterbury the 23rd Feb. 1604 (*i.e.* 1605 N.S.).[169]

'$A \frac{52}{373}$.'

The fact of this will having the testator's mark instead of his signature must not be regarded as a general inability on the part of John Marlowe to write. In those days people who could write frequently made use of a certain mark, peculiar to themselves or their occupation, but in the present case the testator may be regarded as too 'sicke of bodye' to have been physically able to sign his name. He was buried three days after the execution of his will, that is to say, on the 26th January, in St. George's churchyard, in accordance with his wish.

On the 17th March 1605 the poet's mother, Catherine Marlowe, executed a will, which was proved on the 22nd July following, showing that she had died in the interval. The date of her death cannot be traced, nor the place of her burial, although it will be seen that she stipulated that she should be buried by her husband in the churchyard of St. George. This will is of unique interest, as even apart from its connection with Marlowe, it casts so much light upon the home-life and condition of an English household of the period.

This extremely characteristic will also sets at rest, and for ever, the idle tales about the poet being 'the son of a poor Cobler of Canterbury.' John Marlowe's widow, it is seen, must have been left in fairly comfortable circumstances. She kept a maid 'Marye Maye,' and apparently employed besides 'goodwife Morrice' as a nurse or help; she had a store of bed, table, and christening linen; several rings; a small quantity of silver-plate; various gowns; and a wardrobe or 'joyne presse that standeth in the greate chamber'; and besides this, after leaving certain money legacies, has some property to leave to her son-in-law and executor, John Crawford. The will runs thus:

'IN YE NAME OF GOD AMEN. I Katherine Marlowe widowe of John Marlowe of Canterbury late deceased though sicke in bodye yet in perfect memorye I give God thankes doe ordayne this my last Will and Testament written on the 17 of Marche in the yeare of our Lorde

God 1605 in manner and forme as followethe. First I doe bequeathe my soule to God my Saviour and Redeemer and my bodye to be buryed in ye churchyarde of St. Georges in Canterburye neare whereas my husbande John Marlowe was buryed. I do bequeathe unto my daughter Margaret Jurden the greatest gold ringe. I do bequeathe unto my daughter An Crauforde a golde ringe wch my daughter Cradwell hathe wch I would have her to surrender up unto her sister An and an other silver ringe. I do bequeathe unto my daughter Doritye Cradwell ye ringe wth ye double posye. I doe bequeathe unto my daughter Jurden my stufe gowne and my kirtle. I doe bequeathe unto my daughter Crauforde my best cloathe gowne and the cloathe that is lefte of ye same. I do bequeathe unto my daughter Cradwell my cloathe gowne wch I did weare everye daye. I doe bequeathe unto my daughter Jurden one silver spoone and unto her eldest sonne John Jurden one greate silver spoone and unto her sonne William one of ye greatest silver spoones of the sixe and to Elizabethe Jurden one spoone. I doe bequeathe unto my daughter An Crauforde one silver spoone and to her sonne Anthonye one of ye greatest spoones and to John another of ye greatest silver spoones and unto Elizabeth Crawforde one spoone. I do bequeathe unto my daughter Dorytye Cradwell one silver spoone and to her sonne John Cradwell one of the greatest silver spoones. I doe bequeathe unto my daughter Jurden two cushions and unto my daughter Crauford two cushions of Taffate and to my daughter Cradwell two cushions. I doe bequeathe my christeninge linnen as the kearcher the dammaske napkin a face cloathe and a bearinge blanket to bee used equallye betweene them and to serve to everye (one) of theire needs but if my daughter Jurden doe goe out of the towne my daughter An Crauforde to have the keepinge of the same christeninge linnen. I do beequeathe to everye one of them one table-cloathe and the fourthe to goe for an odde sheete that he wch hath the odde sheete may have ye table cloathe. I doe bequeathe unto everye one of my daughters sixe paire of sheetes to bee divided equallye, and in steade of the sheete wch is taken awaye there is one tablecloathe added. I doe bequeathe to everye one of my daughters a dosen of napkins to be divided equallye, beecause some are better then other I doe beequeathe unto my daughter Jurden three payre of pillowecoates and to my daughter Crauforde three payre of pillowecoates unto my daughter Cradwell three payre of pillowecoates one payre of pillowecoates I do bequeathe unto Katherine Reve and unto goodwife Morrice one pillowecoate I doe bequeathe unto John Moore .fortye shillinges and the joyne presse that standeth in the greate chamber where I lye. I beequeathe unto Mary Maye my mayde my red pettiecoate and a smocke. I beequeathe unto goodwife Morrice my petticoate that I doe weare daylye and a smocke and a wastcoate. I doe beequeathe unto goodwife Jurden fortye shillinges. I doe beequeathe unto my daughter Cradwell twentye shillinges. I would have all these portions to bee paied wthin one yeare after my deceasse. I doe bequeathe unto my sonne Crauforde all the rest of my goodes payinge my debts and legacyes and excharginge my funeralls whome I doe make my whole Executor of this my laste Will and testamente. In witnesse whereof I have heereunto set my hande and seale. Wittnesses those names yt are heereunder written and I Thomas Hudson ye writer heereof. The marke of Katherine Marlowe. The marke of Sarai Morrice. The marke of Mary May.

'$A \frac{54}{267}$.'

'Proved in the Archdeacons Court of Canterbury 22nd July 1605.'[170]

Several descendants of Catherine Marlowe's three daughters can be traced in the Canterbury records, but these entries are scarcely likely to interest the public. It may be mentioned, however, that Anthony Marlowe of Deptford, who had also property in the city of London, and to whom some references have already been made, is found early in 1600 to be interested in the new 'Fortune' theatre. In conjunction with other inhabitants of the Liberty of Finsbury he signed a memorial to the Lords of the Privy Council in favour of the said theatre being proceeded with and tolerated.[171]

NOTES

1. *Antiquities of Canterbury.* W. Somner. 1703.
2. *Ibid.*
3. *Ninth Report of the Royal Commission on Historical MSS.*
4. *Canterbury in the Olden Time.* J. Brent. 1860. p. 11.
5. *Perambulations of Kent.* W. Lambarde. 1590. This work contains a copy of the Custumal. Brent (p. 13) says it has been legally proved that 'Kentish men had a well-founded claim of exemption from villenage,' and cites a curious case, 30 Edward I., in confirmation.
6. *Canterbury in the Olden Time,* pp. 14, 15.
7. *Ninth Report of the Royal Commission on Historical MSS.*
8. *Ancient Funerall Monuments.* Weever. 1631.
9. *Calendar of State Papers,* December 22, 1593, pp. 396, 397.
10. *Athenæ Oxonienses.* Anthony à Wood. p. 216.
11. Anthony Marlowe is frequently mentioned in the *Acts of the Privy Council,* the Cottonian MSS., and various official records of the Elizabethan period.
12. *Chorus Vatum* MSS. by Hunter, article 'Marlowe.'
13. *Ninth Report of the Royal Commission on Historical MSS.*; the City Chamberlain's MS. Records, Canterbury, and W. Somner's *Antiquities.*
14. *Antiquities of Canterbury.* W. Somner.
15. Will Department, Archdeacon's Court, Canterbury.
16. *Visitations of the Archdeacon,* Canterbury, etc. MS. particulars furnished by Mr. A. Hussey.
17. *Church Registers of Canterbury.* Edited by Mr. J. M. Cowper.
18. *Church Registers* and *Marriage Licenses of Canterbury.* Edited by Mr. J. M. Cowper. Hasted's *History of Kent,* vol. iii. p. 156, and other Kentish Chronicles, refer to Robert Arthur, Rector of Chartham, doubtless a member of the family. He died March 28, 1454, in the Infirmary of the Cathedral, Canterbury, and was buried in the chancel. 'His effigies and inscriptions are gone; but there remain four shields of arms in brass, one at each corner of the stone: the first and fourth, three bars humette; second and third, a fess between three oak leaves erect.'
19. A Decree of the Burghmote in 1518. See also, *Canterbury in the Olden Time,* pp. 43, 44.

20. *Memorials of the King's School, Canterbury.* Rev. J. S. Sidebotham. 1865. Students had to furnish proof of age before admission on the foundation.

21. Church Register of St. George the Martyr, Canterbury.

22. MS. in Cathedral Library, Canterbury.

23. *Canterbury in the Olden Time. The Miracle Play in England.* S. W. Clarke. No date. Etc. etc.

24. *Canterbury in the Olden Time*, p. 40.

25. *Ibid.* p. 36.

26. *Lives of the Deans of Canterbury.* Mr. J. M. Cowper. p. 46.

27. *Canterbury in the Olden Time*, p. 36. *Handbook for Canterbury.* 'Felix Summerly' (Sir Henry Cole). 1860.

28. *Kentish Gazette*, Canterbury, March 18, 1899. 'Lecture' by Mr. Stanley Cooper, F.R.S.L.

29. *Bunce MSS.*, vol. i. p. 171. In Royal Museum and Public Library, Canterbury.

30 and 31. *Accounts of the King's School*, 1579-80. MSS. in Cathedral Library, Canterbury. These Accounts refer chiefly to the amounts paid to the foundation scholars : '*Stipend. sive Sala. Lᵃ puerorum studen. grammatic,*' for the years ending at the feast of St. Michael. They state that '*Idem denar. per dictum Thesaur. de exit officii sui hoc anno solut. quinquaginta pueris studen. grammatic pro salariis suis ad s. iiij ie pro quolibet eorum per annum.*'

32. *Antiquities of Canterbury.* 'List of Mayors.' W. Somner.

33. *The School-Room Windows*, King's School, Canterbury. A. J. G(alpin). Pamphlet reprint from *The Cantuarian* of November 1898 and of May 1899.

34. *Life of R. Boyle, Earl of Cork.* A. B. Grosart. p. 197.

35. *Dictionary of National Biography*, article 'John Coldwell, Bishop of Salisbury.'

36. *History of Corpus Christi College, Cambridge.* T. Masters. 1831. *Memorials of the King's School.* J. S. Sidebotham.

37. *England as seen by Foreigners.* W. B. Rye. 1865. p. 36.

38. *Pictorial History of England.* 1839. Vol. xi. p. 820.

39. *History of Corpus Christi College.* T. Masters. 1831. pp. 91, 92. Somner's *Antiquities.* 1703.

40 and 41. *History of Corpus Christi College.* T. Masters. 1831.

42. *Lives of the Deans of Canterbury.* J. M. Cowper.

43 and 44. *Itinerary* by Fynes Morysons. 1617. Part 3, p. 151 and p. 19.

45. *England as seen by Foreigners.* Note 7, at p. 183, states, 'In May 1592 the Gravesend tilt-boat, having forty passengers on board, was unfortunately run down by "an hoy" off Greenwich, the Court being there at the time. Most of the passengers were drowned, "at sight whereof (says Stowe) the Queene was much frighted."'

46. *Notes and Queries, passim; Dictionary of National Biography,* article 'Thomas Hobson'; Professor Masson's *Life of Milton.* 1859. Vol. i. pp. 110, 111, and Steele in *Spectator,* No. 509.

47. *Life of Milton.* Professor Masson. Vol. i. p. 111. *Dictionary of National Biography,* article 'Thomas Hobson.'

48. *Athenæum.* 1894, September 1, p. 299. Letter from Rev. Dr. H. P. Stokes and MS. Register of Admissions to Corpus Christi College, Cambridge.

49. *Works of Marlowe.* Edited by Rev. A. Dyce. pp. xii, xiii.

50. Cambridge Matriculation Book, MS.

51. *History of Corpus Christi College, Cambridge.* Rev. Dr. H. P. Stokes. 1898. p. 84.

52. Somner's *Antiquities.* Appendix. 1703.

53. Both in Trinity College and St. John's four students used originally to have one chamber in common, or one Fellow and two or three students. 'Separate beds were provided for all scholars above the age of fourteen.' Dean Peacock's *Observations on the Statutes of the University of Cambridge.* 1841. See also Masson's *Life of Milton,* vol. i. p. 109. 1859.

54. Masters's *History of Corpus Christi College, Cambridge.* 1831. pp. 91, 92.

55. *Ibid.; Dictionary of National Biography,* article 'Benjamin Carrier,' and the MS. Records of King's School, Canterbury.

56. *Memorials of the King's School,* by J. S. Sidebotham ; *History of Corpus Christi College,* by Masters ; and MS. Records of the King's School.

57. *History of Kent,* by Hasted ; and *History of Corpus Christi College,* by Masters.

58. *Eccles. Mem.,* vol. xi. p. 424 ; Thomas Lever's 'Sermon,' as quoted by Strype.

59. Masson's *Life of Milton,* vol. i. pp. 111, 112.

60. *Statutes of Christ's College* in MS. Cf. Dyer's *Privileges of the University of Cambridge* and Dean Peacock's *Observations.*

61 and 62. *History of Corpus Christi College,* by Masters.

63. *The Connoisseur,* October 1902, p. 86.

64. Masson's *Life of Milton,* vol. i. p. 114.

65. *An Apology for Actors.* Thomas Heywood. 1612. Shakespeare Society (reprint 1841), p. 28.

66. 'An Interrupted Performance,' by Rev. Dr. H. P. Stokes, in *The Benedict.* Lent Term, 1899. pp. 3-8.

67. These regulations were occasionally deviated from : *vide* Dean Peacock's *Observations.*

68. *The Cambridge University Grace-Book.* MS. 158¾.

69. Canterbury Cathedral MSS. City Chamberlain's Accounts.

70. *Have with you to Saffron Walden.* T. Nashe. 1596.

71. *Greene's Groatsworth of Wit.* 1592.

72. Masson's *Life of Milton*, pp. 115, 116, furnishes references to several authorities.

73. Masson's *Life of Milton*, pp. 118-120.

74. *Marlowe's Works.* Edited by A. H. Bullen. 1885. Vol. i. p. lxxv.

75. *Purchas's Pilgrimes*, vol. i. p. 440.

76. *The Glorious and Beautiful Garland of Man's Glorification*, by Kett, published in 1585, is an incoherent work of mystical theology. Its dedication to Queen Elizabeth did not save its unfortunate author from the stake.

77. *The Cambridge University Grace-Book.*

78. *Life of R. Boyle.* Dr. A. B. Grosart. 1886. p. 197.

79. This epitaph was discovered on the back of a title-page of a copy of *Hero and Leander*, ed. 1629. Although the lines were first printed by Collier, in his *History of the British Stage*, p. xliv, they are proved to have been in existence anterior to his use of the book, and are therefore not his workmanship. They are subscribed with Marlowe's name. The book now (1904) is in possession of Colonel Prideaux ; it was purchased at Heber's sale.

80. *Tamburlaine* was acted by the Lord Admiral's men in 1587. Greene referred to it in his *Perimedes*, entered in the Stationers' Register, 29th March 1588.

81. Chapman dedicated the drama of *All Fools* and *The Conspiracy of Charles, Duke of Byron*, to Sir Thomas Walsingham, and his continuation of Marlowe's *Hero and Leander* to Lady Walsingham, wife of ' my honoured, best friend.'

82. *Marlowe's Works.* Edited by A. H. Bullen. 1888. Vol. i. p. xxv.

83. *Underwoods.* Ben Jonson. ' Lines to Mr. John Fletcher upon his *Faithful Shepherdess.*'

84. *School of Shakespeare.* R. Simpson. 1878.

85. *Kind Hart's Dreame.* H. Chettle. 1592.

86. *School of Shakespeare.* R. Simpson. 1878.

87. ' Like to an almond tree y-mounted high,' and the five lines following it, also appear in Spenser's *Faerie-Queene*, vol. i. p. 7, stanza 32. Who was the author? The style is Spenserian, but the first part of the *Faerie-Queene* was not published until 1590, and although the two *Discourses of Tamburlaine* do not seem to have been issued in book form until 1590, they had been acted for two or three years previous to that date.

88. Theatrical bills were affixed to the posts which marked the way along the roadside for foot-passengers. Several allusions to them occur in Elizabethan literature and records. In October 1587 Charlwood was licensed for doing 'the only imprinting of all manner of bills for players.' Fleay's *Life of Shakespeare.*

89. *Epigrams*, by Ben Jonson. No. lxxx. 'To Edward Allen.'

90. *Henslowe's Diary*, edited by J. P. Collier. 1841. 'The Shakespeare Society.'

91. *Drummond of Hawthornden*, by Professor David Masson. 1873.

92. *Hero and Leander*. Lines 465 and 470 to 482 were plagiarised by the author of *The Pilgrimage to Parnassus* without acknowledgment.

93. *Pharonnida*. W. Chamberlaine. 1659.

94. *Histrio-Mastix*. W. Prynne. Part I. p. 556. 1633.

95. *Marlowe's Works*. Edited by A. H. Bullen. 1885. p. xxix.

96. Stowe's *Survey of London*, quoted in Dodsley's *Old Plays*. 1725. Vol. i. p. lix.

97. *Ibid*.

98. The original document is now at Westminster, Guildhall : it reads as follows :—RECOGNIZANCE 31 ELIZABETH. *Midḋ. Ses͂. Mᵈ qd. primo die Octobris anno regni dn̄e n̄r̄e Elizabeth R̄n̄e nunce &c. Tricesimo primo Ricŭs Kytchine de Clifforde Inne gēn et Humfridus Rowland de East Smythfielde in cōm pḋ. 'horner' venerunt coram me Willm̄o Fletewode ʒvien̄ ad legem et Recordatore Civite London uno Justit̄ dn̄e n̄re R̄n̄e in Cōm pḋ assign̄ &c. manucepunt p Xp̄oforo Marley de London geñoso vizt : vterg manucaptorŭ pḋict̄ sub pena vigint librͦ et ip̄e p̄ḋ Xp̄oforo Marley assumpsit p se ip̄e sub pena quadragint̄ librͦ de bonis catall terͦ tenementis sŭis et corŭ cujus lͤbt ad opus et usum die dn̄e R̄n̄e levand̄ sub condicione q̄d si ip̄e Xp̄oforo p sonalit̄ comp̄ebit ad pͣ Session de Newgate ad respondend ad via da que ex p̄te dēo dn̄e R̄n̄e vͤsus sum objecientur et non discedet absq licencie curie. Qd tune, &c. Aut alioquia &c.*

99 and 100. 'PROCLAMATION *as to Licenses for Interludes and their Contents*. Given at our Palayce of Westminster the xvi daye of Maye, the first yeare of our Raygne' 1559. 'Imprinted at London in Paules Churchyarde by Rychard Jugge and John Cawood, Printers to the Queenes Majestie. *Cum privilegio Regiæ Majestatis*.'

101. *The History of the Worshipful Company of Horners*. By C. H. Compton. 1882. The Horner's procession has been discontinued since 1768. Horn Fair, held on St. Luke's Day, was abolished in 1872.

102. *Introduction to the Literature of Europe*. 1843. Vol. ii. p. 170.

103. *Marlowe's Works*. Edited by A. H. Bullen. Vol. i. p. 40.

104. *Greene's Groatsworth of Witte bought with a Million of Repentance*. 1592. *Published at the dying request of R. Greene*.

105. *Pierce Pennilesse His Supplication to the Devill*. Thomas Nashe. 1592.

106. *Palladis Tamia : Wits Treasury*. 1598.

107. Dedication to *Hero and Leander*. 1598.

108. *Fragmenta Regalia.* Sir Robert Naunton. 1814.

109. *Life of Thomas Harriot.* By H. Stevens of Vermont, U.S.A. Privately printed. 1900.

110. *A Briefe and true Report of the new found Land of Virginia.* By Thomas Hariot. 1585. A work 'remarkable for the large view it contains in regard to the extension of industry and commerce . . . one of the earliest examples of a statistical survey on a large scale.'— *Edinburgh Review*, LXXI. Cf. *Dictionary of National Biography.*

111. *Literary History of Europe.* Hallam.

112. *Hariot's Life.* H. Stevens. p. 75.

113. The *Dictionary of National Biography* states that Percy allowed Hariott three hundred pounds a year, but H. Stevens shows that this is incorrect. It was eighty pounds per annum, and that was a very large sum for those days.

114. Letter to Harriott in Preface to *Translation of Homer.* By Geo. Chapman. 1616.

115. 'The freethinkers met, including the Earl of Northumberland, Thomas Harriott, Edward Vere, Earl of Oxford, and others,' in Raleigh's house. Nicholas Storojenko's *Life of Greene.* 1881. pp. 36, 37. Grosart's edition.

116. Robert Parsons, or Persons, the Jesuit, author of *A Brief Discours*, 1580, a work more argumentative than logical.

117. Anthony à Wood's *Athenæ Oxonienses.* 1691.

118. *Greene's Groatsworth of Wit*, according to the title-page, was 'published at his dying request.' 1592.

119. See Isaac D'Israeli's account in his *Miscellanies of Literature* of Dr. Samuel Parker's (Bishop of Oxford) attempt, by a posthumous work, to utterly destroy the good name and noble character of Andrew Marvell. D'Israeli points out 'how far private hatred can distort, in its hideous vengeance, the resemblance it affects to give after nature.' The pages of the *Miscellanies*, containing D'Israeli's record of this libel, which its author in 'his cowardice dared not publish, but which his invincible malice has sent down to posterity,' should be pondered over by all believers in posthumous slanders.

120. Henry Chettle's *Kind-Harts Dreame* (1592).

121. *Greene's Groatsworth of Wit.*

122. *A Private Epistle to the Printer*, prefixed to the second edition of *Pierce Pennilesse his Supplication to the Divell*, 1592.

123. 'One of the many crimes laid to the charge of the dramatist Robert Greene was that of fraudulently disposing of the same play to two companies.'—Mr. Sidney Lee's *Life of William Shakespeare*, p. 47, 1898; cf. Cuthbert Cony-Catcher's *Defence of Cony-Catching*, 1592. Isaac D'Israeli, in *Miscellanies of Literature*, says, 'Robert Greene wrote the *Art of Coney-Catching*, or Cheatery, in which he was an adept.' Worse crimes are recorded against him, but his own works,

if they may be believed, make confession of every kind of villainy and meanness. See also R. Simpson's Introduction to *Shakespeare Allusion Books.*

124. *Have with you to Saffron-Walden, or Gabriell Harvey's Hunt is up.* 1596. It should be pointed out that Harvey was then living at Saffron Walden.

125. *Greene's Groatsworth of Wit.*

126. 'Address' prefixed to Greene's *Menaphon*, by Thomas Nashe, 1589.

127. Introduction to *Bartholomew Fair.* By Ben Jonson. 1614.

128. Nashe says Kyd was one of those 'shifting companions that runne through every art and thrive by none.' See Introduction to Kyd's Works, edited by Professor F. S. Boas, 1901, p. xxii.

129. *Shakespeare Allusion Books.* 'General Introduction.' By Richard Simpson. Part II. 1874.

130. *Marlowe's Works.* Edited by A. H. Bullen. p. xliii.

131. *George Chapman.* An Essay. By A. C. Swinburne. 1875.

132. *Specimens of Dramatick Poets contemporary with Shakespeare.* 1808.

133. *Marlowe's Works.* 'Introduction.' By A. H. Bullen. pp. xliv-v.

133a. There was a *Tragedy of Dido* by John Ritwise, son-in-law of William Lilye, acted at Cambridge before Wolsey, and one by Edward Haliwell, of King's College, acted before Queen Elizabeth. Antony à Wood. *Athenæ Oxonienses*, vol. i. p. 35. 1813.

134. *Vide King Henry VI.* Part I. Act V. Scene 3. It runs :

> 'She's beautiful; and therefore to be woo'd :
> She is a woman ; therefore to be won.'

135. On p. 197 of the Appendix to his essay on *George Chapman*, 1875, Mr. Swinburne compares this fragment with Shelley's poem, ' The Question,' which it strangely resembles ' for tone of verse and tune of thought . . . written in the same metre and spirit, that one is tempted to dream that some particles of the " predestined plot of dust and soul " which had once gone to make up the elder must have been used again in the composition of the younger poet, who in fiery freedom of thought and speech was like no other of our greatest men but Marlowe.'

136. This ' Commonplace Book,' the earliest entry in which is dated 1570, belonged to John Thornborough, born in 1551, who was successively Dean of York and Bishop of Limerick. In 1575 Thornborough was chaplain to Henry Herbert, Earl of Pembroke. The book was sold on June 19, 1903, at the Auction Rooms of Messrs. Sotheby, Wilkinson, and Hodge.

137. *Notes and Queries.* Series I., vol. i. p. 469, May 18, 1850.

138. *La Musa Madrigalesca.* By Thomas Oliphant. 1837. pp. 95, etc.

139. See extracts from will of Thomas Baker, in his *Memoirs*. By Dr. R. Masters. 1774. As bearing upon our comments on Baker's manuscript these words from Rose's *Biographical Dictionary* merit attention : 'There is scarcely a work in the department of English History, Biography, and Antiquities that appeared in his time in which we do not find acknowledgments of the assistance which had been received from Mr. Baker.' The works referred to in his list need scrutiny.

140. Kyd's letter and the whole story of this alleged intimacy with Marlowe will be found in the Introduction to *The Works of Kyd*, edited, by Professor F. S. Boas, 1901.

141. MS. in the Privy Council Office. Now published in the *Acts of the Privy Council*, edited by J. R. Dasent, C.B., vol. xxiv., New Series, for 1593, p. 212.

142. *Ibid.* vol. xxiv., New Series.

143. *Ibid.*

144. *History of Kent (Hundred of Blackheath)*. Edited by H. H. Drake. Vol. i. 1886.

145. MS. in Privy Council Office. Printed in *Acts of the Privy Council*, vol. xxiv., New Series, p. 244.

146. *Acts of the Privy Council*, vol. xxiv., New Series.

147. *Memoirs of Edward Alleyn*. J. P. Collier. 1841. p. 25.

148. The name of Anthony Marlowe, otherwise Marler, frequently occurs in connection with Government contracts in the *Acts of the Privy Council*, and many other records of the Elizabethan period. Stowe mentions that he was married to Elizabeth, daughter of William Gonston, Treasurer of the Marine Causes, and that his arms were 'argent, a chevron purpure ; in the dexter canton an escallop, sable.'

149. Journal of Frederick, Duke of Wirtemberg, in 1592, quoted in *England as seen by Foreigners*. By W. B. Rye. 1865. p. 49.

150. *Eastward Hoe.* 1605. Act III. Scene 1.

151. *History of Deptford*. By Nathan Dew.

152. *A Midsummer Night's Dream.* (1593 ?) Act V. Scene 1.

153. *As You Like It.* 1623. Act III. Scene 5.

154. Chapman's Epistle Dedicatory to his continuation of *Hero and Leander* appeared only in the 1598 edition. He tells Lady Walsingham, referring to Blunt's dedication of the first part (Marlowe's) of the poem to her husband, 'This poor Dedication (in figure of the other unity betwixt Sir Thomas and yourself) hath rejoined you with him, my still honoured best friend ; whose continuance of ancient kindness to my obscured estate, though it cannot increase my love to him which hath been entirely circular; yet shall it encourage my deserts to their utmost requital, and make my hearty gratitude speak.'

155. Petowe's continuation of *Hero and Leander* was published in 1598.

156. Ben Jonson quoted, evidently from memory, several lines from *Hero and Leander* in *Every Man in his Humour*, and is reported, in *The Chast and Lost Lovers*, 1651, to have said that Marlowe's mighty lines 'were examples fitter for admiration than parallel.'

157. *The Battaile of Agincourt, Elegies*, etc. By Michaell Drayton. 1627.

158. *The Theatre of Gods Judgements.* By Th. Beard. 1597.

159. *Palladia Tamis: Wits Treasury.* Francis Meres, Maister of Artes of both Universities. 1598.

160. *The Golden Grove.* By William Vaughan. 1600.

161. Compare such lines as these from *The Pilgrimage to Parnassus* :

> 'Though I foreknew that gold runs to the boor,
> I 'll be a scholar though I live but poor.'

Lines 465, 470, and 482 are from *Hero and Leander*, published in 1598, although, as already stated, entered on the Stationers' Books soon after Marlowe's death in 1593. *The Pilgrimage*, although not published until 1606, was written and recited apparently six or seven years earlier.

162 and 163. *Memoirs of T. Baker.* By R. Masters. In his will Baker states of those MSS. (now in the British Museum) that 'twenty volumes in folio of my own handwriting . . . were conveyed to him,' *i.e.* to Robert Harley, Earl of Oxford.

164 and 164a. To refute Warton's assertion, in his *History of English Poetry*, that ' Marlowe had no systematic disbelief of religion, and that the Puritans had construed his slight scepticism into absolute atheism,' Ritson, in his coarse *Observations* on that work, referred to the Baine's libel in the Harleian MSS. Ritson referred to MS. 6853, but that Professor Boas refers to is MS. 6848. The ' Disputation' bears the latter number also, whilst the 'Kyd' letter is numbered 6849. The paging of these MSS. has been altered recently at the British Museum.

165. *The Freemen of Canterbury*, 1903, and the *Register of St. George, the Martyr, Canterbury.* Both edited by J. M. Cowper.

166. *Register of St. Dunstan, Canterbury.* Edited by J. M. Cowper.

167. *Transcripts from Wills.* Archdeacon's Court, Canterbury.

168. *Canterbury Marriage Licenses*, 1903. Edited by J. M. Cowper.

169. *Transcripts from Wills.* Archdeacon's Court, Canterbury.

170. *Ibid.*

171. *Life of Edward Alleyn.* By J. P. Collier. 1841. p. 58. Cf. *Acts of the Privy Council.*

THE BIBLIOGRAPHY OF
CHRISTOPHER MARLOWE

COMPILED BY JOHN H. INGRAM

THIS is the first Bibliography that has ever been published of the Works of Christopher Marlowe. It cannot be expected that it is exhaustive, but it will afford a good basis for any further effort in the same direction. Some of the items included may be deemed to be of little value, but it is very difficult to determine where and in what respect a publication may become useful, either to the bibliographer or general inquirer. Amongst the many works which have been consulted during the compilation of this section of the book grateful notice may be drawn to Mr. W. Heinemann's *Bibliography of Marlowe's Doctor Faustus*; to the very useful *Indices to Periodicals* issued by *The Review of Reviews*, and—above all, for their valuable references to review and magazine articles published during the last century—to those most useful aids to students, the *Indices to Periodical Literature* issued by Dr. W. F. Poole, the pioneer of such publications, and by his collaborator, Mr. W. J. Fletcher, M.A., etc.

COLLECTED WORKS

THE WORKS OF MARLOWE. Edited, with a Life of the Author, by E. G. Robinson, in 3 vols. London. 1826. 8°.

THE WORKS OF CHRISTOPHER MARLOWE: with some account of the Author, and Notes, by the Rev. Alexander Dyce. 3 vols. London. 1850. 8°. Reprint, 1858. 8°.

—— *A new edition*, revised and corrected, in 1 vol. 1865. 8°.

—— *Another edition*, in 1 vol. 1876. 8°.

THE WORKS OF CHRISTOPHER MARLOWE. Edited, with Notes and Introduction, by Lt.-Col. Francis Cunningham. London. 1871. 8°.

—— Edited by A. H. Bullen, B.A., in 3 vols. 'The English Dramatist' Series. London. 1884-5. 8°.

THE POEMS OF Greene and MARLOWE. Edited, with Memoirs, by Robert Bell. London. No date [18—]. 8°.

—— *Another edition.* 'Bohn's Standard Library.' 1876. 8°.

THE DRAMATIC WORKS OF CHRISTOPHER MARLOWE. Selected with a Prefatory Notice, Biographical and Critical. By P. E. Pinkerton. A volume of Selections only, in 'The Canterbury Poets' Series. 1885. 8°.

SHAKESPEARE'S ZEITGENOSSEN UND IHRE WERKE. Von F. M. von Bodenstedt. Berlin. 1858-60.

Lilly, Greene, und MARLOWE *die drei bedeutendsten Vorläufer Shakespeares,* with a German translation of their plays, und ihre Dramatischen Dichtungen. 1860. 8°.

MARLOWE'S WERKE. Historisch-Kritische Ausgabe von H. Brey-mann und A. Wagner. 1885-1889. 8°.

CHRISTOPHER MARLOWE. 'The Best Plays of the Old Dramatists.' 'The Mermaid' Series. Edited by Havelock Ellis, with a general Introduction by J. A. Symonds. Unexpurgated edition. London. 1887. Reprint, 1903.

—— Théâtre. Traduction de F. Rabbe, avec une préface par J. Richepin. 2 tom. Paris. 1889. 8°.

SEPARATE DRAMATIC WORKS

Although presented on stages about 1587 *Tamburlaine* was not entered in the Stationers' Books until August 14, 1590: it was published the same year. The title-page of the first edition runs thus :—

TAMBURLAINE THE GREAT, who from a Scythian Shephearde by his rare and woonderfull Conquests, became a most puissant and mightye Monarque. And (for his tyranny and terrour in Warre) was tearmed the Scourge of God. Divided into two Tragicall Discourses, as they were sundrie times shewed upon Stages in the Citie of London. By the right honorable the Lord Admyrall, his servauntes. Now first and newlie published. London. Printed by Richard Jhones: at the

Signe of the Rose and Crown neere Holborne Bridge. 1590. 4°.

TAMBURLAINE THE GREAT. *Another edition*, but with the following new half-title:—*The Second Part of the bloody Conquests of mighty Tamburlaine.* With his impassionate fury for the death of his Lady and love faire Zenocrate: his fourme of exhortacion and discipline to his three sons, with the maner of his own death. 1590. 4° and 8° editions.

—— —— With, some slight variations in the title-page, such as 'Monarch' instead of 'Monarque,' and 'most stately shewed' for 'shewed.' Both first and second parts. 4° and 8°. 1592. Woodcut.

—— —— Printed for Edward White, and are to be solde at the little North doore of Saint Paules church, at the sign of the Gunne. 1605. 4°. Another edition of the Second Part, printed by E(lizabeth) A(llde) for Ed. White, etc. 4°. 1606.

> NOTE.—Langbaine, *Account of English Dramatic Poets*, p. 344, mentions an 8vo edition of 1593, but no copy of it can be traced, nor can any edition of 1597, mentioned by German writers, be found.

—— —— Being a reprint of the edition of 1590, in the 'Englische Sprach- und Literaturdenkmale des 16, etc. Jahrhunderts.' Herausgegeben von Karl Vollmöller. Heilbronn. 1885. 8°.

The drama of *Doctor Faustus* was entered in the Stationers' Books on January 7, 1601, but the earliest edition yet traced is the quarto of 1604, thus:—

THE TRAGICALL HISTORY OF DOCTOR FAUSTUS. As it hath been Acted by the Right Honorable the Earle of Nottingham his servants. Written by Ch. Marl. London. Printed by V. S. for Thomas Bushell. 1604. In Bodleian Library only.

—— *Another edition*, styled *The Tragicall History of the horrible Life and death of Doctor Faustus.* Written by Ch. Marl. Imprinted at London by G. E. for John Wright, and are to be sold at Christ Church Gate. 1609. 4°. Unique copy in Town Library, Hamburg.

—— —— Printed by G. E. for John Wright. 1611. 4°. Sold at Heber's sale. Woodcut on title.

THE TRAGICALL HISTORY OF DOCTOR FAUSTUS. *Another edition.*
Printed for John Wright, and are to be sold at his shop
without Newgate, at the Signe of the Bible. 1616. 4°.
Woodcut: Faust and the Devil.

—— —— With new Additions. Printed for John Wright, etc.
1619. Unique copy in the Rowfant Library.

—— —— With new Additions. 1620. 4°. Woodcut on title.

—— —— With new Additions. 1624. 4°.

—— —— With new Additions. 1631. 4°. Woodcut of Faustus
invoking the Devil.

—— —— Printed for W. Gilbertson; with new additions as it is
now acted, with severall new scenes, together with the actors'
names. 1663. 4°. Woodcut.

—— —— In vol. i. pp. 1-85 of *Old English Plays.* 1814. 8°.

—— —— In vol. i. pp. 1-88 of *Old Plays*, being a continuation
of Dodsley's 'Collection.' London. 1816.

—— —— Reprint of the edition of 1624.

—— —— Edited with a biographical sketch of the author, notes,
etc., by W. Oxberry. 1818. 12°.

—— —— In *The Works of the British Dramatists*, with Notes,
etc., by John S. Keltie, F.S.A. Edinburgh. 1870. 8°.

—— —— With Introduction and Notes by W. Wagner. In 'The
London Series of English Classics.' 1877. 8°.

—— —— In 'The Clarendon Press' Series as *Old English Drama*,
containing Marlowe's *Doctor Faustus* and Greene's *Friar Bacon*.
Edited by A. W. Ward, M.A., etc. 1878. 8°.

—— *New editions* of *Old English Drama* reprint, in 1887, revised
and enlarged 1892, and again 1901. 8°.

—— *Another edition.* To which is added Goethe's *Faust*, from the
German by J. Anster. In 'Morley's Universal Library.' 1883. 8°.

—— —— In 'The Excelsior' Series. 1887. 8°.

—— —— Edited with a Preface, Notes, and Glossary, by Israel
Gollancz, M.A. In 'The Temple Dramatists.' 1897. 12°.

—— —— 'Seen through the press by John Masefield. Decorated
by Charles Ricketts.' 1903. 8°.

Doktor Faustus. Übersetzt von W. Müller. Mit einer Vorrede
von L. A. von Arnim. Berlin. 1818. 8°.

Christopher Marlowe's Doctor Faust . . . und die alte englische
Ballade von *D. Faustus.* Deutsch von A. Böttger. Leipzig.
1857. 8°.

Le Faust de Christopher Marlowe, traduit par F. V. Hugo. Paris. 1858. 12°.

Marlowe's Faustus, in Band 3 of 'Shakespeare's Zeitgenossen und ihre Werke.' Von F. W. von Bodenstedt. Berlin. 1860. 8°.

Marlowe's Faust, die älteste dramatische Bearbeitung der Faustsage. Uebersetzt und mit Einleitung und Anmerkungen versehen von Dr. A. von der Velde. Breslau. 1870. 8°.

Die innere Stellung Marlowe's zum Volksbuch vom Faust. Von Dr. W. Münch. 1879. 8°.

Het oudste Faust-Drama. Marlowe's Tragische-Historie van Dr. Faustus. Vertaald, etc. R. S. Tjaden-Moddermann. Gröningen. 1887. 8°.

Doktor Faustus. Oversat af A. Halling. Studien fra Sprog-og Oldtidsforskning, etc., No. 35. Copenhagen. 1891. 8°.

Faustus. Notes ; A Supplement to the Commentaries on Marlowe's *Tragicall History of D. Faustus*, by H. Logeman. *Recueil de Travaux.* Université de Gand. 1898. 8°.

Marlowe's Faustus. With Notes, by A. Riedl. Berlin. No date. *Neue Ausgabe.* Salzwedl. 1874 (?).

The Tragical History of Dr. Faustus. By Christopher Marlowe. 'Rudolphi and Klemm's English Library.' Zürich. 1881. 16°.

Marlowe's Doctor Faustus. Treuer Abdruck der ersten Quart-Ausgabe. 1604. Herausgegeben von H. Breymann. 1884. 8°.

> NOTE.—Mr. W. Heinemann, in his ' Bibliography of Marlowe's *Faustus*,' 1884, says, in *the Serapeum*, 1847, vol. viii. p. 175, Budik mentions an 8° of 1612, and that Peter refers to it in his *Lit. der Faustsage*, Leipzig, 1851, and elsewhere. There is, or was, probably a copy of this edition in some German library. Herr Peter also refers to a Quarto of 1651, and Van der Velde and Dr. Engel also mention it, in their works on the *Faustsage*. Other editions, unknown to English authors, of 1622, 1626, 1636, and 1690 are referred to by Arturo Graf, in his *Studii Drammatici*, Torino, 1878.

The Rich Jew of Malta had been performed at least as early as 1591, with Alleyn as ' Barabas,' and was licensed for printing on May 17, 1594, but the first known edition of it, which was edited by the dramatist, Thomas Heywood, is the following :—

THE FAMOUS TRAGEDY OF THE RICH JEW OF MALTA. As it was played before the King and Queen, in His Majesties Theatre at Whitehall, by her Majesties Servants at the Cockpit. Written by Christopher Marlo. London : printed by J. B. for Nicholas

Vavasour, and are to be sold at his Shop in the Inner-Temple, neere the Church. 1633. 4°.

THE FAMOUS TRAGEDY OF THE RICH JEW OF MALTA. *Another edition*, in R. Dodsley's 'Collection of Old Plays.' Vol. viii. 1780. 8°.

—— —— In vol. i. of 'The Ancient British Drama.' 1810. 8°.

—— —— Reynell and Son, London. 1810. 8°.

—— —— With a Biographical Sketch of the Author, Explanatory Notes, etc., by W. Oxberry. 1818. 12°.

—— —— In new edition of R. Dodsley's 'Collection of Old Plays,' vol. viii. 1825. 8°.

Der Jude von Malta, translated by E. von Buelow. In 'Alt-Englische Schaubühne.' 1831. 8°.

Edward the Second was entered in the Stationers' Books on July 6, 1593, a few days after its author's burial. For many years the first known issue of the work was a Quarto of 1598, but in 1876 a copy of an edition of 1594 was discovered in the Royal Library, Cassel. The title-page reads thus:—

The troublesome raigne and lamentable death of EDWARD THE SECOND, *King of England: with the tragicall fall of proud Mortimer.* As it was sundrie times publiquely acted in the honourable citie of London, by the right honourable the Earl of Pembroke his servants. Written by Chri. Marlow Gent. Imprinted at London for William Jones, dwelling neare Holborne conduit at the Signe of the Gunne. 1594. 4°.

—— *Another edition;* after *proud Mortimer*, the title reads, 'And also the life and death of Piers Gaveston, the great Earle of Cornewall, and favorite of King Edward the Second, as it was publiquely acted by the right honorable the Earle of Pembroke his servauntes. Written by Chri. Marlow Gent. Imprinted at London by Richard Bradocke, for William Jones, dwelling neere Holbourne conduit, at the Signe of the Gunne.' 1598. 4°.

—— —— 'Printed at London for Roger Barnes, and are to be sould at his shop in Chauncerie Lane, over against the Rolles. 1612.' 4°.

—— —— 'As it was publiquely Acted by the late Queenes Majesties Servants at the Red Bull in S. Johns streete. Written by Christopher Marlow Gent. London. Printed

for Henry Bell and are to be sold at his Shop at the Lame-
hospitall Gate, neere Smithfield, 1622.' 4°.

The troublesome raigne and lamentable death of EDWARD THE SECOND,
King of England : with the tragicall fall of proud Mortimer.
Other editions, in 'Select Collection of Old Plays,' vol. ii.
1744, 12°, and 1780, 8°, and 1825, 8°.

—— *Another edition,* in 'The Ancient British Drama,' vol. i.
1810. 8°.

—— —— in 'The Works of the British Dramatists,' edited with
Notes, etc., by J. S. Keltie. Edinburgh. 1870. 8°.

—— —— With an Introduction and Notes by W. Wagner. Har.-
burg. 1871. 8°.

—— —— Edited, with Introductory Remarks and Notes, by
F. G. Fleay. London. 1873. 8°.

—— —— With Introductory Remarks : Explanatory, Grammatical,
and Philological Notes, etc., by F. G. Fleay. In 'School and
College Classics.' 1877. 8°.

—— *Other editions.* Edited by O. W. Tancock. 'Clarendon
Press' Series, 1879 ; third edition, 1899. 8°.

—— *Another edition.* 'English Historical Plays,' arranged for
acting, by J. Donovan, vol. i. 1896. 8°.

—— *Other editions.* Edited, with a Preface, Notes, and Glossary,
by A. W. Verity, M.A. 'The Temple Dramatists.' 1896 and
1902. 16°.

Edward the Second. Translation by J. A. Webster. English and
Greek, Act v. Scenes 1, 5. Gaisford Prize. Oxford. 1898.

Eduard II. Translated by E. von Buelow. 'Alt-Englische
Schaubühne.' 1831. 8°.

Although *The Massacre at Paris,* a drama chiefly relating to the
St. Bartholomew massacre, is regarded as by Marlowe, the
published text is scarcely worthy of the parentage ascribed to
it. From a fragment of a MS. copy of scene xix., apparently
intended for use in a playhouse, J. P. Collier, in his *History
of English Dramatic Poetry,* vol. iii. p. 134, first edition, printed
a number of passages, to show how corrupted the accepted
text was. Doubtless the play was obtained for publication by
means of some actor's faulty memory. Although Henslowe
records in his Diary that the actors played the *Massacre* for
the first time on the 3rd January, 1593, the only old edition
known of it is :—

THE MASSACRE AT PARIS: With the death of the Duke of Guise. As it was plaide by the right honourable the Lord High Admirall his Servants. Written by Christopher Marlowe. At London, Printed by E[lizabeth] A[llde] for Edward White, dwelling neere the little North doore of S. Paules Church at the signe of the Gun. No date (*circa* 1600?). 4°.

Of *Dido*, only one early edition has been traced. The play was apparently left by Marlowe in an incomplete state, and Nashe, always on the look-out for a commission, patched it together by means of some absurdly ludicrous passages. Marlowe's handiwork is prominent all through the drama, but is disfigured by Nashe's blotches. The title-page reads thus :—

THE TRAGEDIE OF DIDO, QUEENE OF CARTHAGE: Played by the Children of her Majesties Chappell. Written by Christopher Marlowe and Thomas Nashe, Gent. . . . At London. Printed by the Widdowe Orwin, for Thomas Woodcocke, and are to be solde at his shop, in Paules Church-yeard, at the signe of the black Beare. 1594. 4°.

THE REIGN OF KING JOHN, although now included only in the Works of William Shakespeare, is sometimes ascribed to Marlowe, and he probably helped in revising the old play on this subject, to fit it for audiences of his times.

In revising and improving the older plays on the TROUBLESOME REIGN OF KING HENRY VI., Marlowe certainly had a hand, as has been referred to in the course of this work, but as his share in the work cannot be separated from his coadjutors', it is needless to enter into the bibliography of the subject.

Lust's Dominion ; Or, The Lascivious Queen, A Tragedie ; although published in 1657, as by Christopher Marlowe, Gent., is certainly not by him. It is believed now to be by Dekker, Haughton, and Day, and Mr. W. W. Greg suggests that as 'it is an alteration of an older play,' Marlowe may have had a hand in it. It is, however, impossible to discredit him with any portion of this work.

There is no need to refer to any other of the dramatic works ascribed to Marlowe.

POETIC WORKS

THE RAPE OF HELEN.   Translated by Marlowe, from the Greek
of Coluthus, 'into English rhyme in the year 1587,' says T.
Wharton, *Hist. of Engl. Poetry*, vol. iii. p. 433, ed. 4°, on the
authority of the Coxeter MSS. No copy has yet been discovered.

OVID'S ELEGIES.   The earlier editions of this translation are undated.   Presumably the first is that bearing the title-page,
'*Epigrammes and Elegies*. By J. D. and C. M.   At Middleborough.'   Although this 12mo book bears the foreign
imprint, Mr. C. Edmonds, in his preface to a reprint of it,
states his belief that it was printed by W. Jaggard, the printer
of *The Passionate Pilgrime*, 1599, and other pirated works.
The Epigrams are by Sir John Davies.   The translation,
which was attributed to Marlowe, was of only a portion of the
Elegies, and bears a second title-page, '*Certain of Ovid's
Elegies*.   By C. M[arlowe].   At Middleborough.'   Date of
publication was probably 1596.

—— *Another edition*, bearing a similar imprint, '*Epigrammes and
Elegies*, by J. D. and C. M.   At Middleborough,' and also
undated, is considered to have been printed abroad.

All Ovid's Elegies: 3 Books.   By C. M., is a later and complete
translation of the whole of the *Amores*, issued with the Epigrams of Davies, as before.   This is supposed to be the book
which, with works by Marston, Bishop Hall, and others, was
condemned by Archbishop Whitgift at Canterbury, in June
1599, to be burned.   W. C. Hazlitt considers this to be the
work which 'continued to be printed with Middleborough on
the title, and without date, as late as 1640.'

CERTAINE OF OVID'S ELEGIES, translated by Christopher Marlowe, was a reprint of the old copy found at Isham, and was
produced under the editorship of Mr. Charles Edmonds.
1870.   4°.

LUCAN'S FIRST BOOKE.   'Translated line for line by Chr. Marlow.
At London.   Printed by T. Short, and are to be sold by
Walter Burre at the Signe of the Flower de Luce in Paules
Churchyard.   1600.'   4°.   This is the only known early
edition.   The 1600 edition of *Hero and Leander* included
Lucan's First Booke on the title-page, but the latter work does

not appear in any known copies of the book. The translation is dedicated 'To his kind and true friend, Edward Blunt,' by Thomas Thorpe, the notorious piratical publisher of *Sonnets by W. Shakespeare*. The translation, although not published until 1600, had been entered on the Stationers' Books, 28th September 1593.

HERO AND LEANDER. By Christopher Marloe. London, printed by Adam Islip, for Edward Blunt. 1598. 4°. Although not published until five years later, this poem was entered on the Stationers' Books on 28th September 1593 as 'A book entitled *Hero and Leander*, being an amorous poem devised by Christopher Marlowe.' Another 4to edition issued in 1598 refers to Chapman's continuation. The title-page reads: '*Hero and Leander*: Begun by Christopher Marloe; and finished by George Chapman. *Ut Nectar, Ingenium.* At London, printed by Felix Kingston, for Paule Linley, and are to be solde in Paules Churchyarde, at the Signe of the Blacke-beare.'

—— *Another edition*, in all respects similar, save that it was stated to have added *Lucan's First Booke*, which is only known separately, and to be 'printed for John Flasket,' instead of for Kingston, was published in 1600. 4°.

—— —— without the reference to Lucan, appeared in 1606. 4°.

—— —— 'imprinted for Ed. Blunt and W. Barret,' was published in 1609. 4°.

—— —— 'printed by W. Stansby for Ed. Blunt and W. Barret,' was issued in 1613.

—— —— 'printed by A. M. for Richard Hawkins: and are to be sold at his Shop in Chancerie-Lane, neare Serjeants Inne.' 1629.

—— —— 'printed by N. Okes for William Leake, and are to be sold at his shop in Chancery Lane neare the Roules.' 1637.

—— —— Begun by Christopher Marlowe and finished by George Chapman. Printed from that of 1637. 'Observations, etc.' Published by C. Chapple. 1820. 8°.

—— —— with critical preface by S. W. Singer, being vol. viii. of the 'Select Early English Poets.' 1821. 12°.

—— —— with decorations by C. Ricketts and C. Shannon. London. 1894. 8°.

HERO AND LEANDER. *Another edition*, issued as a broadside and
titled 'A most excellent Ditty of the Lovers promises to his
beloved' (by C. M.), was issued about 1650. Folio.

This broadside was reprinted in 'The Roxburghe Ballads,'
vol. i. p. 205. London. 1869.

On the 14th April 1598 was entered on the Stationers'
Books—*The Second Part of Hero and Leander conteyning their
further Fortunes* by Henry Petowe. 4°. Some account of this
book, 'the first fruits of an unripe wit, done at certaine vacant
howers,' as its writer styles it, has been given in our account
of Marlowe, who, of course, was personally unknown to
Petowe.

THE PASSIONATE PILGRIME. By W. Shakespeare. At London.
Printed for W. Jaggard, and are to be sold by W. Leake, at
the Greyhound in Paules Churchyard. 1599. This little
anthology, which had for a second title, in the middle of the
book, *Sonnets to Sundrie Notes of Musicke*, was only partly by
Shakespeare (some of the poems being by Barnfield, Marlowe,
and others) and was fraudulently ascribed to him by the
publisher. The book contained the first known publication
of Marlowe's *Passionate Shepherd to his Love*, but minus the
fourth and sixth stanzas. In 1600 the song reappeared in
'England's Helicon,' another anthology, but without the sixth
stanza, and was reprinted in 1653 by Isaak Walton, in his
Complete Angler, in its present form. Since that time the song
has been published in innumerable shapes, forms, and places.
The present volume is the first work in which a contemporary
version of the verses, from an Elizabethan Commonplace
Book, formerly belonging to John Thornborough, Bishop of
Limerick, has been given to the public. It contains many
variations from any of the known publications. The music
to which the song was sung was discovered by Sir John
Hawkins in an Elizabethan manuscript, and is given in
Boswell's edition of Malone's *Shakespeare*, and in Chappell's
collection of *National English Airs*. In Chappell's *National
Songs*, vol. ii. p. 139, the originality of the tune is fully
discussed. Sir Walter Raleigh wrote two *Replies* to the
poems, and Donne, Herrick, and others imitated it in various
pieces.

The FRAGMENT, beginning 'I walked along a stream,' first appeared,

as far as is known, in the 1600 edition of ' England's Parnassus '
(where it was given in the *Description of Seas, Waters, Rivers,
etc.*), over the name of Ch. Marlowe.

Dialogue in Verse was first published in the ' Alleyn Papers,' edited
by J. P. Collier for the 'Shakespeare Society.' The MS. was
stated to have been found amongst the Dulwich College
papers, written as in prose on one side of a sheet, with the
name ' Kitt Marlowe ' inscribed on the back in a modern hand.
The lines are obviously not by Marlowe, although they have
been reprinted in every edition of his poems, since their
publication by Collier.

A sonnet and two pieces of verse, described as by *Ignoto*, followed
the *Epigrams* of Sir John Davies, in two of the Middle-
brough editions of Marlowe's *Ovid*, and are reprinted in all
the collections of his poems. They are certainly not by
Marlowe.

The Latin Epitaph on Sir John Manwood, although first printed
by J. P. Collier, *History of the English Stage*, is doubtless
by Marlowe.

REFERENCE BOOKS, REVIEWS, ETC.

Allot, R. ' England's Parnassus.' Collection of poems by Shake-
peare, Marlowe, etc. 1600.

All the Year Round. ' Faust on the Stage.' Comparison between
the dramas of Marlowe and Goethe. Vol. xxiii. London.
1879. 8°.

Athenæum. Review of A. H. Bullen's edition of Marlowe's Works.
No. 2977, pp. 634-5. 1884.

Atlantic Monthly. Review of Bullen's edition of Marlowe's Works.
Vol. lvi. pp. 851, etc. Boston, U.S. 8°.

—— ' The Legend of Doctor Faustus.' Vol. ii. pp. 551, etc.
Boston, U.S. 1858. 8°.

Beeching, H. C. Review of Bullen's edition of Marlowe's Works.
The Academy, vol. xxiv. p. 265, and vol. xxvi. p. 315. London.

Bibliographer, The. ' The Bibliography of Doctor Faustus,' by
W. Heinemann. London. 1882.

Blackwood's Magazine. ' Doctor Faustus,' vol. i. pp. 388, etc. ;
' Edward II.,' vol. ii. pp. 21, etc. ; ' Jew of Malta,' vol. ii.
pp. 260, etc.

Boas, F. S. 'New Light on Marlowe.' *Fortnightly Review*, vol. lxxi. p. 212, etc. London.

—— 'Shakspere and his Predecessors.' London. 1895. 8°.

—— 'The Works of Thomas Kyd.' Introduction and 'Contemporary Documents relating to the charge of Atheism against Kyd and Marlowe,' pp. cviii-cxvi. Oxford: The Clarendon Press. 1901. 8°.

Bodenham, J. 'England's Helicon, or, the Choicest Flowers of our Modern Poets, with their Poetical Comparisons.' Selections from Shakespeare, Marlowe, etc. London. 1600.

Bodenstedt, F. M. von. 'Marlowe und Greene als Vorläufer Shakespeare's.' Braunschweig. 1858. 8°.

Book Lore. 'Marlowe and his Works.' By J. H. Slater. pp. 98-101. In this paper it states that F. Archer is reported to have been executed at Tyburn for the murder of Marlowe, but no authority is given for the report. London. 1887.

Borman, E. 'Geistesblitze, etc., über Bacon-Shakespeare-Marlowe.' Proving, according to this writer, that the author of *Novum Organum* wrote the works ascribed to Shakespeare and Marlowe. Leipzig. 1902. 8°.

Bradley, A. C. 'Marlowe,' in 'Ward's English Poets.' Vol. i. p. 411, 2nd edition. London. 1883. 8°.

Braga, T. 'Lenda do Dr. Fausto.' 'Estudos da Edade Media.' pp. 89-114. Porto. 1870. 8°.

British Stage. Account of Marlowe's death from Burial Register. January 1821.

Broughton, J. Useful and numerous MS. Notes in British Museum copy of Marlowe's Works. 1826 (Robinson's) edition.

—— Five useful and suggestive articles on C. Marlowe, in *Gentleman's Magazine*. London. 1840-41.

Carpenter, Bishop Boyd. 'The Religious Element in Marlowe's *Faustus*.' *Sunday Magazine*, xxix., July, 442.

Chappell, William. On 'The Passionate Shepherd.' 'National English Airs,' 1869; 'National Songs,' ii. 139, 1838-40; 'Popular Music of the Olden Times.' 2 vols. 1855-59.

Choate, J. B. 'Wells of England,' p. 166. Boston, U.S. 1892. 8°.

'*Cornwall, Barry,*' *vide* B. W. Procter.

Courtney, W. L. 'Death of Marlowe.' Poem. *Universal Review*. Vol. vi. p. 356. London. 1890. 8°.

Collier, J. P. 'The Poetical Decameron.' 2 vols. Much biblio-graphical information about Marlowe in various parts of this work. 1820. 8°.

—— 'Memoirs of Edward Alleyn,' pp. 8, 11, 18, 50, 59. Refer-ences to Marlowe. Printed for *The Shakespeare Society*. London. 1841. 8°.

—— 'History of English Dramatic Poetry and the Stage.' London. 1831. 8°.

—— Edited by. 'Diary of P. Henslowe.' For *The Shakespeare Society*. London. 1845. 8°.

> *N.B.*—As the above works, written or edited by J. P. Collier, contain many fraudulent statements, they must all be regarded with scepticism.

Collier, W. F. 'History of English Literature,' p. 167. London. 1861.

Craik, G. L. 'Literature and Learning of England.' Series 11, vol. iii. 1845. 12°.

Cowper, J. M., Edited by. 'Church Registers' and 'Marriage Licences' of Canterbury. Contain many entries relating to the Marlowe and Arthur families.

Canterbury. Various dates local journals.

—— 'Roll of the Freemen . . . of Canterbury, 1392 to 1800.' Canterbury. 1903. 8°.

Crofts, Ellen. 'Chapters in the History of English Literature, Chap. viii., pp. 171 to 194, on Marlowe. Edinburgh. 1884. 8°.

Dawson, G. 'Shakespeare and Other Lectures.' Marlowe's 'Faustus,' p. 342. Edinburgh. 1888.

Deighton, K. 'Marston, Marlowe,' etc. 'Conjectural Readings' London. 1894. 8°.

Dews, N. 'History of Deptford.' Marlowe, pp. 122-25. Dept-ford. 1883. 8°.

Dowden, E. Fortnightly Review. Critical article on Marlowe, vol. xiii. pp. 69-81. 1870.

—— 'Transcripts.' 431.

Dunham, ——. 'Literary and Scientific Men of Great Britain,' vol. ii. pp. 49, etc. 'Lardner's Cabinet Cyclopedia.' 1830.

Eckstadt, Vitzthum von. 'Shakspere and Shakespeare.' Written to prove that Francis Bacon wrote the dramas of Shakespeare and Marlowe. Stuttgart. 1888. 8°.

Eclectic Magazine. Marlowe, vol. lxxvi. pp. 24, etc.

Edinburgh Monthly Magazine. 'Marlowe's *Faustus.*' Signed 'H. M.' vol. i., No. iv. Edinburgh. 1817. 8°.

Every Saturday. Vol. ix. pp. 670.

Elze, K. 'Notes on English Dramatists.' Halle. 1889. 8°.

Engel, Dr. E. 'Christopher Marlowe' in 'Geschichte der Englischen Litteratur,' pp. 136-41. Leipzig. 1883. 8°.

Faligan, E. 'De Marlovianis Fabulis.' A thesis exposing many of the fables about Marlowe. Paris. 1887. 8°.

Filmore, L. Translation of Goethe's *Faust*, with an Appendix, containing an account of and quotations from Marlowe's *Faustus* (Smith's Standard Library). London. 1841. 8°.

Fischer, R. 'Zur Kunstentwicklung der Englischen Tragödie bis zu Shakespeare. Strassburg. 1893. 8°.

Fleay, F. G. 'Life of Shakespeare,' pp. 235, etc. Showing the co-operation of Shakespeare with Marlowe. London. 1886. 8°.

—— 'History of the London Stage.' London. 1890. 8°.

—— 'Biographical Chronicles of the Drama.' 2 vols.—vol. ii. London. 1891. 8°.

Foard, J. F. 'Joint authorship of Marlowe and Shakespeare.' *Gentleman's Magazine*, February, vol. cclxxxviii. pp. 134, etc.; vol. xxi., New Series, February, pp. 158, etc.

Fraser's Magazine. Review of Dyce's 'Marlowe,' vol. xlvii., pp. 221, etc., January to June 1853.

Friswell, J. H. Varia. 'Dr. John Faustus,' pp. 79-104. London. 8°.

G[alpin], A. J. 'The Schoolroom Windows.' At the King's School, Canterbury. 1899. 8°.

Gildon, C., *vide* Langbaine, G.

Grant, Ch. 'The Two Fausts.' Comparison between Marlowe's and Goethe's works. *Contemporary Review*, pp. 1 to 24. 1881.

Grinsted, T. P. 'The Relics of Genius.' Concerning the grave, etc., of Marlowe, pp. 215, 216. London. 1859. 8°.

Hales, J. W. 'Folia Literaria.' As to the date of 'Hero and Leander,' p. 167. London. 1893. 8°.

Hayward, A. 'Faust : a Dramatic Poem,' translated. References to and quotations from Marlowe's *Faustus*, pp. 223, etc. 2nd edition. 1834. London. 8°.

Hazlitt, W. 'Dramatic Literature of the Age of Elizabeth.' 2nd edition. London. 1821.

Hazlitt, W. 'Lives of the Poets,' by S. Johnson, completed by W. H., vol. i. pp. 191-4. London. 1854.

Hazlitt, W. C. 'Shakespeare's Times.' London. 1902. 8°.

Heinemann, W. 'Bibliography of Marlowe's *Dr. Faustus,*' reprinted from *The Bibliographer.* A very carefully compiled pamphlet. London. 1884.

Herford, C. H. Marlowe's 'Source of his *Tamburlaine.*' *The Academy,* No. 598, p. 265. London. 1883.

Horne, R. H. 'The Death of Marlowe: a Tragedy.' This has passed through various editions. 1870. 8°.

Hunter, J. Chorus Vatum. Addl. MSS. 24488, fol. 372-80. In British Museum. Much original research in these MSS.

Ingram, J. H. 'Marlowe and his *Doctor Faustus.*' Critical, biographical, and vindicatory. *Rose, Shamrock, and Thistle Magazine.* Edinburgh. 1865 (?).

—— 'A New View of Marlowe. Illustrated. *The Universal Review.* London. July 1889.

—— 'Shakespeare's Associates.' *The Key.* London. April 23, 1864.

Johnson, E. G. Review of H. Ellis's edition of 'The Mermaid' Series. *The Dial,* (ch.) No. 58. p. 97. 1887.

Langbaine, G. 'Lives and Characters of the English Dramatic Poets.' Continued by C. Gildon. London. 1699. 'Marlowe.'

Larnier, S. 'Shakespeare and his Forerunners.' 2 vols. London. 1902.

Lee, Jane. 'Transactions of the New Shakspere Society,' pp. 11, etc. Very useful as showing the co-operation between Shakespeare and Marlowe. 1876.

Lee, S. 'Another New Fact about Marlowe.' *Athenæum.* 18th August 1894. No. 3486. pp. 235-6.

—— 'Marlowe, Christopher,' in vol. xxxvi. *Dict. of Nat. Biog.* 1893.

—— 'Life of Shakespeare,' pp. 57, 60-64, 90, 393, 399 refer to Marlowe and his works, and his influence on Shakespeare. 1898. 8°.

Leitner, P. von. 'Ueber den Faust von Marlowe.' In *Jahrbücher für Drama,* etc., 1 Band. Leipzig. 1837. 8°.

Leutbecher, Dr. J. Ueber den Faust von Goethe,' pp. 135-140, refer to 'Der Dr. Faustus von Marlowe.' 1838. 8°.

Lewis, J. G. 'Christopher Marlowe: Outlines of his Life and Works.' The first separate work on Marlowe. Canterbury. 1891.

Limström, C. J. 'Doctor Faustus' af C. Marlowe. Ofversättning med inledning, pp. 26, etc. Upsala. 1839. 4°.

Literary World. Review of Bullen's edition of Marlowe's Works, vol. xv. p. 325. Boston, U.S.

Lowell, J. R. 'Old English Dramatists': Marlowe, etc. London. 1892.

—— *Harper's Monthly Magazine*, vol. lxxxv. p. 194.

Lowell, R. S. T. 'Marlowe and his Times.' *The Nation*, vol. xl. pp. 423, 445.

Lyceum. 'A Literary Tercentenary,' vol. v. p. 40, October 1893; and vol. vi. p. 209. 1894.

Malone, E. 'History of the English Stage.' 1790. 8°.

—— 'Life of Shakespeare.' London. 1821.

Manly, J. M. 'Specimens of the Pre-Shakespearian Drama.' Boston. 1897. 8°.

Meissner, A. 'Die Englischen Comödianten zur Zeit Shakespere in Oesterreich,' respecting *Doctor Faustus* performances at Vienna, etc. Frankfurt (?). 1883. 8°.

Meyer, E. 'Machiavelli and the Elizabethan Drama.' Weimar. 1897. 8°.

Mézières, A. 'Prédécesseurs et Contemporains de Shakspeare, Paris. 1863. Deuxième édition, pp. 110-156.

Minto, W. 'Characteristics of English Poets,' p. 230. London. 1874.

Morley, H. 'English Writers': Marlowe, vol. ix. p. 245, and vol. x. p. 111. 1864-7. 8°.

Münch, Dr. W. 'Festschrift . . . Deutscher Philologen, etc., zu Trier,' pp. 108-138, über 'Die innere Stellung Marlowe's zum Volksbuch vom Faust.' Bonn. 1879. 8°.

National Review. 'Shakespeare's Contemporaries.' p. 962. February 1903.

Nicklin, J. A. 'Marlowe's Historical Play, *Edward II.*' and his ' *Gaveston.*' *Free Review*, December, vol. cccxxiii.

Norton, E. 'Marlowe and his Times.' *Harvard Monthly*, vol. i. p. 50.

Notes and Queries. Nearly every volume of this invaluable publication contains material of interest and value concerning the life and works of Marlowe. 1849, etc. *In progress.*

Notter, F. 'A full account of Marlowe's *Faustus*' in *Monatsblätter der Allgemeinen Zeitung.* Augsburg. 1847. 4°.

Percy, J., Bishop of Dromore. 'Reliques of English Poetry,' edited by Hales, J. W., and Furnivall, F. J. 1868. 8°. New edition, vol. i. pp. 220, etc. 1876.

Plowman, H. The Theatre, vol. xxv. p. 8.

Procter, B. W. 'Essays, etc., on English Tragedy,' vol. ii. pp. 98-101. Boston, U.S. 1853. 8°.

Richardson, A. S. Appleton's Journal, vol. vi. p. 347.

Rogers, F. 'Tamburlaine the Great.' *Academy*, vol. xxxiv. p. 244.

Saturday Review. 'Memorial to Marlowe,' vol. lxxii. p. 318.

—— '*Faustus* as arranged by Poel,' vol. lxxxii. p. 36.

Scheible, J. 'Der Schatzgräber in den . . . Mittelalters. Erster Theil, pp. 229, etc. 'Die Sage von Dr. Faust.' Stuttgart. 1846. 16°.

Schipper, J. 'De versu Marlowii.' Bonn. 1867. 8°.

Sidebotham, J. S. 'Memorials of the King's School, Canterbury.' Canterbury. 1865. 8°.

Simpson, J. 'Eminent Men of Kent.' 'The First of the English Dramatists.' pp. 109, 110. London. 1893.

Simpson, R. 'Shakespere Allusion Books.' General Introduction, etc. New Shakspere Society. Very useful for citation of proofs that Shakespeare and Marlowe worked in conjunction, etc. London. 1874. 8°.

—— 'School of Shakespere.' 2 vols. London. 1878.

S[mith], G. B. 'Christopher Marlowe.' *The Cornhill Magazine*, vol. xxx. pp. 329, etc. 1874.

Songs of England and Scotland. 'The Passionate Shepherd': variations in and 'Replies' to. Vol. i. pp. xxix, 5-9, 287-90. London. 1835. 2 vols. 8°.

Spectator, vol. lxvii. p. 381.

Stoddard, R. H. Review of A. H. Bullen's edition of Marlowe's Works. *Dial* (ch.) v. 197.

Stokes, D.D., Rev. H. P. 'History of Corpus Christi College, Cambridge.' London. 1898. 8°.

—— 'Another New Fact about Marlowe.' *Athenæum*, p. 299, September 1, 1894.

Swinburne, A. C. 'A Study of Shakespeare.' London. 1880. 8°.

—— 'George Chapman: an Essay,' pp. 51, etc. 1875.

—— *Encyclopædia Britannica*, 'Marlowe,' vol. xv.

—— 'Poems and Ballads': Second Series. 'In the Bay,' stanzas

8 to 40 refer to Marlowe, and incidentally to Shelley. London. 1878. 8°.

Swinburne, A. C. 'Astrophel and Other Poems.' Four quatrains for a Memorial to Marlowe, pp. 121, 122. London. 8°.

Symonds, J. A. 'Shakespeare's Predecessors.' pp. 581, etc. 1884.

—— '*The Mermaid*' Series. General Introduction. 1887. 8°.

Taylor, Bayard. Translation of Goethe's *Faust*, vol. i. Appendix iii. on Marlowe's *Faustus*, with quotations. 2 vols. Boston, U.S. 1870. 8°.

Temple Bar. 'Faustus,' vol. xcviii. p. 515.

Tycho-Mommsen, Dr. 'Marlowe and Shakespeare.' Treats of Marlowe's blank verse, and gives translations from his dramas. Eisenach (?). 1854. 8°.

Ulrici, H. 'Ueber Shakespeare's Dramatische Kunst,' vol. i. 151. Halle. 1839. 8°.

United States and Democratic Review. 'The Two Fausts.' Vol. xiii. pp. 315-23, New Series. New York. 1843.

Valentine, E. A. N. Poem on C. Marlowe. *Critic*, xxxv., October 1888.

Verity, A. W. 'Marlowe's Influence on Shakespeare.' 'The Harness Essay Prize.' Cambridge. 1886. 8°.

Villemain, A. F. Cites the finest passages of *Faustus* in *Journal des Savants*. Mars 1856.

Ward, A. W. 'English Dramatic Literature to the death of Queen Anne,' vol. i. p. 173. 2 vols. London. 1875.

Warner, ——? *Library*, vol. xvii. 9714.

Wharton, J. 'History of English Poetry,' vol. iv. p. 313. New edition, edited by W. C. Hazlitt. 1871.

Whipple, E. P. 'Literature of the Age of Elizabeth.' Boston, U.S. 1869. 8°.

Yung, E. et Alglave, E. 'Les trois Faust.' Marlowe-Lessing-Goethe. *La Revue Politique et Littéraire*. Paris. 1877. 4°.

INDEX